The Content Machine

The Content Machine

Towards a Theory of Publishing from the Printing Press to the Digital Network

Michael Bhaskar

ANTHEM PRESS
LONDON · NEW YORK · DELHI

Anthem Press
An imprint of Wimbledon Publishing Company
www.anthempress.com

This edition first published in UK and USA 2013
by ANTHEM PRESS
75–76 Blackfriars Road, London SE1 8HA, UK
or PO Box 9779, London SW19 7ZG, UK
and
244 Madison Ave #116, New York, NY 10016, USA

British Library Cataloguing-in-Publication Data
A catalogue record for this book is available from the British Library.

Library of Congress Cataloging-in-Publication Data
Bhaskar, Michael.
The content machine : towards a theory of publishing from the
printing press to the digital network / by Michael Bhaskar.
pages cm
Includes bibliographical references and index.
ISBN 978-0-85728-111-1 (pbk. : alk. paper)
1. Publishers and publishing. 2. Publishers and publishing–History.
3. Electronic publishing. 4. Frames (Information theory) I. Title.
Z278.B48 2013
070.5–dc23
2013034708

ISBN-13: 978 0 85728 111 1 (Pbk)
ISBN-10: 0 85728 111 9 (Pbk)

This title is also available as an ebook.

CONTENTS

ACKNOWLEDGEMENTS

Many thanks to everyone who read drafts and commented on them. In particular thanks go to Sharon Achinstein, Roy Bhaskar, Chris Bunn, Iain Millar, Angus Phillips, Padmini Ray Murray and William St Clair for their thoughtful and invaluable comments. Digital publishing is alive with conversation and the many chats, Twitter debates and, yes, the odd beery discussion at the Frankfurt Book Fair, have helped shape this book. Thanks to Stephen Brough and Andrew Franklin of Profile Books for letting me write this book – they along with my colleagues at Profile are what the spirit of publishing is all about. The staff of the British Library, which was essential to my research, proves what an irreplaceable institution it is. Tej Sood at Anthem has championed the book with style and judgement throughout, for which I am hugely grateful. Rob Reddick and everyone else at Anthem have handled the process with serious aplomb. Lastly, thanks above all to Danielle for everything.

The technology of the book publisher is so out of date, he hardly has a technology.

J. G. Ballard

Publishing is not evolving. Publishing is going away. Because the word 'publishing' means a cadre of professionals who are taking on the incredible difficulty and complexity and expense of making something public. That's not a job anymore. That's a button. There's a button that says 'publish', and when you press it, it's done.

Clay Shirky

Introduction

USEFUL MIDDLEMEN

What's the difference between these words before and after they are published? Is publishing a tangible moment? Can you point to the instance when words pass from being unpublished to published? What is publishing anyway?

We're not short of descriptions and opinions. For John Thompson, publishers are 'merchants of culture' (or as Ned Ward said of the eighteenth-century publishing magnate Jacob Tonson: 'Chief Merchant to the Muses'); for Gary Stark, they are 'entrepreneurs of ideology'. Cass Canfield, president of Harper & Row and one of a generation of great American publishers including Bennet Cerf and Jason Epstein, was more lyrical still: 'I am a publisher – a hybrid creature: one part star gazer, one part gambler, one part businessman, one part midwife and three parts optimist.'

A common theme is the Janus-faced publisher, who has one eye on culture, the other on commerce. The writer and critic Raymond Mortimer argued publishing is 'at once an art, a craft and a business', echoing Émile Zola's formulation of the visual artist as both poet and worker. Richard Nash sees publishing as 'the business of making culture', while the editor Diana Athill views publishing as

> a complicated business which has to buy, sell and manufacture or cause to be manufactured. What it buys and sells is products of people's imaginations, the materials for making books, and a variety of legal rights. What it manufactures is never the same from one item to the next. (Athill 2000, 6)

Hunter S. Thompson thought publishers a combination of business nous and ineptitude, people 'notoriously slothful about numbers, unless they're attached to dollar signs'. Many have been unkinder. The children's writer Maurice Sendak was even more strident: 'publishing is such an outrageously stupid profession. Or has become so [...] nobody knows what they're doing. I wonder if that's always been true?' The philosopher A. J. Ayer was caustic: 'If I had been someone not very clever, I would have done an easier job like publishing. That's the easiest job I can think of.' So was Goethe, who saw publishers as 'cohorts of the devil'. Suffice to say, publishing has long been open to interpretation.

Perhaps, unsurprisingly, the clearest commentator is Oscar Wilde, who said with unmistakable brevity, 'A publisher is simply a useful middleman.'[1]

Hustlers and Humanists, or Why We Need a Theory of Publishing

Publishing isn't like most industries. It busies itself with questions of intangible value and moral worth. Nor is it exactly like the arts or sciences, as it obsesses over balance sheets and profit margins. Publishing is weird. Books are amenable to an industrially scaled analysis: given sufficient resource allocation any number of copies can be made available to produce steadily increasing returns. Yet they are also exclusive cultural or experiential phenomena, like fine art or ballet, whose limitations of distribution are part of their symbolic and financial value propositions.

Publishing is the primal creative industry *qua* industry.[2] It was the reproductive potential of the printing press, the first technology to mass produce and widely distribute cultural and intellectual items, which threw up new modes of organisation around the workshop, the humanist printer and 'typographical fixity'. The spread of printing across Europe was astonishingly rapid and ignited revolutions in religion, science and education (Eisenstein 1980). Arguably, more than anything else, printing, publishing, created modernity itself. Even before Gutenberg, in medieval *scriptoria* and the great centers of ancient learning, there were still many

---

1 See Thompson (2010), Stark (1981) and Nash (2012). For Cass, see *New York Times* (1986); for Hunter S. Thompson, see http://www.theguardian.com/books/2005/feb/21/huntersthompson (accessed 21 August 2013); for Sendak, see Brockes (2012); for Ayer, see Knowles (2008); for Goethe, see Esposito (2013); for Wilde, see Cole (1989).

2 This has been an issue. As publishing became ever more industrial throughout the nineteenth century, the gentlemanly world of book publishing found itself in something of an identity crisis, at once thinking itself above the machinic and labour connotations of industry, at the same time keen to embrace the productive potential of technology. While most opted for the latter, some, like William Morris's Kelmscott Press, based themselves wholeheartedly on a rejection of 'industry' (Stetz 2007).

functions of publishing; after all, books (or scrolls) were still produced. Publishing occupies a unique place in cultural history, and we should ask what affect this had on other creative industries.

So we have a strange practice, but also an ancient proto-industry acting as a template for one of the fastest growing areas of the contemporary economy. Now we also have an industry in crisis.

Perverse as it may seem, even setting digital media aside, publishing is in crisis. Publishing, famously, is always in crisis. The present one has some nasty symptoms. Across the industry consolidation has been rampant. New working methods and cultures have displaced gentlemanly Old World orthodoxies. Bricks and mortar retailers fight for survival, particularly in Anglo-American cultures.[3] Costs, inevitably, keep rising. Alarming macro-trends, like the decline in long-form reading, the rise in alternative media and audience time pressures, only worsen. Trade publishers see their mid-lists hollowed; academic publishers face pressure from higher education spending cuts, while educational publishers encounter increased competition across their markets.

Then along came the digital challenge. Centralising power, eroding value and breaking publishing's time-worn business models with parvenu ease, publishers have been caught in a race to catch up, scale up and tool up. Trade publishers are trapped, like traditional computer manufacturers, between powerful upstream producers (i.e. authors, agents) and downstream distributors and retailers, like Amazon and Barnes & Noble. Profit lies in the efficient coupling of the two, creating a structural vulnerability now exposed by the web.

Self-publishing – whether for the callow novelist or seasoned academic – has never been easier, raising strategic questions not just for the industry but about what it means to publish in the first place. Publishing can be difficult for outsiders because it is already intensely competitive. In few sectors is there an equivalent expenditure of intellectual capital on such low financial returns. In short, in few fields do equivalent levels of talent work flat out for, by the standards of many globally scaled industries, such meagre pickings. From old media giants to nimble web native start-ups, new entrants are nonetheless circling. It remains to be seen what difference merged entities like Thomson Reuters and Penguin Random House will make or how publishers will grow in emerging markets. The calculus is changing in the digital world with its low barriers to entry, fast growth rates and direct consumer relationships.

---

3 Exhibit A, in this regard, is the collapse of the major book chain Borders in 2011.

Over the centuries change was the norm for publishers, whether they liked it or not. Somehow book sales kept on rising. Yet this masks missed opportunities – by, erroneously, defining their role as makers of books, publishers have straitjacketed themselves, missing new formats ripe for publication and so backing themselves into a corner. Perhaps this is an inevitable result of specialisation and market segmentation. Perhaps not. Either way, publishers need a more informed idea of their role, allowing them to focus on core competencies in difficult times while building a more expansive notion of their activities. In future they might react more nimbly to technological change and see it as an opportunity, not a threat. Ignoring big questions is easy but leaves publishers without a clear identity when having one has never been more important. Lacking definition leaves publishers horribly exposed to the whims of history and technology.

On a more theoretical plane, our concept of mediation is troubled. In the now standard textbook on communication studies Denis McQuail (2010) lists some of the metaphors for mediation: as a window, a mirror, a filter, a gatekeeper or portal, a signpost, guide or interpreter, as a forum or platform, a disseminator, an interlocutor. Mediation, like publishing, is conflicted and elusive. A theory of publishing is a theory of mediation, of how and why cultural goods are mediated. It is the story behind media, rather than the story of a medium itself (like books or words), and has a big role to play in our understanding of communications.

Publishing is an activity, a mode of production; it is difficult labour. At the same time, it is about judgement, taste, aesthetics and the exercise of reason, the considered deployment of resources, financial or otherwise. It is anything but straightforward. Nonetheless, most books on publishing, the history of the book or cultural studies are premised on an unexamined understanding of publishing. Publishing has been thoroughly explored, both historically and in the present, but not adequately theorised.

People will always communicate. More books, by far, are published than ever before. On the one hand, we have a human need, a booming sector and, with the Internet, a general flourishing of communications unprecedented in history. Long-form reading isn't going away, it's in a golden age. We also have an industry, a set of standards and way of life under threat. What's going on here? We need to go beyond folksy descriptions, untested assumptions, industry propaganda and workmanlike dictionary definitions to really *get* publishing. We need to test those assumptions and see what, if any, conception of publishing stacks up.

We need greater clarity. Publishing is often equated with making something public. Is that enough? Does publishing always need to be commercial and what is its relationship to profit making and capitalism? Does publishing work with or against technology and technological change, and how? Dissenting pamphlets and the *Financial Times* web app, Bach sonatas and *The Sims* are all published material. How can that be? In order to understand publishing, how it might survive and thrive in a period of unparalleled challenge, we need to appreciate why it was a problem before digital technology.

Beyond the theoretical or strategic questions, this is important. Publishing really matters. It's at the heart of our literature and our learning, our civil society, our public spheres and political discussions. Publishing carries forward our sciences and powers our culture. Publishing isn't a passive medium; it is a part of our lives and societies, shaping them, guiding them, sometimes even controlling them. Rarely looking inward, publishing helps define our world. Over the centuries that classic combination of hustler and humanist has had an outsized impact. That should be worth a closer look.

In my view a theory of publishing must account for the following:

- The public and institutional character of publishing, explaining what makes something public;
- The role of publishing as an act of mediation;
- Divergent historical understandings;
- Divergent media forms published;
- Facets such as (financial) risk, the relationship to content and market making;
- Publishing's past and how it informs its engagement with digital media in the present.

The Argument

My argument suggests firstly that publishing is far from simple. Despite employing hundreds of thousands, even millions of people around the world, quite what constitutes publishing isn't nearly as easy to nail down as might be thought. How do video game or music publishing compare with book publishing for instance? How indeed does publishing's long history and rich present-day diversity fit in with our notions of what it might be?

Digital publishing, an example of what Clayton Christensen (1997) would call 'disruptive innovation', has only made things more difficult. Now anyone can publish or be a publisher, what does it really mean to publish? Reams of material discuss how digital technology has impacted publishing but pundits and executives alike often focus on the most superficial, short-term developments. While apparently important subjects like ebook formats and digital marketing tactics are certainly of interest, they miss the wider and more fundamental questions arising from the Internet's structure. The foundations of scarcity and intellectual property, the role as a gatekeeper, connector and mediator, are all under assault from forces often misunderstood by contemporary publishers.

Until publishing has a clear sense of how the technological landscape translates into a business dilemma measured in decades, the entire practice as it is presently constituted will shrivel. Publishing won't go bust or dramatically exit stage left as some digital proselytisers seem to think; publishing will slowly contract and retreat into its own irrelevance. For those of us who believe publishing plays an important, useful role in the world neither option appeals.

The core of my argument builds a theory of publishing on four key terms: framing and models, filtering and amplification. They are the real content machine. My premise is that publishing can never be divorced from content. Wherever you find publishing, you find content. It follows that a theory of publishing grows from a theory of content, and this is where framing and models come in. Content is framed – packaged for distribution and presented to an audience – according to a model. The concept of framing and modelling comes with considerable baggage and detail, crucial to a full understanding of how publishing works, which I explore in Chapters 3 and 5 respectively along with questions about the relationship of publishing to technology and commerce.

The real heart of publishing, however, lies in filtering and amplification. Publishing is about selection. Even self-publishers filter; after all, they pick work to publish, namely their own. At its most inclusive publishing is a marginal filtering process. If there were no filtering process we would be simply dealing with the medium itself, rather than the publishers working within that medium. The whole framing process is really designed to amplify texts. Publishing is about scaling up from creating a single instance to multiple copies. The model is why you want to scale up, why you want to amplify (typically, but as will be demonstrated, far from exclusively because of money). If publishing is anything, if public content means anything, it lies in the idea of amplification.

Lastly, I connect this theory or 'system' of publishing to the maturing digital landscape. Points made earlier in this introduction are addressed directly. The shift to market making, the growth in new models of intellectual property, the idea of curation and strategies drawn from web native organisations are all explored as possible answers to the challenge of digital networks. My aim is not to apply the theory in an instrumental way, so much as to tease out the broad implications for the general drift of publishing. If there is one thing this argument aims to do, it is to make clear that publishing is tricky.

Readers looking for contemporary or digital arguments should concentrate on Chapters 2 and 6. Most of my forward-looking comments about market making, publishing as a service, open licences, lean publishing, curation and the New Publisher can be found in Chapter 6. Those looking for the main argument about publishing, content, media and economics should focus on Chapters 3, 4 and 5. Naturally, the author believes the best way of reading the book is the old fashioned way – from beginning to end.

By 'publishing' I principally mean book publishing. However when we close off meanings of publishing and limit our understanding to books or text, we have an impoverished sense of the role. In fact, we can't easily distinguish between this or that publishing. In this argument, 'publishing' walks a tightrope between a narrow focus on books and the wider world of 'content publishing' generally, oscillating between the two.

A Theory of Publishing?

The study of books and publishing is now a permanent and respectable feature of the scholarly landscape. In the past few years alone, publishing studies has made enormous strides in explaining this mercurial practice. To name just a few of the prominent writers in the area, John Thompson (2005, 2010) explores in detail the patterns and undercurrents of Anglo-American publishing; Albert Greco (2005, 2007) investigates the complex economics of publishing firms and book markets; Claire Squires (2007) elucidates the productive aspects of marketing in contemporary publishing; and writers like Miha Kovač (2008), Angus Phillips and Adriaan van der Weel (2011), alongside a host of bloggers, offer insights into the digital revolution. Yet there are still gaps in our knowledge and focus. The otherwise indispensable *Oxford Companion to the Book* (2010), for example, has only a token entry on 'publishing', focused on its financing role, which shows how strides in book history don't necessarily translate into a greater appreciation of publishing – without which the history of books would be unrecognisable.[4]

The state of publishing knowledge has, despite these advances, long been bemoaned. Its status as an academic discipline has remained unclear, at times undeveloped, caught between larger and more established areas of study, like the history of the book and media studies. In the 1980s, literary critic John Sutherland called our understanding of publishing a 'hole at the centre of literary sociology' (Sutherland 1988, 576). He was quite clear that it wasn't so much historical knowledge that was lacking but a more theoretical view: 'publishing history, though it flourishes with extraordinary juvenile vigour, lacks binding theoretical coherence' (Sutherland 1988, 576). He went on to state the case – the project of this study – more clearly still:

> Publishing history [...] would seem less in need of antlike collaboration than a new theoretical base from which to proceed. That base is alien to the inherited text-centric and canonically exclusive theories on which academic English, for instance, founds itself. And without theoretic formulation, the publishing history enterprise very quickly founders on intractable hard cases. (Sutherland 1988, 588)

Much has changed since Sutherland was writing, not least the publication of the above-mentioned research, but, as with everything in publishing, change happens more slowly than might be supposed. Theoretical forays, so common in cultural and media studies, are still relatively rare. Richard Nash's (2013) essay 'The Business of Literature' is a rare and welcome example: polemical, lyrical and thoughtful, Nash depicts publishing as a radical agent involved not just in the making of books but in capitalism and modern culture. Simone Murray (2006) could, nearly twenty years after Sutherland, complain of a precariousness of identity in publishing studies; where it might be critical and research intensive, it frequently remains vocational or anecdotal.

This study, following recent work on publishing, aims to build on such 'publishing theory'. For some, the term and idea will be anathema.

---

4 Of course, there is a wealth of information about publishing contained in the *Companion* (2010), but indirectly as it relates to the book.

Theory has too many negative connotations as obscurantist, dated and muddle-headed, too far removed from the cut and thrust of publishing. Certainly the attempt here is to outdo no one in the unintelligibility stakes. Instead my aim is to salvage what's useful from theory; to say, 'yes, a common-sense understanding of publishing is perfectly acceptable most of the time, but there is value in more difficult and nuanced views'. Take the figure of the author (or rather, the Author) as an analogy. Once everyone knew what an author did – they wrote books, end of story. Then along came some difficult questions. The American New Critics W. K. Wimsatt and Monroe Beardsley started to argue it was the words and readers' interpretations that mattered; the author's intentions were irrelevant to our understanding of literature. Roland Barthes took the notion one step further, famously proclaiming the Death of the Author and the primacy of the reader in constructing meaning.

Michel Foucault (1980) took a different line in this 'decentring' of the author. What, he asks, is an author's work? If you take anyone's collected papers, could this be called their *œuvre*? If we accept someone is an author, then is everything they wrote, all the scraps, receipts and trivial ephemera part of the *œuvre* as well? What constitutes an author's work is, on reflection, more complicated than we might have thought. In response Foucault goes on to describe the 'author function'; authors essentially have two identical names, their 'real-life' name and their authorial name, which serves to group a body of works. Thus, even a group of texts almost certainly not written by the same person are grouped under an author function, as we do with names like Hippocrates or Hermes Trismegistus.

For much of history many works, like epic poems, didn't require an author at all, they were part of a shared heritage. Then, in the seventeenth and eighteenth centuries, it became more and more common to ask 'who wrote it?'. This increased authorial emphasis coincides with the growing legal apparatus of intellectual property; once writers could own their texts, they needed an author function to brand them. Ultimately Foucault (1980) thinks the author function regulates our system of discourse into parcels sorted by author, part of our 'bourgeois' era marked by individualism, property and commerce.

The point is not whether Foucault et al. were right or wrong, but that their work enriches our understanding of authorship. It does justice to the incredible complexity of the world. We can take or leave the arguments, but we can't take or leave the sense that maybe authorship isn't as straightforward as just writing books, that readers as well as writers create meaning and societies as well as individuals are responsible for producing categories like authorship in the first place.

We don't need a publishing theory to slot in as some half-baked adjutant to literary theory. We do, however, need a publishing theory to explain, at a critical juncture, something of what publishing is and does.[5] In the words of the publishing consultant Mike Shatzkin (2012), '[T]rying to explain publishing, or even understand it, remains a great challenge.' We should keep rising to it.

This is a work of synthesis. It builds on many of the ideas I've heard from publishing thinkers circulating on countless blogs, in tweets, at conferences, in journals, books and other fora about where the industry is headed and how it should respond to the digital challenge. This book places them in a more detailed historical and theoretical framework. It looks at not just what we mean by publishing but the relationship between print and digital publishing and how they inform one another. I am indebted to powerful works in a range of fields: publishing studies and industry commentary, of course, but also the history of the book, media and communication studies, cultural and literary theory, business studies and economics, history and biography, sociology and the extensive but still emergent literature on digital media. This is a resolutely interdisciplinary and synergetic study. It remains a sketch, an essay in Montaigne's sense of an attempt, a try, part of a debate not some definitive analysis. It is by necessity broad in scope and I readily accept the need for local refinements and revisions.

My position is both that of researcher and practising digital publisher. I hope this gives me both a bird's-eye and a ground-up view of the changes occurring in publishing.[6] Seeing publishing change from within, and occasionally trying to push it forward, has been exhilarating and endlessly informative. At their plain office desks, digital publishers have felt the excitement and risk of a new frontier, a journey whose destination is unknown. Those studying publishing are fortunate; it is an unusually open and self-referential industry. Publishers, perhaps due to their literate backgrounds, are more likely than most to think about, interpret and communicate what they do, why and how. This book is

5 An alternative title might adapt that of the sociologist Göran Therborn's (2008) *What Does the Ruling Class Do When It Rules?*: what do publishers do when they publish?

6 Bruno Latour (2005, 33) argues, 'As a rule, it's much better to set up as the default position that the inquirer is always one reflexive loop *behind* those they study', which leaves this author in the strange position of chasing his own tail.

partly industry self-commentary, without, I hope, buying wholesale into the day-to-day beliefs and self-descriptions of a loquacious, intelligent and interest-protecting industry. Reflexivity and self-consciousness have been constant companions.

I also steer clear of too much crystal-ball gazing, a mug's game. The future of publishing is one of the major themes, but that doesn't equate to saying *x* or *y* is the future of publishing. Long-term trajectories, certain probabilities at most, are discussed, although I don't shy away from normative and strategic conclusions. As with any good hypothesis, there should be testable goals. Needless to say, those still reading for a business analysis of publishing, complete with simple answers about what publishers should do in a networked world, will be disappointed. This is not to say that the work isn't useful; it just isn't useful in a '10 Steps to Publishing Success' sort of way. If there is a magic formula, I wish I knew it. My focus is on the *longue durée*: publishers as cultural and informational hierophants, the big questions about commerce, technology and the impact of digital media. There is no end of writers telling publishers what to do, and this volume aims for more nuance, rather than a publishing-by-numbers approach. The analysis is focused on what we can broadly call 'traditional' publishers. The executives at Twitter or Amazon, for example, hardly view the future with the existential angst of dead tree publishers – as they like to call them in Silicon Valley. I believe publishing, traditional and new, dead tree and digital, is important and still offers incalculable value to content, content producers and the world generally. Despite the excitement and advances of digital technology it would be a great loss if dead tree publishers became dead publishers.

Chapter 1

THE PROBLEM OF PUBLISHING

Imagine a publishing house. Here are the editors reading manuscripts before debating their virtues at an acquisitions meeting. We have the production department, sales, marketing and publicity; editorial managers with their proofreaders, copyeditors, text designers and typesetters; the art department with their large screens and colour printers. We have the C-suite executives and interns, secretaries and strategists, office managers, HR, contracts, the IT team and the legal counsel; we have an army of freelancers, from off-site readers to the man who delivers coffee. The large off-site machinery of distributors, sales agents and support services lies out of view, but remains essential. Departmental boundaries at a publisher's have, in recent times, become rather blurred; marketing and publicity, for example, share responsibility for managing the company's social media accounts. More or less, though, there is a clear workflow, a critical path winding its way through the organisational structure.

A manuscript navigates the path, beginning as a rough Word document. It ends as a complete text, gleaming from the attentions of many skilled editors and designers, produced as a handsome hardback with an eye-catching jacket, with excellent sales placements, favourable notices in major broadsheet newspapers, excited chatter on the web and a strong early showing in the bestseller lists. Somewhere on the journey it was published. Which department, which person did the publishing? One might be tempted to say the publisher, *ex officio*; only she really spends most of her time smoothing personnel issues in her large editorial team and wooing big name authors with big plans and bigger advances. One could say the editor, the individual responsible for bringing the book to the house, who sculpts the text and makes critical calls on its presentation. However, they didn't design the book, produce it or get it into the shops or people's consciousness. Do publishers need to commission, finance or distribute books to be publishers? Must they do it all and in what order? Can you only do a couple of tasks? Must you own a book to publish it?

The point is, of course, no one publishes the book – publishing, that strange textual alchemy, happens through the entire organisation and is the sum of its activities. Publishing is the peculiar, elusive, above all emergent property of publishers. So what kind of emergent property is it?

Before we can begin, we need to consider what publishing is. Before digital came along, there were several fault lines to publishing. First, the definitions and usages of the word 'publishing', for instance, continually shift and tug against each other. Second, the historical situations of publishers, still understood as 'publishing' today, can in no way be dealt with as a single category. Third, we need to go beyond book publishing to the spectrum of 'publishings', and ask what this multimedia status implies. Lastly, we need to analyse the operations of publishing, find those aspects often thought identical to publishing, and see if they really are. If we can establish that these functions are not reducible to publishing as a whole, we have an aporia, a 'black hole' at the heart of an activity that employs millions around the world with a history stretching back hundreds, even thousands of years. An odd situation. By tracing each of these strands we can start to see a theory of publishing, not as a strange and unwieldy imposition but an accessory to this vital area of our cultural and intellectual lives.

What's the Problem?

Particle physics might require a unified field theory – but publishing? Publishing consultant Brian O'Leary suggested as much at the Books in Browsers conference in San Francisco, arguing for 'a unified field theory of publishing' (see O'Leary 2011b). Theories explain the world, resolving apparent anomalies. They are testable against parts of reality. Presupposed is the idea something needs explanation in the first place. As a profession, in some senses analogous to plumbing or teaching, or an industry, analogous to the motor or drinks industry, publishing doesn't seem to require a theory or an explanation as such. Most industries or trades are more or less self-explanatory. No one is offering unified field theories of the beverage industry. Why would you need one for publishing?

O'Leary (2011b) constructs his theory in response to a new problem: the impact of digital technology on publishers. He sets out to critique the 'container model of publishing', whereby publishers fill 'containers', or books, with content, and then sell them. In digital settings, this model breaks down because traditional containers don't work in the freely moving world of browsers and code – we need to start instead with content and its context ('the critical admixture of tagged content, research, footnoted links, sources, audio and video background, even good old title-level metadata' (O'Leary 2011b)). Rather than seeing context as secondary to discrete physical units, it is at the forefront of a publisher's work in disseminating texts through convergent, digital, open, free, remixed and interactive spaces. Put simply O'Leary's field theory suggests that, with the advent of digital, what was a container industry should become a context industry.

It is a good theory. Yet it begs a question. Does publishing only need a theory post-digital? What's more, is it really a theory in the first place? A theory of publishing has to explain what publishing does in the digital age – O'Leary explains what it could do, he outlines a strategy, but he doesn't ask if the container model fully explains publishing *before* digital. In fact, publishing's problems are as old as publishing.

Publishing was never simple. Take an example, which will be explored in more detail below. What, exactly, is the difference between a published and an unpublished work? If I leave manuscripts lying around in public, does that in some way constitute publishing? There have long been separations between printing and publishing, and indeed, separations between the many acts now considered core to publishing. Publishing floats somewhere above the production and dissemination of books, neither printing nor distribution, sales, art, copyediting or copyright owning exactly, but a strange conceptual amalgam of all or none of them. The closer one looks the more publishing dissipates into a non-activity with blurred limits. While the Internet poses an existential challenge to publishing, even prior to the web publishing was existentially challenged. We don't just need a unified field theory for digital publishing, but for publishing in general.

To borrow Raymond Williams's (1983) term, publishing is a 'keyword'. Williams saw keywords as problems, concealing contradictions and alternative meanings. Culture is a prime example of a keyword that awkwardly straddles meanings referring to either art or society, deeply connected to both. If keywords are about connections with other keywords, collectively forming a complex, then note some of Williams's selections with the word 'publishing' in mind: aesthetics, art, capitalism, career, civilisation, commercialism, communications, consumer, creative, culture, educated, expert, fiction, industry, intellectual, literature, mass, media, mediation, popular, society, technology, wealth and work amongst others.

A more recent project (Bennett, Grossberg and Morris 2005) to update the list reveals yet more associations: audience, celebrity, commodity, consumption, copy, discourse, economy, education, information, knowledge, management, market, network, representation, sign, text, value, virtual and writing. Intensely, unstably connected, publishing often lacks what Williams called 'that extra edge of consciousness' (Williams 1983, 24). Designating 'publishing' and 'publish' keywords isn't consigning them to a language game, but to argue problems in language stem from real historical situations. To understand publishing, we must first understand its difficulty.

The Word Itself

The English word 'publish' predates the invention of the printing press by at least seventy years, if not more if its delay in reaching England is taken into account. The earliest use registered in the *Oxford English Dictionary* (*OED*) is from 1382 in the Wycliffite Bible: 'It is yhrd and with solempne word puplyschid in the halle of the kyng.' Books and cultural products have less historic importance than the wider sense of to make public, to declare or to announce something, a use more about sending a message than pertaining to an industry. Another example in the *OED* is from Lytton Strachey's *Queen Victoria* (published in 1921): 'For the Queen, far from making a secret of her affectionate friendship, took care to publish it to the world.' This refers to publishing as projecting an act or emotional state directly – there is no sense of an intermediary. Queen Victoria would not be a publisher in any colloquial use of the term. Most early uses were about not concealing things, a lineage in which publishing is hardly a positive act so much as a lack of secrecy.

The word 'to publish' stems from the Anglo-Norman *puplier* and the Middle French *publier*, loosely meaning to make public or known, to announce or to proclaim; both words trace back to the Latin *puplicare*, meaning to make public property or place at the community's disposal. The word's history is embedded in European public life. In post-classical Latin, it also meant to denounce and had a meaning 'to confiscate'. Roger Chartier records how the word meant to read a work in public in France: 'the older meaning of "publication" as a "public" reading of a work before the prince, lord or institution to which it was dedicated' (Chartier 1995, 33).[1]

Another significant thread is institutional, typically relating to ecclesiastical, juridical or political bodies (the church, the law and the state). Thus one would publish a will, a libel, wedding banns or monarchical edicts, in a manner and meaning that has changed little over the centuries. Compare Shakespeare's will as recorded in 1616, 'And doe Revoke All former wills & publishe this to be my last will & testament,' to that of Robert Maxwell, quoted in the *Financial Times* in 1992: 'I, Robert Maxwell, residing at Heddington Hill Hall, Oxford, England, do hereby make, publish and declare this codicil to my last will and testament.' Both wills invoke publishing in a purely institutional way, outside of which the usage has no bearing – that is to say, the institution itself presupposes and contains the publishing. Publishing is an action only within the broader context and so can be seen in terms of a service or function within it, something reflected in history. For example, in early modern England, royal and ecclesiastical publishing, from proclamations to bibles, psalters and catechisms, were the two most valuable monopolies granted to publishers. In the later Elizabethan period, the two were effectively merged in the lucrative position of Royal Printer (a post dating back to 1541–42) allowing for close control of official publishing.

Only at the third level of the definition of 'publishing' do we come to an industry sense, as a process '[t]o prepare and issue copies of (a book, newspaper, piece of music, etc.) for distribution or sale to the public. Also: to prepare and issue the work of (an author)'. This leaves open interesting tensions, for example, between issuing music (sound) and books (text) and also procedural questions, such as what issuing copies involves at a granular level. The inclusion of author, bracketed, is also instructive, as it implies that acts of publishing are fundamentally distinct from those of authorship, or creation, even as the authorship connection ties us to ideas of individuality and textuality. This differentiation is alive in recognisably modern form in Thomas More's *Dialogues Heresyes* (1529), written just beyond the incunabula phase of the printed word: 'I am now driuen [...] to this thirde busyness of publishynge and puttynge my boke in printe my selfe.'

---

1 It would be helpful to contrast this history with that of other languages (e.g. for *Verleger, editore* and *éditeur*).

Publishing is here distinct from both authoring and bookselling, sufficiently removed from writing for authorial involvement to be remarkable, even explicitly seen as different from 'putting into print', which wasn't clear at the time. Quite unlike the usage in Strachey (1921), More's publishing becomes active, conscious and purposeful, contrasting with a more passive use at 3b: 'To make generally accessible or available for acceptance or use (a work of art, information, etc.): to present to or before the public; *spec.* to make public (news, research findings, etc.) through the medium of print or the Internet.'

Print and text are tacitly privileged. Why should this be when modern publishing is so much more multi-form?[2] Only at this third level does the idea of medium come into play; we saw at first glance a near unmediated sense of publishing; yet in every understanding regarding content, mediation is key. Part of the issue with 'making public', perhaps the most commonly understood definition of publishing,[3] is that it doesn't bring mediation to the fore – the act of making public is almost assumed to just happen, as if it didn't require a medium, or the process behind that medium, through which it happens.

At a fundamental level all dictionaries and definitions are circular, yet in many instances publishing is beset with a particularly vicious circularity. Publishers publish; to publish is to make something public. We immediately hit the stumbling block of the insufficient conception of 'making public'. In his 1755 *Dictionary*, Dr Johnson followed a prototype of the public (or 'publick') argument, defining 'publish' as '[t]o put forth a book into the world'. Characteristically commonsensical, yes, but it is a definition with the same ambiguity over what constitutes 'putting into the world' in the first place. Johnson, too, is caught in unhelpful vagueness.

Here's a brief thought experiment: you write a novel, and leave it on a park bench. Is this a published novel? Let's say you print 1,000 copies, leaving them on 1,000 park benches. How about now? Or how about a publisher buys it, takes out masses of adverts, but literally no

---

2 Of course the *OED* can hardly be treated as infallible, but its foibles and blind spots are nonetheless interesting, as Williams (1983) recognises.

3 With different emphases, see, for example, Angus Phillips and Giles Clark: '"To publish" is commonly defined as "to make public"' (2008, 1); Richard Guthrie: 'Publishing is a process by which human communication is made public' (2011, x); and John Feather: 'Publishing, as it is generally understood, is the commercial activity of putting books into the public domain' (2005, 2).

one buys a single copy? In what sense has that work been published? At what point does a letter or email pass from private correspondence to public, published text? One hundred or 100,000 recipients? Or is the idea of putting a numerical value on being public absurd, and if so, what conceptual distinction should we make instead? If I post the email on the Internet, we can assume it has been published, but then, if nobody views it, how is it more public than an email sent to 100 people? Is being public a state of being – the state of being public in itself – or is it epistemological, the state of being known, or even being known to have been published?

Simply to say 'making something public' specifies virtually nothing. One way of thinking about this is to follow John Thompson's (2010) distinction between making a work *available* and making a work *known* to the public. Another is to approach the notion of public. However, this runs into a wall of arguments about what the public is, where it comes from, what influence it exerts, who constitutes and controls it, and so on. Social theorists like Pierre Bourdieu (2005) and Bruno Latour (1993) have, in different ways, suggested the idea of a 'public' is imposed on the world, not an innate feature of it. By saying publishing is axiomatically connected to the public, we create as many problems as we resolve. The discussion masks the inherent conceptual plasticity of 'public', a contested word if ever there was one. A definition of publishing needs a better sense of what becoming public really involves.

Returning to the *OED* and its senses of 'publishing', we find a shorter and more recent etymology: '1. The action of making something publicly known; official or public notification; promulgation, public announcement; 2. The action or business of preparing and issuing books, newspapers, etc., for public sale or distribution; an instance of this.' At the first point, we return to the institutional thrust, where publishing is embedded in and dependent upon certain social bodies, although crucially here incorporating Thompson's (2010) idea of knowing; reception is equally important. Cultural products, however, are not referenced at the first level. In the second half of the definition, we see print media still in the ascendancy and with a new modifier – 'business' – introducing an explicitly commercial bent for the first time. In other contexts this takes pride of place,[4] like this description

---

4 Unsurprisingly, 'business' is a central theme in those books that analyse the modern publishing industry. However it is important to recognise that publishing is not, and should not be, exhausted by this understanding, and is conditioned by those other understandings.

in Merriam Webster: 'the business or profession of the commercial production and issuance of literature, information, musical scores or sometimes recordings, or art.' Commercial involvement, management structure and their companion, financial risk, are utterly central to this definition, perhaps reflecting its North American origin. This capitalist connection contrasts with the non-market entities of church, law and state. We have a multifaceted and conflicted public character.

With no mention of production, copyright, content or styles of publishing, an emphasis on public but no clear idea what that means, a sense of social institutions, although a double sense failing to illumine that public character, European and Latinate origins, dictionary definitions of publishing edge towards extreme circularity.[5] Study the dictionary long enough and any word has a 'complex of senses', to once again quote Raymond Williams (1983). I am interested in the specific complexity of publishing.[6] Having worked through layers of meaning and historical residue we are left with a good deal of semantic friction and a strange beast indeed.

Such etymological and lexicographical analysis sketches many of the main conflicts characterising the problematicity of publishing. Statistical tools give added weight. While I do recognise its limitations, the Google Ngram Viewer is particularly helpful.

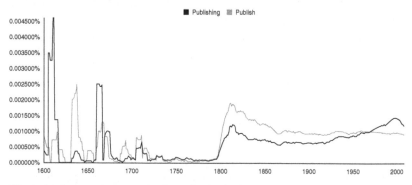

(Vertical axis: usage instances; horizontal axis: time)

The above graph charts uses of 'publishing' against 'publish' from 1600–c.2010. Note fluctuations in the seventeenth century,

---

5 Take the More (1529) quote from above.

6 Obsolete usages are also useful, notably *OED* II 7. 'To populate (a country, etc.); (refl.) to reproduce, multiply, breed'; similar to 'peoplish', another old word. While there is no space in this book to elaborate, this comes closest to my theory of what constitutes the core of book publishing.

although with fewer books published and no discernible trends there are limitations to what this tells us. Publishing and publish are out of phase. In the 1640s, when there was a large spike in book releases and, of course, political turmoil in the English Civil War (Barnard and McKenzie 2002; Feather 2005), so there is a spike in use of the word 'publish'. Most of the eighteenth century is perhaps unexpectedly fallow; the age of the coffee house and, in the typical Habermasian scheme, the public sphere has few mentions of either word until the 1790s when there is an explosion of both. This corresponds to a second significant spurt in novels published in the UK (Moretti 2007),[7] hinting at a connection between the novel form and publishing. Around this time, the modern publishing house, including Thomas Longman and John Murray, emerges from other sections in the value chain. Unstable and ill defined in the seventeenth century, structural evolution and generic formation allow both 'publishing' and 'publish' to enter the lexicon in forms corresponding to contemporary usage. Through the crises of the seventeenth century they emerged from institutional uses. Lastly, note 'publishing' overtakes 'publish' in the mid-twentieth century. Did the industry, as it expanded, consolidated and professionalised, become more monolithic and of greater importance in the minds of writers and readers?

Predating the normalisation of 'publish' and 'publishing', there is a strong relationship between these words and 'book', although use of 'book' rises rapidly around the time Moretti (2007) sees the first boom in novel publications in the mid-eighteenth century, displacing an easy association between 'book' and 'publishing'.

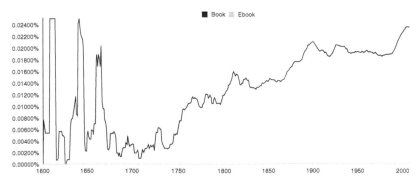

(Vertical axis: usage instances; horizontal axis: time; mentions of the word 'ebook' are so infrequent as to seem nonexistent)

---

7 Using the Ngram Viewer is an example of the kind of 'distant reading' favoured by Moretti (2007).

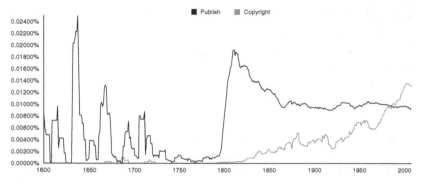

(Vertical axis: usage instances; horizontal axis: time)

Intriguingly 'copyright' is now more widely used than 'publishing'. 'Copyright', as we shall see, is important in publishing, but seems to have superseded it even before the rise of open-source software and the Internet instigated a wave of soul searching. Other publishable media have encroached on traditional book-publishing territory.

The history of 'publishing' and 'publish' reveals an activity wherein the more one looks the more one sees a protean concept marked with clear associations including books, novels, print media and media generally, public or announcing functions, institutions and power, business and money; but these associations, especially the grey area around the idea of 'making something public', are left loose and unexplained. Words and usages change over time. They do so for good reasons. As with investigations of all such keywords, far from learning what publishing is or does, we are left with unanswered questions.

Instances from History

Thanks to its long and not undistinguished record one might be tempted to say that publishing as an industry has a greater sense of history than other creative fields. In my experience this is not the case. Memories are short; today's worries are paramount. However, examining moments in publishing history reveals how, despite superficial similarities, there has never been an obvious thing called 'publishing'. Here I look at three historical examples in terms of how they break apart simplistic ideas of publishing.

1. Anton Koberger (1440/1445–1513): Koberger was a *bona fide* Renaissance man, a scholar, printer, publisher, merchant, entrepreneur, civic leader, reader, aesthetic visionary and regional magnate. Koberger was born to Nuremberg burgomeisters and, like Gutenberg,

trained as a goldsmith. He ran probably the largest printer of the fifteenth century, publishing works from the likes of Boethius, Duns Scotus, Thomas Aquinas, St Augustine and St Jerome. In the fifteenth century, publishing and printing were virtually interchangeable, with the functions of actually producing a book eliding with the act of publishing it, although binding, distribution and bookselling were all, usually, distinct. Koberger embodied this elision but with some variations; for example, he sometimes worked as only a printer, while at other times he operated as publisher and bookseller (or market maker). Today he is best remembered for producing one of the most important incunabula, the *Nuremberg Chronicle* (*Liber Chronicarum*) by Hartmann Schedel. A lavish, full-colour example of a medieval world history, including, among much else, detailed histories of German cities illustrated by over 2,000 woodcuts. Koberger would often publish on his own account, but not in this instance. Two wealthy and enlightened businessmen, Sebald Schreyer and Sebastian Kammermeister, instigated the project, and bore the cost of production and sales risk. Koberger made print and typographical decisions;[8] his vast number of presses (24, at a time when most printers had one or two) and a hundred artisans made him the most industrious printer in Europe. For his most famous work, Koberger was far from a publisher in the modern sense; he did not commission, own, market or sell the *Nuremberg Chronicle*, which places him in the same position as a modern-day printer.

Such was the scale of Koberger's operation we can safely associate him with printing. Yet according to Febvre and Martin, he was 'the most powerful publisher of his day' who 'bought out [...] at least 236 books, most of them of the first importance' (Febvre and Martin 2010, 124). Unusually he kept a bindery under the same roof as his presses. He cultivated many local connections, and published books specifically for local ecclesiastical markets and university curricula; he created a vast network of sellers and scouts through all the great German cities and as far afield as Budapest, Bruges, Florence and Paris.[9] He acted as a mentor to figures like the humanist printer Jean Amerbach, was a friend and collaborator of Erasmus, and godfather to Albrecht Dürer.[10] He owned paper mills, was an appointee of the municipal Great Council

---

8 See Morse Library (2003).

9 He commanded an apprentice, Busch, to find the best-learned manuscripts on his sales tour of Italy (Febvre and Martin 2010).

10 Eisenstein (1980) sees the presence of Koberger as crucial in the development of Dürer's art and by extension a whole new type of Renaissance artist, a market-playing entrepreneur (*Economist* 2011).

and became one of the richest men in Nuremberg. He was not simply a printer then, but someone with diverse interests, embedded in the Northern Renaissance, risking large amounts of capital on innovative industrial processes, organisations and cultural products. He was productively enmeshed in the religious, legal and pedagogical institutions of his time and region in that characteristically ambiguous way of publishers, at once a supplicant supplier and a social and intellectual equal, with a deep knowledge of theology and scholastic philosophy.

Koberger is an extreme instance of fifteenth-century publishing. On the one hand, he is a maker of objects, albeit in advanced fashion. He prints rather than involve himself with too many decisions and he works for hire. On the other, he is a scholar and aesthete, publishing the finest works of philosophy in new forms on his own account, building large distribution networks and actively making markets, as in his instrumental role in establishing the early Frankfurt Book Fair. This duality cuts across most printers of the time; they tread a tightrope between artisan craft and textual learning, work for hire and trading on their own account. Copyright is largely an irrelevance. Cash is not. We can thus say that Koberger, as a prototypical early publisher, is more printer than anything; but the sheer act of printing in those early days was often enough to make someone a publisher without exhausting the idea of publishing.

2. Henry Herringman (1628–1704): Early British publishing was largely focused on London, and had nothing to compete with the scale of Koberger. The earliest British printers like William Caxton and Wynkyn de Worde followed the model of blended publishers and printers. Herringman is one instance of where publishing made a decisive break with the production of print. In Koberger's time, intellectual property was weak and ill defined where it existed at all; piracy was common and ownership of a text was an uncertain status to say the least. Under such circumstances it's no surprise we rarely find publishing without the anchoring effect of the press. Henry Herringman, initially a Restoration printer and bookseller, was one of the first to make the break, turning England's unique publishing landscape to his advantage. Tightly controlled by the Company of Stationers guild, printing was regulated by successive Licensing Acts from 1662. There was an institutional and legal structure in place allowing a measure of tradable intellectual property (IP) known as 'rights in copies'.[11] As

---

11 This grew out of the Company of Stationers' Court of Assistants. Company members could claim their rights in a work, much like the Company Register, which 'allowed' books for publication.

early as 1565, Masters of the Company were holding rights in copies independently of printing them, becoming owners of IP they neither produced, distributed or sold, but nonetheless accruing benefits from that ownership (Feather 2006). At the time, many of the most profitable works like bibles or books of statutes were held as monopolies, granted by the Crown to select publishers from the Company of Stationers and over which they held a budding copyright.

Herringman, initially working in this context as a bookseller and publisher, had got out of the business of printing or selling books by 1684. He bought rights in many of the key writers of his day, including poets like Milton and Donne, dramatists like Middleton and Jonson, and most successfully of all, John Dryden, who had possibly worked for Herringman in the 1660s. Feather (2006) argues this is an example of a modern publishing relationship: Herringman viewed Dryden as a good long-term investment, with backlist potential, widespread popular appeal in the short term and literary value. Dryden defined the literary age, and having Herringman as a backer didn't hurt. Herringman's experience, connections and proven ability to sell books would have been valuable to Dryden before he eventually left Herringman in 1678, around the time he published *Oedipus*. Herringman was also involved with three others in financing the fourth folio edition of Shakespeare. He bought copyright early in translations of Horace's *Lyrics*; and he acquired the entire copyright estate of another publisher, Humphrey Moseley. From the 1680s Herringman had a considerable, if not unrivalled, portfolio of *belle lettres*, either bought from other copyholders or direct, enabling him to jettison his retail business in 1684 and become Master of the Company of Stationers a year later.

Herringman was new. His business model of buying rights, repackaging books and extracting value over the long term will be recognisable to many publishers today. He was foremost an owner of copyrights, a rentier capitalist, who dealt with the intangibles of intellectual property and financial instruments to net gains and build a business. Unlike Koberger, Herringman is so instinctively a publisher because he built a firm on copyright, even if the scale of printing was much smaller in the UK with only 72 presses in the whole country (Barnard and McKenzie 2002). Herringman built lists over the long term when the presence of piracy meant others couldn't. Indeed, the very concept of lists makes more sense in the context of Herringman than Koberger. Herringman was an early mover in the gradual shift towards a total separation of publishing from other steps in the circulation of books, by establishing ownership of copyright as the centrepiece of a practice closer to merchant banking than artisanal manufacturing. One of the more active publishers of his age, Herringman was constantly looking for new ways to extract value from old or under-published texts, a hallmark of publishing instinct. He also provided a model for other owners, including families from whom he bought inherited copyrights for his already extensive collection.[12] This is publishing not as a maker of books or markets, but as the owner and judicious investor of risk capital.

3. The Game: By the early nineteenth century, publishing had become a recognised activity on either side of the Atlantic, spurred on by the rise of superstar writers like Byron, Scott and later Dickens. The market for these products was increasingly global and voracious, which, in the absence of an international copyright regime until the 1880s, meant working on a very different basis to the burgeoning intellectual property market Herringman so skilfully exploited. Rather publishing in America turned into what participants called 'The Game', a reprinting race to market in which a publisher's greatest asset was their ability to print text at astonishing speed, beating other pirated editions and buying a fleeting window of monopoly.

Industrial printing techniques meant works could be printed much faster than on traditional hand presses, just as demand was (unevenly) rising thanks to growing literacy and disposable income. Major antebellum publishers like the Careys and the Harper brothers knew that if they got hold of a manuscript first, they had a brief window before others piled in with cheap pirated reprints. Everything was about getting the book out first: often they would have an agent working in London whose purpose was not to buy rights so much as secure a manuscript first, which would then be sent express to the United States. The Carey's agent, John Miller, offered £100 for the manuscript of *Nicholas Nickleby*, which was then couriered by the new steamship, the *Great Western*, before being rushed off the presses to cash in on the exclusivity.

Publishers would employ multiple printers working all hours to get books ready. Henry Carey, for instance, employed 30 presses to print

---

12   Gaining a detailed purchase on the exact economics at work is not always easy: 'There is still no satisfactory model of the economics of the London trade which usefully structures the dense and complex relationships between writers, printers, booksellers and readers during the hand-press period' (Barnard and McKenzi 2002, 553).

editions of Byron's *Don Juan* in 36 hours in 1826. By the mid-1820s the Harpers developed a noticeably slick and sizeable printing operation, occupying a large printing house on Cliff Street in New York. Dirty tricks were common, printers were bribed to give up manuscripts; price wars were instigated against imported British editions; reviewers were bribed to read from a certain edition; texts would even be changed in order to claim copyright on a new work. In metropolitan centres like New York and Philadelphia pirated editions would sometimes appear within hours of initial publication. On his American tour of 1842 Dickens railed against the practice as outright theft.[13] The reprint formed an ecosystem of publishing with effects that rippled outward from the first release, extracting new layers of value and finding new audiences with each new version:

> A Dickens novel might appear first in a good quality reprint by Carey or some other respectable firm; then in a cheap piracy of that reprint; then in chapbooks; then in serialised forms; then in provincial newspapers; then in 25¢ 'rail-road' editions; and finally as chapters printed on railway timetables. (Johns 2009, 303)

Moreover the system was highly profitable. Between 1824 and 1826 the Careys made the vast sum of $500,000. It also led to extreme instability and ultimately collapsing prices, margins and sales.

Eventually a truce was called and an informal compromise, known as the 'Courtesy of the Trade' or the 'Harper Rule', was put in place. Despite not altogether eradicating the Game it introduced a degree of stability – even though it would take decades to establish a formal international rights system the Harpers, for example, profitably introduced America to giants of contemporary British writing like the Brontë sisters, George Eliot, W. M. Thackeray and indeed Charles Dickens. The transatlantic reprint trade contrasts strongly with Herringman and Koberger. For the former, the emergent forms of copyright were central to his business model; for the latter, it was the ability to produce books in large quantities amid general print scarcity. Neither condition held for Americans like Fletcher Harper. Even at this relatively advanced stage in publishing history, they were, like news or reprint publishing, about speed of delivery. Piracy has a long history bound up with notions of law, commerce, creativity and inclusion, but not usually publishing. Yet here, contrary to

---

13 The Harpers, having taken Scott's *Peveril of the Peak* off the boat before it even docked saw editions on the bookstalls in only 21 hours, comfortably beating the Careys (Tebbel 1987).

the idea that publishing is based on copyright, publishing is largely about piracy, and that idea of making public is about speed, not ownership or simply a matter of printing books. In spite of (or because of) this it was an exciting time in American publishing producing many familiar names: John Wiley, Charles Scribner and George Palmer Putnam in New York, Henry Houghton, Charles C. Little and James Brown in Boston.

From Nuremberg to New York, there can be no history of publishing, only publishings. For a start, we might ask to what extent people can realistically be considered publishers *avant la lettre*. We would also be surprised if publishing hadn't drastically changed. These three episodes offer examples that are all recognisably book publishing, but have distinct operational modes and rationales. Different goals, identities and economics are in play. They demonstrate what historically elusive and strangely evolved creatures publishers must be. What common ground do they share that we can call publishing? History of the book scholars have long recognised this troubled history.[14] Using this genealogy we can ask: is publishing in fact a series of disjunctures factitiously grouped under a common term, mistakenly aligned out of an interest in books? Perhaps we should no more compare them than we do typographical blacksmithing and social media marketing.

Publishing Media

Books and publishing make a comfortable combination. However, a great deal of publishing's complexity lies in its traversal of media forms. If we can publish sound, image and text, what does that imply about publishing? Given the products are so different, what level of equivalence can we establish between them? An analysis of other media offers new perspectives on what it means to be published. Over the past forty years, desktop and web publishing have become increasingly important, but I regard them as belonging in the chapter on digital challenges. Equally, there are such variations within the book publishing industry, between say an STM textbook and a historical romance, one can barely call them a single business. I don't underestimate these differences, but focus instead on uses of the term beyond books.

1. *Music publishing* started in much the same way as book publishing: print publishers cranked out print matter disseminated through a

---

14 'The word "publisher" is anachronistic, except for the last century, and conceals a tissue of complex relationships between the roles of patron, printer, stationer and bookseller' (Adams and Barker 2006, 50).

network of resellers, dominated by monopolies in places like England and Venice. In the eighteenth century, there emerged a series of prominent German music publishers like Breitkopf & Härtel, who published composers including Haydn, Mozart, Beethoven, Liszt and Mendelssohn. In the nineteenth century, publishers like Chappell & Co. of Bond Street in London took up a similar role. By the end of the nineteenth century, action had shifted to New York's notorious Tin Pan Alley (or West 28th Street, if you prefer), where a crowded riot of music publishers mingled with the Broadway vaudeville community to find and circulate the hottest tunes. Recorded music quickly transformed the industry, leaving most of the power, not to mention glamour, in the hands of the recording industry, leading to a fundamental split between publishers and record companies.

Music publishers, the largest of which is currently Sony/ATV, occupy a distinct place in the music industry as a result. Whereas book publishers are typically the primary intermediary and certainly the product's obvious business manager, music is controlled by both record companies and publishers, who act as a kind of rights controller. Publishers collect royalties, usually either mechanical (referring to sales of CDs and the like by a record company), performance (for example, from ringtones and the radio) or the growing area of synchronisation (where music is played alongside moving images).[15] Bands are paid to promote products, licence ringtones, or write for films; and publishers conduct this process helped by an architecture of national licensing bodies. Tension emerged between record companies and publishers, as the former looked to secure airplay for their unit sales model, while the latter remained opposed, seeing revenue opportunity missed and, worse, business undermined. The controversial practice of payola (paying radio stations to play a song, rather than vice versa under a publishing model) is unsurprisingly anathema to publishers and outlawed by the industry.

Recorded music sales entered a crisis after the launch of file-sharing service Napster in 1999. According to industry body the IFPI, worldwide sales were down 30 per cent 2004–2009. Publishers and artists usually split revenues 50/50, and with this collapse in the CD market publishers

---

15 'While mechanical royalties have diminished along with the physical sales of recorded music, both performance and synchronisation royalties have increased since the turn of the millennium' (Wikström 2009, 93). The value of this can be seen in the high price paid by Sony for EMI's publishing division, higher than the cost of EMI the record company. See Novak (1984).

have managed to claw back some of their old status as the industry's principal movers, even in some areas owning master recordings, a traditional stronghold of record companies (Wikström 2009).

Music publishing isn't about selling units. Instead it resembles a large amalgam of a book publisher's rights department and a library collections agency, a characterisation that nonetheless distorts its enormous position in the wider field of music. One way of thinking about how this contrasts with a basic conception of book publishing is to compare purchasing a book in a shop as a published product and hearing a song on an advert, again, a published product. Hearing music in this sense is intangible not only in the physical sense, but also in a more philosophical sense. To hear music broadcast is to experience something beyond the control of the subject, experienced fleetingly and in concert with other media. Ontologically, experientially and even economically the two products are incommensurable: yet both are published. Music publishers, unlike book publishers, are rarely involved in the creative process or the production, packaging, distribution and positioning of works. Yet they earn massive revenues spreading music to new areas and in new forms, following a business model very different to the recorded music industry, which is the most obvious counterpart to book publishing. Two axes are at work here, first, in the nature of the product published, and second, in the practices constituting publishing.

2. As with music, when it comes to *video games* the alterity of the thing published is striking. Again, lazy associations with print publishing are untenable. Video games are interactive and visual, like film incorporating music, actors, production departments and vast development budgets – a single triple-A game often costs upwards of $40 million to produce, astronomical sums alien to even the largest book publishers.[16] Indeed, the video games industry resembles the Hollywood studio system as much as a book or music publisher. Creative teams called studios are responsible for producing games either funded or licensed by a publisher, large commercial organisations that are acquiring studios in ever-greater numbers. Such a structure is not wholly unfamiliar to book publishers: a primary

---

16 These expenditures are reflected in earnings: Activision Blizzard's *Call of Duty: Modern Warfare 3* made over $1 billion in its first week of sales. Such figures are found virtually no where else in publishing and mark out video games as one of the strongest commercial growth areas of contemporary pan-platform publishing – global revenues are projected at $68 billion for 2012, 10.3 per cent growth, year on year. See Caron (2008).

creator, the author or studio, deals with an asymmetric intermediary, the publisher, who manages various aspects of 'making the work public' including distribution, marketing, publicity and sales. Despite being a digitally native industry this principle of organisation has proved remarkably resilient in an era of allegedly seamless distribution – witness *Angry Birds* creator Rovio's use of publisher Chillingo, an intermediary whose almost sole function was to bring the game to an Apple employee's attention, a small act responsible for seeding the game's phenomenal success (Cheshire 2011).

Free-to-play gaming is an important part of the industry. It relies on a select band of die-hard fans for monetisation. Recently a line of products known as massively multiplayer online games exploded the unit sales ideal by creating virtual, ongoing worlds complete with geographies, histories and even fully convertible currencies. Here what is being published is not so much a discrete product as the wholesale simulation, maintenance and monetisation of a reality. On the other hand, a simple ludic game like *Pong* involves only basic interactions and no graphics by current standards. Yet it is a game just like the highly evolved *Skyrim* or *World of Warcraft*. This is a gulf indeed – there is almost nothing in common here except interactivity. Interactivity itself is what's published.

3. *Newspaper, periodical and magazine publishing* dates back to at least 1665 in the UK – and earlier still elsewhere, if you include *acta diurna* in ancient Rome, *tipao* in China, medieval almanacs, news sheets, *gazetas* in Italy, *Zeitungs* in Germany. Their long, initially close, history and shared reliance on text has created superficial similarities between the book and newspaper industries. Writers, printers and readers once occupied a common network of inchoate news and book publishing. Newspapers pioneered many developments in print, including faster, wider distribution, more efficient typesetting and the process of industrialisation that so spurred print volumes from the turn of the nineteenth century. As with other forms of publishing we note a separation between content production and commercial arms; typically a magazine or newspaper has an editor responsible for content and a publisher responsible for business matters. There is, however, a blurring between outside and inside, similar to when a games publisher buys a studio. Newspapers are filled with outside input – they are half content producers, half content buyers, as per book publishers. Newspapers purchase and package material from newswires, freelancers, photographers, video teams and picture agencies.

Content licensing and syndication from and to third parties are important for the industry. So not only do they confuse lines between internal/external content generation, but they are enmeshed in a contorted formation of business models.

Newspaper or magazine publishing is cut four ways – between commercial concerns and symbolic imperatives (on broadsheets couched as a desire to report the facts), but also between a split audience – readers and advertisers, for whom that audience is the product. This is reflected in the revenue split, with the newspapers earning 57 per cent of their revenues worldwide from advertising (OECD 2010). Newspaper publishing sits across two value chains as a result, not so much looking for sales as third-party revenues; in this case sales, or success, is not just correlated with unit sales volumes but also perceived advertiser value:

> The traditional role of newspaper publishers is to intermediate between content producers (journalists), information users, and advertisers and other attention seekers. Publishers select, check, integrate and package information, on the one hand, and they aggregate demand for information into audiences on the other. They distribute information and sell 'access to audiences' to advertisers acting as intermediaries in a two sided market. Finally, yet importantly, they spread the costs of information production and distribution over a large number of users and advertisers, and consequently make information not only physically but economically accessible to users. (OECD 2010, 56)

Although there are some games publishers looking at sponsorship or ad models, few book publishers work on anything like this basis. Cost structures reflect the stance – only 24 per cent of expenditure is on editorial or content-related activity, with the rest spent on items like marketing, distribution, promotion and production. This tends to run against newspaper protestations of the expense of news-gathering operations, something underlined by their traditionally healthy margins. Unlike games or music publishing newspapers have an innately topical yet wholly undefined product: news. Also unlike them is an institutional status as supplementary to a prior social structure, taking us back to those early usages. A trade magazine about, say, flower arranging, exists as a service to the edifice of flower arranging and must buy into its codes, mores and values for its ability to publish to that audience. Publishing the news brings a raft of selection and framing dilemmas beloved of media theorists, a generic fuzziness present but less noticeable in other forms of publishing.

Publishing spans media. Take again the example of a song played in an advert. The sounds themselves are experienced through the media of either radio or television, transmitting the media of sound; both are broadcast, yet the music is there via publishing. Thus sound is simultaneously broadcast and published. But publishing sound in this way doesn't quite work – somehow the immediacy and presence of sound in any form, doesn't cohere with our notions of publishing. It is too active, live and interventionist.[17]

The communications theorist Bernard Miège (1989) contrasted what he called 'publishing logic' with 'flow logic' or a broadcast model.[18] If publishing logic is about selling discrete units of content with a royalty for creators, flow logic is about continuous programming and mass audiences. They both share one feature which has, over the past ten or fifteen years and well after Miège (1989) described them, proved utterly transformational: the web. As we will see, if Miège (1989) is to fully account for digital convergence we need to re-evaluate publishing logic. Worth highlighting, too, are their respective sizes in terms of revenue. According to the OECD, 2009 newspaper revenues capped $164 billion; all books across consumer, STM and education were $112 billion; video games were $55 billion, while recorded music was $27 billion and films $85 billion (although the last two are not clearly publishing).

Mahler's *Ninth Symphony*, a *Harry Potter* puzzle, *Le Monde*, a book of Lucien Freud paintings and *Grand Theft Auto*: these are all published, despite having different cultural registers, stylistic features, media formats, business models, audiences, organisational systems, types of creator, temporal and geographical roots. What conception of publishing makes these strands cohere? Or have we falsely grouped a set of disorderly practices?

What Publishing Is Not

To dispel myths about what publishing might be, we must establish core activities. We have to ask, is this or that element always part of

---

17 Audiobooks are a halfway house – at one level they are sound, at another just another format of a text like a paperback or an ebook. They are sufficiently close to a book to easily absorb the associations of 'book publishing' rather than 'music publishing'.

18 The newspaper press has a logic of its in Miège's (1989) system, somewhere between the other two.

publishing? If the answer is no, the activity isn't integral. Publishing is irreducible to that element. Immediately this begs the question of whether there could ever be unchanging integral parts of such a social, evolving activity. Social constructivists would argue against: publishing under their rubric would simply be the clustering of activities that reflects the arbitrary character of all social entities.

By demonstrating what publishing is not the argument presupposes a realist view of publishing as a consistent, intelligible and historically coherent thread of practice. This is not to essentialise publishing, but to interpret it as a comprehensible, continuous but nonetheless changing *system*. This method reveals the modularity of publishing, picking and choosing functions to produce utterly different organisations and outputs. Clark and Phillips make this point:

> Publishers can choose which elements of the value chain they undertake themselves, and which are outsourced to third parties. For example, while commissioning new titles is usually done in-house, copy-editing and proofreading are typically carried out by freelance editors. The key elements of the value chain are the acquisition of intellectual property, editorial, design and production, marketing, and sales, and most publishers will control these functions directly. Publishers can look to combine stages of the value chain and, for example, editorial, design and production may be combined into one function. (Clark and Phillips 2008, 68)

First, note the modularity of how the value chain's links can be swapped in and out of house at will. Secondly, consider the 'key elements', which arguably hold for modern book publishing but can't for transhistorical and transmedia conceptions of publishing.

We can immediately disassociate publishing from both the primary creation of content and the production of a print product (or moving to the digital realm, even the production of code). Writing a book, as Thomas More (1529) implied, is not the same as publishing it. The boundary between printing and publishing was, as we saw in the early days of print, unclear, yet even here there is a distinction – sometimes Koberger was simply the printer, otherwise he was the publisher; sometimes the closeness of the two would make them inseparable at first glance, but there is nonetheless a demarcation between publishing and cast metal.

Distribution is another constant. However, again, this has always been separable. In the fifteenth century, distribution was in the hands of itinerant journeyman booksellers carrying stacks of unbound manuscripts from town to town. As with printing, lines were often blurred: publishers would keep networks of agents across the main bookselling centres of Europe, running their own cross-border distribution networks. As we saw with Herringman, publishing also had significant crossover with bookselling itself – the printing workshop, publishing house and bookshop were often the same place in the first centuries of printing. Contemporary publishers like Random House and Macmillan own distribution arms distinct from their publishing operations, the profitability of which relies on contracting to third parties. Distribution has always been part of bringing products to market, but it may or may not be part of the process of publishing. In itself then, this raises a problem discussed earlier – simply making something available – distributing it – does not in itself constitute publishing even if it is a necessary condition for it.

In his discussion of the music industry, Patrick Wikström (2009) calls it a 'copyright industry', for him a more accurate term than either 'creative' or 'cultural' industry. Placing intellectual property as the major constituent of publishing is tempting for several reasons. The stock of contracts, what John Thompson (2010) calls a publisher's 'intellectual capital', is one of its prime assets. Separable from either printing or distribution, holding intellectual property has been central to the trade. Arguably publishing consists of a copyright market, a view neatly tying together all the forms of publishing that share this element. However, as the example of early American publishing shows, this, too, is insufficient.

Publishing often occurs without a framework of intellectual property rights, or at least ignores such a framework, not only in the fifteenth century but today, and not just on the Internet. In countries with weaker notions of IP, publishing is routinely undertaken by those not in possession of rights. Licences like Creative Commons or Open Access are by no means exclusively digital phenomena. They are predicated on copyright but challenge some of its business assumptions. While copyright has become bound up with publishing, it is wrong to traduce publishing to copyright. Doing so removes a large amount of historical, contemporary and indeed future activity from the aegis of publishing. Adrian Johns (2009) persuasively argues that piracy has a creative and ambiguous history; publishing and piracy overlap.

Having dealt with some commonly outsourced features we can confidently skip other regularly outsourced elements like design, copyediting or proofreading. They may be essential parts of the value chain but are not at the conceptual core of publishing, as they cannot account for all forms of publishing. Many aspects of how publishers engage content, from editorial development and outside readers through to final checks on quality, aren't intrinsic to the act of publishing.

Regardless of the flavour of publishing in question, it does not comprise the value chain but is an element of it. Like proofreading, publishing is itself a node on the value chain, as well as in some sense comprising the value chain.

In recent years, marketing and publicity have grown in prominence, becoming core competencies for Anglo-American publishers. At root, marketing and publicity returns us to the idea of market making, whereby a publisher creates and finds audiences for a work – publishing as the means by which works come to attention. Marketing and publicity, like copyright, are shared across all forms of publishing, and as with copyright are attractive building blocks for a theory of publishing. Like copyright they are ultimately too limiting and suffer a conceptual failure. Marketing and publicity functions are usually separate from the thing being marketed or publicised, whereas publishing and the thing published are part of the same process. That is to say, publishing is part of the creation of a work, whereas marketing and publicity are ancillary and after-the-fact processes, the increased role of marketing in content decisions, strategies and indeed creation notwithstanding (Squires 2007). If we can safely modularise and disconnect marketing and publicity – in any case often undertaken by specialist out-of-house agencies – can we disconnect market making in a broader sense? Not so easily. We have found something core. In addition, the above argument depends on a seemingly obvious incorporation of content as an essential part of the mix: without content, there is no publishing. In order to publish, you need something to publish. Another core element.

Commissioning, or the acquisition of content, would logically follow as a core area of publishing as well. Yet, even commissioning varies greatly, some publishers commission from scratch, others work with agents, others have a blend of strategies. Different sectors come with different biases in commissioning. Some rely on reading, others on quantitative research; some on contacts, some on legacies or existing brands. Some commissioning is about contract publishing, others about learned societies. Some commissioners are in-house, others academics on editorial boards. Nor is commissioning a universal category – some publishers are obliged for reasons of ownership, contract or expediency to publish certain works, the commissioning element taken out of their hands. Content acquisition is not always 'commissioned' as such but frequently bought after submission. Equally many publishers are repackagers or reprinters of content. While it might seem an unproblematic cross-form element of publishing commissioning is in fact highly variable. The whole gamut of editorial or creative input can tell us no more than that publishing involves content.

If we accept the modular thesis, that the precise constitution of a given publisher is a historically contingent assortment of roles, then might we think of publishing as a content-dependent management exercise? Publishers are the overseers of a process resulting in cultural products entering the public realm, but that process need not be specified in advance. This managerialism operates in an abstract sense, conflating publishing with what publishers claim to be. Thus publishers may choose to work on commissioning and publicity while outsourcing production and distribution; this no more means those are fundamental than if the situation was reversed, as it often was in the incunabula period. If we break down the traditional processes of the book – papermaking, publishing, text creation, printing, binding, bookselling and distribution – publishing is simply the initiating or controlling influence. The point is publishers are managers, coordinators or catalysts. Supple enough to satisfy a constructivist view of social organisation, like the definition of publishing as 'to make public' this view ultimately doesn't help. It can't tell us what impact publishing has on texts and effectively aligns publishing as just one activity among many, but essentially undifferentiated from them. Saying publishing is whatever we call publishing is a circular and superficial way of apprehending the world. If we maintain publishing has a discrete identity, as I do, then this view cannot hold.

Lastly, let's examine the claim that publishing is a service. Going back to connections with prior institutions like the church or state, we can view publishing as a service industry providing them with the materials they needed. Bible and theological publishing developed as a service to the church.[19] Another example is the development of science into a discipline complete with the apparatus of a modern institution:

---

19 Furthering this line of thought, we can view the history of schisms and reformulations of orthodoxy in Christian thought as driven by publishing as well.

centres of power and productivity such as research universities and laboratories beginning in Germany; a codified system of accepted best practices – the scientific method; august bodies to validate claims, like the Royal Society; and of course a network of communications (publications) tying it all together. *The Proceedings of the Royal Society* has a continuous publication history dating back to 1800, around when the systematisation of science began taking modern form;[20] the first publication of *Nature*, to this day the world's most cited journal, dates back to 1869, when the professionalisation of science in the UK started apace. It published the great scientists of the day like Thomas Huxley and Herbert Spencer, both of whom were part of an informal dining society, the X Club, whose members shaped late nineteenth-century science.

Both publications might thus be seen as services, parasitic but supportive, contained but contributory, to their wider institutional space. Here publishing is part of the production of discourse and knowledge as socially constituted and institutionally founded. We see this today in the ongoing service relationship of academic publishing to the academy – the culture of research benchmarking initiatives and 'publish or perish' academic career paths is serviced by an insatiable, not to mention highly profitable, academic publishing industry. University departments become writing factories, spewing out research to be published in a welter of expensive journals paid for by those same universities.

There are two issues here. Publishing is not simply an appendage. *Nature* wasn't just a sideshow to the business of science in the late nineteenth century; it was deeply engaged in its professionalisation, systematisation and growth, just as its prestige still makes it a power broker in the scientific community, allocating funding, setting research agendas and making careers. The many debates surrounding printing's role in the Reformation make clear the act of publication has profound implications far beyond simply being a service, as with Luther and his allies. Far from subservience, publishing is symbiotically involved with entities like church and state.

Plenty of publishers are, of course, unconnected to any institutions: trade or consumer publishers. When publishers became recognisably

---

20 The *Philosophical Transactions of the Royal Society* meanwhile has a continuous publication history dating back to 1665, the longest of any scientific journal in the world, although it is just predated by the *Journal des Sçavans* as the first example of modern scholarly publishing.

distinct so, too, did the Romantic artist, brilliant, individualistic and answering only to a sublime aesthetic. Arguably publishing poetry is a service to poets, or poetry. Publishers do sometimes publish solely because they see intrinsic worth. As editorial director at Faber & Faber, T. S. Eliot was primarily interested in what he saw as the poetic value of submissions, not their commercial character. We might also say, well, publishing is just a service to authors. But then we just push the question back, as we would then surely ask: if publishing is a service to authors what kind of service is it and what does it do?

What do we have left? Content. Market making. Making public. An element of risk perhaps, not necessarily, but commonly, financial. Any theory of publishing must connect these dots, all of which span the history of publishing and its different forms, definitions and possibilities.

Why We Need a Theory of Publishing

This survey makes no claims to being exhaustive. The purpose is to create trouble, to suggest a greater underlying level of complexity than might first appear, not elaborate on the many histories, forms, practices and uses of publishing. Set out is an aporia requiring explanation. Suffice to say, most publishers aren't plagued by philosophical doubt. They get on and do the job.

This doesn't mean there isn't a problem. Even if we isolate contemporary book publishing, its modularity means its core whittles down to a few abstract and confused notions still requiring explanation. Aside from this or that activity or this or that product, what is the driver, the common factor? Inevitably, the closer one looks the more problems arise and the more publishing becomes, to return to Williams (1983), a keyword, with multiple, elusive connections to other problematic concepts.

Publishing is neither clear, easy or adequately accounted for. We have little sense of how its different usages, histories, modalities and internal functions blend to form divergent, emergent and slippery acts of intermediation. Before the advent of digital we still needed a grand unified theory of publishing.

Chapter 2

THE DIGITAL CONTEXT
AND CHALLENGE

A sense that the written word is seeing the greatest transformation since Gutenberg is, despite becoming a cliché, not unwarranted. Not only are books and publishing experiencing the most profound transition since the dawn of the press but our entire communications paradigm is witnessing arguably the greatest change in history. Moreover we are still in the early phases of digital technology. Over the coming decades it will undoubtedly evolve in unexpected ways. To paraphrase Zhou Enlai on the French Revolution, even by the end of the present century it will be too soon to tell regarding the digital revolution. The impact has been felt across sectors and publishing is no exception. Such technologies beg the questions what is a book and what does publishing it mean?

In response has been the ballooning of what author Ewan Morrison (2012) calls a 'speculative meta-practice',[1] a series of discussions across conferences, blogs, email lists, seminars, industry consortia, newspapers and consultations, and indeed in books like this, dissecting the emergence of digital publishing in minute detail. Every move by publishers, retailers, start-ups and technology firms has been closely scrutinised. For a number of years the joke was that the best way to make money in digital publishing was to host a conference. In such changeable conditions adding to this debate in long form is doomed. In the space of a week, for example, the iPad transformed digital tablets from a small niche to a mainstream product pursued by all major technology manufacturers. My intention is therefore to avoid speculative meta-practice as much possible, moving beyond immediate concerns. Using contemporary examples, I seek to pick out the underlying trends and tendencies, those truly transformational factors and the deep patterns driving the challenge set by digital publishing.

---

1 See Morrison (2012).

Most visibly, the digital revolution has manifested itself for book publishers in terms of ebooks. As Thompson (2005, 2010) has pointed out, the ebook is only the culmination of changes in the publishing workflow since the 1980s – books only become print at a late stage in the publication process. Most of the actual work on them already takes place in digital formats. Nonetheless ebooks have exercised publishers a great deal. Yet they are neither the most interesting nor the most challenging part of the digital transition. Significant effort ensures ebook behaviour mirrors print. The standard business model for ebooks is, like print, based on unit sales, while the standard workflow, and indeed product, echo those of print books. The only difference is an ebook's immateriality. Nonetheless, moving to the 1s and 0s of binary code caused a host of problems, despite, in many ways, not being such a momentous shift after all.[2]

Desktop publishing's (DTP) early entrance proves digitisation and dematerialisation alone are incapable of disrupting publishing. Rather, the growth of digital *networks* is key. The sociologist Manuel Castells has written extensively on the rise of a 'network society' where changing social formations and advancing digital technology create new cultural forms. The network society is fundamentally altering our communications, creating 'mass self-communication' and convergence, the phenomenon of all media merging in one digital system. The impact of this integration could hardly be more profound. Network topology creates an informational economy, shrinking geographic coordinates, changing patterns of productivity and work, a media and society very different to that of the mid-twentieth century. Networks are about connections, data transferral, linkages, paths and webs of contact. Digital networks represent a vast increase in the capabilities of networks generally and we are still absorbing their consequences.

We can't make straightforward distinctions between media forms, technological environments and social structures. Today, this means sketching the consequences not just of a digital age but more importantly, a network age. An ebook without a network, without a distribution channel, is scarcely more radical than a printed book. An ebook on the open web has a near infinite capacity to be copied and shared,

---

2 In the words of McGuire and O'Leary, 'We are now effectively replicating this ["paper-based"] model for digital: Publishers send files to distributors and retailers, who sell those files to readers, who download them onto various devices and read them when and where they like' (2012, 2).

instantaneously, around the world. The difference is stark. As Castells puts it, 'The emergence of a new electronic communication system characterized by its global reach, its integration of all communication media, and its potential interactivity is changing and will change forever our culture' (Castells 1997, 357). He implies the network does not only reshape the distribution of content; it reshapes content – and us – as well.

To understand the digital challenge we need to uncover the relevant network effects emerging from the Internet (whose name says it all: the network of networks) and ask how they up-end publishing. This chapter looks firstly at histories of communication technology to make the case for a 'digital network', rather than just a digital view. It examines how content might evolve, before looking at the architecture of the network as a means of understanding the real problems of digital: disintermediation and a destabilised copyright. Publishers have hitherto worried about operational problems including digital supply chains, new product creation, commercial terms, contracts, new staff, IT infrastructure and web marketing. They have played down the other two. By and large the initial confusion around digital publishing has abated. Operational factors have been controlled, clear growth strategies laid out, worries managed.

Eventually the network will start to tell. If, as the previous chapter argued, publishing was existentially challenged before digital, then that challenge just got bigger. At its heart lies a deceptively simple and unthreatening question:

If anyone can be a publisher, what makes you a publisher in the first place?

The Origins of Digital Publishing

Publishing has always been about technology, be it papermaking, post-medieval metallurgy or coding HTML 5. When Gutenberg first assembled the press, he brought together a wide ensemble of technologies, processes and ideas for possibly the first time. Technology shapes and drives publishing in a complex interplay of possibilities and reactions, not so much one leading the other as a mutually accommodating dance (see Chapter 4 for more detail). If this is technological determinism, it is of the softest kind. Remarkably the press was relatively stable for the first 350 years of its existence. Presses from the late eighteenth century would have been recognisable to craftsmen in fifteenth-century Mainz.

Change was on its way. In 1800, the polymath and statesman Lord Stanhope produced the first fully iron press, one achievement among many in a career littered with discovery and invention.

Following this, the innovative German printer Friedrich Koenig moved to London in 1804 where he demonstrated his fast steam-powered presses, which he then sold to John Walter, editor of the *Times*, for use on the newspaper.[3] Thereafter change occurred more rapidly and hasn't slackened. In 1843, American Richard M. Hoe invented the rotary printing press and begun lithographic printing, which really took off in 1873 with the arrival of offset lithographic printing, and was followed by hot metal typesetting in 1886. Productivity increased with each new technology, driving printing prices down and potential circulation up.[4] Further innovations continued throughout the twentieth century, including screen printing, dot matrix printing and in the 1970s inkjet printing, which coupled with the PC initiated a revolutionary expansion in the scope of print. Having been static for hundreds of years, printing has come a long way. Yet the fundamental principles behind printing – text and images copied to paper – remain the same. It was an ensemble of technologies starting around the 1940s that would rupture the reign of the press.

The origins of modern computing and digital technology lie (largely) in World War II and Allied attempts to break the 'unbreakable' Nazi code – Enigma – at Bletchley Park in England. Alan Turing and others developed massive and complex machines to vastly increase available computing power[5] based on a series of mathematical, logical and technical breakthroughs. After the war activity shifted to John von Neumann's team at Princeton's Institute of Advanced Studies and Bell Labs in New Jersey, the research arm of AT&T, where the transistor was invented in 1947. A semiconductor acting as an electronic switch, the transistor inscribes binary code, 1s and 0s, in electronic form and is the basis for the panoply of electronic devices we know today. Refinements were made at Bell Labs, Texas Instruments and Fairchild Semiconductors through the 1950s. Slowly computers became part of life – at least, if your life prominently featured big business, government

---

3 Newspapers were much more prevalent in the United States at the time, but thanks to the steam-powered press circulation increased rapidly after its introduction.

4 These breakthroughs are by no means exhaustive. See Howard (2009) for more detail.

5 Hitherto a computer was a person.

agencies or research universities. The UNIX operating system (again from Bell Labs) came in 1969, while 1971 saw the first microprocessor, followed in 1975 by the first microcomputer. Digital technology only went mainstream a couple of years later, notably with the launch in 1977 of the Apple II from a young company founded by Steve Jobs and Steve Wozniak,[6] followed in 1981 by IBM's launch of the PC (personal computer) and then the Apple Macintosh, strikingly, in 1984. From an expensive, rare and unwieldy technology based on punch cards and requiring vast amounts of energy the computer had become, in twenty years, if not ubiquitous then unremarkable. The power of digital technology was evident, but, without a network, without connectivity, the potential for radical disruption was circumscribed.

Since the late 1960s, however, a parallel series of developments had been occurring. The Pentagon's elite research arm ARPA (Advanced Research Projects Agency) created a network of computers, switched on in 1969, the year UNIX was first released. In 1973, two computer scientists, Vint Cerf and Robert Kahn, wrote the underlying protocols of the Internet: TCP/IP (Transmission Control Protocol/Internet Protocol). The key point about TCP/IP is a principle of data packeting, where all information is standardised into units or packets of data, but the network remains utterly neutral as to what the packets contain. It was fundamentally open and designed to avoid central control. These features are, thanks to Cerf and Kahn, ingrained in the Internet and go some way to explaining its disruptive potential. From these beginnings the Internet grew among specialists with some interesting results, such as USENET, a discussion forum based on UNIX emerging from Duke University in 1980, and the first Internet worm, or self-replicating piece of software, from Cornell computer scientist Robert Tappan Morris in 1988.

Only with the now legendary creation of the World Wide Web (WWW) in 1990 by CERN physicist and computer scientist Tim Berners-Lee did the Internet become mainstream. For many years the WWW and the Internet have been synonymous in the public mind, but in fact the WWW sits on top of the Internet which comprises many other layers and types of data traffic. Berners-Lee created a series of protocols and mark-up languages to make the Internet more useable and useful, including HTML (Hypertext Markup Language) and HTTP (Hypertext Transfer Protocol). When in 1993 Marc Andreessen, a young computer scientist at the University of Illinois

---

6 Also the year in which Microsoft was founded.

at Urbana-Champaign, released Mosaic, the first web browser, the pieces were in place for an explosion in Internet use, which grew at phenomenal rates through the 1990s and hasn't stopped since. As of 2012 there were 2.2 billion Internet users, while by 2008 another information technology – mobile phones – saw subscriptions pass 50 per cent of the global population and growing fast (Castells 2009).

These developments in widespread digital computing and connectivity are the poles around which the network society revolves. Their development is heavily intermeshed. A relevant sub-strand to these narratives is the growth of desktop, web and digital book publishing, which like print facilitate replication. Their specific manifestations led to the possibilities and threats now facing contemporary book publishers. Desktop publishing (DTP) started in the 1980s, when computers and software reached levels of sophistication able to match traditional typesetting. MacPublisher was released in 1984; PageMaker followed in 1985 from the Aldus Corporation, which was named after Aldus Manutius, the early Venetian publisher. It was the chairman of the Aldus Corporation, Paul Brainerd, who coined the phrase desktop publishing. The legacy of PageMaker lives on in Adobe's InDesign (PageMaker used Adobe's PostScript language and Adobe acquired the software in 1994). Quark, its great rival, also lives on. The use of publishing was always indicative: this was software not just for creating documents. The simple what-you-see-is-what-you-get (WYSIWYG) interfaces of early programs running on MS-DOS or Mac OS had a fatal flaw – distribution – waiting to be solved by the Internet and web publishing. Everyone now had the means to create *and* disseminate content at the click of a button, a complete transformation from the Gutenberg era.

Michael Hart, founder of Project Gutenberg (which aimed to digitally store and circulate out-of-copyright texts), invented the ebook some years earlier, in 1971. In 1993, Digital Book Inc. was founded to sell ebooks on floppy discs and was followed by publishers like Voyager, which sold ebooks on CDs. Simultaneously, the 1990s saw the release of early ereaders and the formation of the E Ink Corporation at the MIT Media Lab, building on technology first developed at Xerox's Palo Alto Research Center in the 1970s. E Ink's resourceful use of charged microcapsules overcame objections over glare and eyestrain many felt when reading on screens. By the late 1990s, the outlandish valuations and frothy initial public offerings

(IPOs) of the dotcom boom were in full flow. Publishers were caught up in the enthusiasm. Jeff Gomez describes the trajectory:

> Back in 1999 electronic books, or ebooks as they became known, were not only going to change everything but they were also going to *replace* everything. Because of this, heady predictions were made during the Internet goldrush of the late 1990s; printed books and the ink-on-paper experience were rapidly on their way out, and digital delivery and consumption would soon be commonplace. The publishing industry was soon going to be rocked to its very foundation, and only a small handful of its original players would be left after the sea change. Traditional publishers were out-dated relics about to be sunk.
>   It didn't happen. (Gomez 2008, 117)

Companies like Accenture and PwC forecast large ebook revenues in just a few years and publishers jumped on the bandwagon. All this overlooked the truth that in the 1990s ebooks were a solution without a problem. They were never likely to be commonly adopted when there were issues over device and bandwidth availability, crude digital rights management (DRM) and even general confusion about their name. There was what the blog *Teleread* christened 'the Tower of eBabel' – a morass of competing, incompatible and confusing ebook formats. What little content was available was far too expensive.

Premature maybe. The next decade would show the form was not without promise. In 1994, a financial software engineer called Jeff Bezos founded a web-based book-retail service, Amazon, which embedded bookselling in networked environments. The 1990s had seen several abortive ereaders including the Cybook, the Rocketbook and a curious failure from Apple called the Newton tablet. By the 2000s, developments pointed to a resurgence in the ebook space: the launch of Microsoft Reader in 2000; iTunes in 2003, and with it the mainstream idea of paid-for downloads; Google's mass book digitisation programme in 2004; and the web 2.0 phenomena from around 2004–2005. There was increasing digital engagement, usage and media consumption throughout the decade, paramount to which was an agreement on a standard ebook format, the epub, and in 2007 the launch of Sony's eReader and store. In 2007, Amazon, by then perhaps the world's pre-eminent bookseller, as well as one of the world's leading technology firms, launched a new device, the Kindle, on 19 November in New York. Developed in secret by ex-Apple executives headed by Gregg Zehr at a facility in Cupertino called Lab126 (Brandt 2011), the Kindle led digital reading into the mainstream. Despite unpolished looks and a high initial price point of US$399, adoption of the device was driven by an aggressive strategy pricing all bestsellers at US$9.99, followed by speedy device iterations, service improvements and price drops. By 2010 the Kindle was widely assumed to be the world's most popular ereading device, although Amazon refused to give figures. That year saw the launch of the next major development: the Apple iPad.

The early phase of digital technology, the network society and digital publishing is at a close. Digital networks and the possibility of digital publishing have long roots and architectures translating into a specific set of questions for publishers.

Changing Content

Before examining network effects on publishing, consider how content, which will be examined in greater detail in the next chapter, is changing. With its scale and variety, a web page (or any portion of electronic text) is obviously a very different beast compared to a printed page.[7] Publishers' businesses were optimised for a particular flow of content (printed text and images) and so changes in the nature of content represent an adaptive challenge. Moreover the phenomenon of convergence described by Castells (2009) sees all media merging, facilitated by Cerf and Kahn's Internet neutrality, questioning divisions between different types of publisher both within the world of books and between media. In a world of convergent new media, it may no longer make sense to simply print books.

Digital content is dematerialised. It is binary code. There is no 'meatspace' object. While the Internet itself relies on an extensive physical hardware of fibre-optic cables, data centres and switching points, digital content is part of a programme. When combined with a network this

---

7 Roger Chartier (1995, 18) mapped some of the differences relatively early: 'To read on a screen is not to read in a codex. The electronic representation of texts completely changes the text's status; for the materiality of the book, it substitutes the immateriality of texts without a unique location; against the relations of contiguity established in print objects, it opposes the free composition of infinitely manipulable fragments; in place of immediate apprehension of the whole work, made visible by the object that embodies it, it introduces a lengthy navigation in textual archipelagos that have neither shores nor borders.'

has important effects. Copying becomes effortless, instantaneous and achieved with perfect fidelity, in a stroke hurdling the major historical barriers to circulation. Content is malleable, updateable, transferable. It has geographic simultaneity. It becomes fluid. Dematerialisation alone doesn't allow all of these properties, but on the web – in the network – they are there. Many reading and distribution systems are designed to limit this historically strange state of affairs and recreate the limited copyability of the print book, underwriting an economics of publishing unwelcoming to the infinite copying of text.

The dematerialisation of content doesn't just affect the value chain in terms of publisher bottom lines but also in the value perception of readers – minus the physical object, which readers have long assumed was what they paid for, prices look high. Print costs, however, are only a small percentage of a book's cover price; the rest comprises author advance, publisher fixed costs, discretionary marketing spend, retailer discount and so on, meaning the opportunity for dramatic reductions in price aren't easy, despite consumer expectations.

Digital text behaves differently. Hyperlinking is one example.[8] While to some extent hyperlinking has always existed in the form of references to other works (Cope and Phillips 2006), the hyperlink, an integral part of the web, creates interlinked documents. Google used the total structure of hyperlinks as a means of gauging the importance and relevance of web documents, indexing them according to a complex algorithm that sees the hyperlink as the central element of the network. Hyperlinks allow referencing, dispersing attention, as well as tying documents together. Kevin Kelly (2011) and Nicholas Carr (2011) both talk about the Internet and the hyperlink as creating a vast uber-text, an endless sea of content. Whereas printed text is contained, copyability and the potential for hyperlinking allow books to become part of the network. This is a 'docuverse',[9] 'streams of words rather than monuments' that culminate in 'the complete universal library, all books, in all languages' (Kelly 2011) networked together in a never complete textual flow. Kelly's vision is of free or exceptionally

---

8 Adriaan van der Weel (2011) gives another example, seeing the difference between text and digital text as one of the mark-up that necessarily surrounds and conditions digital text.

9 Originally coined by Ted Nelson, the philosopher and technologist also responsible for the phrase 'hypertext'.

low-cost access, collaborative authorship, textual proliferation and total connectivity both to and within the docuverse.[10]

Perhaps, in his view, the book will simply fade, and the web will remain. Units of attention represented by the book remain consistent. Infinite content and hyperlinking there may be, infinite attention there is not. Whereas Kelly is optimistic, Carr (2011) worries about the never-ending, never-finished nature of digital text. He sees some benefits in keeping reference works constantly updated, but also troubles. The lack of completeness is a problem. Published text becomes editable. We are possibly witnessing the beginning of the end for 'typographical fixity', a foundation on which modern knowledge, case and constitutional law and arguably civilisation have been built. This has downsides. How can publishers work with this great knot of content? What is their role? As we shall see, faced with such a scenario it's not traditional purveyors of content that flourish but creatures of the network, inherently optimised to work with the grain of digital media.

Text has become one item on a menu of multimedia and interactive forms – items well outside the purview and skill set of publishers, expensive to produce and difficult to sell through existing channels. As we have seen, both interactivity and multimedia goods have a publishing history, but one clearly demarcated from book publishing, at least, until digitally driven convergence started blending forms of content and interaction. So-called 'enhanced ebooks' or book apps come with video, audio, new graphical elements, more material and slick touch interfaces. Classics like T. S. Eliot's *The Waste Land* (published by Faber and Touch Press, 2011), Jack Kerouac's *On the Road* (Penguin, 2011) and Mary Shelley's *Frankenstein* (Profile Books and inkle studios, 2012)[11] have been reinvented for a digital age, remixed with multimedia and re-organised for touch screens. Apps like *Journey to the Exoplanets* (published by Farrar, Straus and Giroux, 2011), the *Human Body* (Dorling Kindersley, 2011) and *The Solar System* (Faber and Touch Press, 2011) have redefined reference works by creating experiences impossible in the static media of print. In this environment almost anything is possible; the limits are those of imagination, and more tellingly, time and money.

Since the earliest days of the web, a new genre of literature has grown in the margins of creative writing. Variously called electronic

---

10   As with Foucault's (1980) polysemous society, in many ways Kelly's (2011) vision is already present, for what is the Internet but an interlinked docuverse chunked down into units known as websites?

11   Disclosure: *Frankenstein* was a project I worked on.

literature, interactive literature, new media writing, network fiction or locative narratives, with connections to both video games and digital art, they contain graphics and images, are digitally produced, interactive and multimedia. They can be cross-platform, multiply authored, geo-locative and dynamically and algorithmically produced (so-called generative text).[12] These dithyrambic works are profoundly different experiences to print artefacts, even ones as experimental with form as, say, Mark Z. Danielewski's (2000) *House of Leaves* or Jonathan Safran Foer's (2005) *Extremely Loud and Incredibly Close*. Publishing has not made significant strides into the subculture of electronic literature, generally a fairly self-referential and difficult body of work despite, or more likely because, of its attempts to redefine the written word. As multimedia and interactive elements are more commonly fused into traditional books and publisher workflows, electronic literature has a chance to increase its visibility. Readers are becoming more comfortable with digital goods. Large potential markets grow before our eyes. One of the leading critics of the form makes a bold prediction: 'digital literature will be a significant component of the twenty-first century canon' (Hayles 2008, 159).

Writing for and on digital platforms has history in East Asia, where digital literary content quickly found a huge audience. Japan has a unique environment for mobile communications where the major national carrier, NTT DoCoMo, released Internet enabled phones for the general consumer, a service called i-mode, earlier than elsewhere (in 1998).[13] This lead to a new genre called *keitai-shosetsu* (mobile fiction) written for mobiles. Mawkish, romantic and highly sexualised, written in a clipped vernacular, read largely by teenage girls, the genre was started in 2003 by a story called *Deep Love*, which subsequently became a film, a TV series, a manga comic and, not least, a print book; in short it was a phenomenon. By 2007, half of the top 10 bestselling books in Japan were originally *keitai* fiction.[14] Not only is the content distinctive but it is originated through community websites with a unique culture of

---

12 *Inanimate Alice*, begun by novelist Kate Pullinger and digital artist Chris Joseph in 2005 and still going, is an excellent example, as is *Underbelly* from Christine Wilks (2010), winner of the inaugural New Media Writing Prize.

13 Japanese mobile technology now suffers from the 'Galapagos effect' whereby its technology is increasingly isolated due to early decisions, which simply creates greater difference which further increases its uniqueness and so on (Ito, Okabe and Matsuda 2005).

14 See www.keitaishosetsu.com

noms de plume, readers and writers interacting and distinctively Japanese archetypes like the *otaku* and *kawaii,*[15] with a democratic business model wherein popularity drives publishing. *Keitai* fiction is a new genre of writing that blends cultural and technological forms, an artistic community-based expression optimised for small screens and shrinking attention spans.

In China web-based novels, known as 'original fiction', also became a mainstream force. As with everything in China, the scale is astounding. By 2011, some 195 million people, or 40 per cent of China's Internet population that year, were reading original fiction, which had become a high-growth 5 billion yuan industry powered by major players like the world's largest telecoms giant, China Mobile.[16] As in Japan the writing is community based, working on a freemium model via portals.[17] Popular work is upgraded to pay-as-you-go VIP areas, and beyond that specialist print publishers package the most viewed novels. A site like Shanda Literature, which even has its own ereader, claimed 1.46 million writers, over 10 million users per day and 70 million unique users per month in 2012. The writing is distinctive, centring on historical fantasy and romance, quickly changing format – *Legend of Immortal,* originally a novelised fantasy, for example, had a major TV series and an online game. Despite small payments for stories, some writers make a decent living. *China Daily* (2011) cites Huang Wei earning 1 million yuan per year from original fiction. Both *keitai* and original fiction represent new ways of writing and a new end product – these are stories born and raised on the web, with a language, register, topicality and appearance designed for online platforms. They exist in a space between nineteenth-century serialised fiction, pulp teen comics and cheap Australian soap operas, but with an inescapably digital genesis and delivery. While neither form has truly taken off in the West,[18] it demonstrates how specialised storytelling modes within digital culture can quickly enter the mainstream.

Digital humanities and transmedia storytelling further indicate how book content has started to break the confines of print. Content is an embodied form of knowledge. The growth of new disciplines like the

---

15 *Otaku* are obsessive geeks, often interested in manga and anime, while *kawaii* signifies a generalised and distinctively Japanese form of cuteness.
16 See *China Daily* (2011).
17 The combination of free and paid for elements in a service.
18 Mobile fiction, often delivered via SMS, has some purchase in both Germany and South Africa.

digital humanities, whose outputs are data sets, websites or software, challenges the monograph and by extension the edifice of scholarly publishing (and even the architecture of knowledge itself). Suddenly the fusty academic press has no choice but to introduce products utterly alien to the old enterprise. Publishers of journals find themselves facing digitally generated forms of knowledge and struggle to successfully publish them. Likewise, across the creative industries, marketing and primary content blur to produce what I have elsewhere called 'paracontent', that is, that which is both part of the experience of a work yet also outside it, often in other media formats that support and publicise that work (Bhaskar 2011). Paracontent taps into the notion of transmedia storytelling, where stories exist across and through a variety of media, the whole greater than the sum of its parts (Jenkins 2008). Paracontent explicitly registers how different elements of a transmedia work have different goals, part marketing, part primary product.

We need only glance at the web to see varieties of publishable content are proliferating. Print has an inherent limitation on its copyability and multimedia facility. Digital has neither. Print has high barriers to entry. Digital barriers are negligible. Relationships in print happen at a remove. In a digital world they are more direct and immediate. Digital delivery and content creates opportunities for innovative, skilled and agile entrants to the market, even as they can add cost and complexity to old business practices. As many of the examples show however, this isn't an insuperable problem. In Japan, the energies and audience of *keitai-shosetsu* gave new life to a sclerotic print market.

In the long run these changes, the loss of fixity, creation of a docuverse and new masterpieces of a digital age, may be the deepest and most important of all. Changing content represents a challenge to publishers, but with investment and vision it can be met. Far graver are structural features of the network, which transform not just products but the entire rationale for publishers in the first place.

Network Effects

Discussions of the Internet have to deal with both its relative newness and constantly developing nature. First, the browser-based web was heralded as the future; a decade later the same web was declared dead thanks to growing non-web data traffic and a new generation of browser-bypassing connected devices (Anderson and Wolf 2010). Conclusions are at best interim. Network effect is used here in the broadest sense, to include all kinds of properties of digital networks. Of course, publishing and indeed any human endeavour have always relied on networks – of people, capital, goods and knowledge – but traits of digital networks are particularly marked. We have a twin movement of centralisation and fragmentation, centrifugal and centripetal forces working through a shared architecture, each an effect of it, each feeding into and driving the other. Everything on the Internet shares this pattern of centralisation and fragmentation, not just publishing or media.

Centralisation

In the early days of the Internet, the so-called 'California Ideology' imbued the technology with a sense of utopian promise: it would herald an opening and levelling where great visionaries would craft new democratic and libertarian social and aesthetic forms. Yet centralisation has increased. Just a few websites and device manufacturers dominate the landscape of digital culture. Far from being unpredictable, it is a feature of the network embodied in the notion of the 'Highlander Principle' (taken from the film's tagline 'There can only be one'). There can only be one tablet, search engine, online store and social network. One service occupies a space to the exclusion of all others, thereby becoming enormously powerful in key verticals. There is some competition, but digital big business displays a remarkable degree of centralisation.

Google has an estimated 67 per cent market share for global online search enquiries.[19] Despite seeing significant inroads from its rival Apple and the rise of smartphones and tablets, Microsoft still has nearly 90 per cent of the market for operating systems. Facebook is double the size of the next 14 social networks put together.[20] Even after an aggressive push from other OEMs Apple still has 57.6 per cent of the global tablet market as of 2012[21] while between them Apple and Google have a near duopoly on smartphone operating systems. Amazon has around 70 per cent of the global ebook market and in many territories enjoys overwhelming superiority in online bookselling, just as for many years Apple's iTunes utterly dominated music downloads. The *New York Times* has reported on how tech firms marry hardware and software to create seamlessly locked experiences in emulation of Apple's

19 See Thibault (2010).
20 See http://www.ebizmba.com/articles/social-networwebsites (accessed 1 March 2012).
21 See Miller (2012).

integrated approach.[22] Lines of ownership and market share are not clear cut, but there is nonetheless an obvious pattern of centralisation whereby mega-nodes become the prime brokers of the network. The tendency is towards monopolistic or oligopolistic dominance in a vertical.

Each actor in this West Coast drama has a clear incentive to promote centralisation – on their products and services. Despite the Internet's openness digital technology centralises. Lock-in occurs everywhere. Think of the QWERTY keyboard, one interface decision enshrined as essential despite the possibility of better alternatives. Philosopher and computer scientist Jaron Lanier (2011) gives the example of the MIDI musical encoding, the *de facto* standard for all digital music. He asks, is this the best encoding, is it desirable all our music takes one form? It hardly matters as we're already locked in. Our systems are designed to play this and only this format. Lock-in makes life easy, but means you can't get out. The phenomenon relies on path dependence, whereby past decisions condition future options. If computers and behaviour require a QWERTY keyboard then we can't easily change, just as if we already have an Amazon account it's much easier to continue purchasing from Amazon than start with a new retailer. Lanier (2011) points out that although digital technology offers almost unlimited creative potential it also allows lock-in to spread faster and more fully than ever before.

Studying the mathematics of network topology is currently in vogue and we are beginning to better understand the deep ramifications of network design. One means by which networks centralise is through their ability to add value through centralisation. The most famous explanation is Metcalfe's Law, originally applied to the telephone network. It states the value of a network is proportional to the square of the number of users on the network. In essence, the more people on a network the more valuable it becomes. Immediately we see why Facebook is so much bigger than its rivals – your friends are more likely to be there and so its utility increases. Centralisation helps centraliser and user. Metcalfe's Law has been joined by Reed's Law and Beckstrom's Law, which look at networks in terms of the value added to each interaction on the network provided by the network. Common to them all is the

---

22 Viewed in this light Big Tech's corporate strategy becomes clear – they are all playing for total platform dominance, hence Google in browsers and operating systems (Chrome), Apple in retail (the Appstore), Amazon in tablets and cloud computing and app stores (the Kindle Fire), Microsoft in search engines (Bing). Everyone in a patent war; everyone in market segments outside their original competencies.

sense that utility and network size are connected. Beyond a certain point networks will inherently and exponentially increase as value accrual is dispersed among the network, incentivising those outside to join. Strong mathematical frameworks have been established to demonstrate this as an inherent feature of all networks, although significant debates remain. An associated feature is the 'bandwagon effect' – the more people to have done something the more people do it in future.[23] The more iPhones out there the more people buy iPhones. The logic of conformity takes over when things have happened before or reach scale.

Legal scholar Jonathan Zittrain (2008) sees these powerful network effects as having a further driver in the form of rogue elements on the Internet pushing users into closed but protective systems. Both the Internet and the original PC are 'generative' technologies, which is to say, technologies allowing third parties to build on them without prejudice. They encourage diversity and supersede closed proprietary online services like Minitel or Compuserve by being more usable, adaptable and capable. However with the spread of malware and cybercrime, the web's open architecture becomes a liability: the web has 'tightly coupled networks of data flows that can pass both the latest world news and the latest PC attacks in adjoining data packets' (Zittrain 2008, 56). Most users aren't interested in a system's generativity so much as their security. So-called 'tethered appliances' that are umbilically linked to a centralised service, and so closed from new, unapproved applications, have grown in response. Even web 2.0 services like Facebook are tethered insofar as ultimate control remains with the platform, not the user. Tablets, smartphones and family-oriented gaming devices all accelerate the trend, threatening many beneficial features of our emergent digital ecosystem. As people gravitate, for better or worse,[24] to closed and tethered systems it only increases lock-in and centralisation on those systems.

To go with the Highlander Principle, and what Zittrain (2008) has called the 'Fort Knox Problem', we have the Wu Cycle. Tim Wu (2011),

---

23 Another associated network effect is the 'cluster effect' usually associated with geographical business and innovation clusters like Silicon Valley (appropriately) or the City of London. Clusters of products or services, like Google's suite of tools or Amazon's devices and services also create a cluster effect where the value of each is increased by the presence of the others, so encouraging centralisation.

24 Unquestionably worse for Zittrain (2008). Not only is the generativity nullified but perfect legal enforcement, enabled in such systems, could give rise to mass censorship, total surveillance, immediate injunctions and absolute regulability.

another legal scholar, proposes a gestalt running through the commercial patterns of communications technology over the last 150 years: 'the Cycle'. Communications technologies start decentralised and idealistic before quickly becoming dominated by monopolistic corporations. 'Without exception,' he writes, 'the brave new technologies of the twentieth century – free use of which was originally encouraged, for the sake of further invention and individual expression – eventually evolved into the "old media" giants of the twenty-first, through which the flow and nature of content would be strictly controlled for reasons of commerce' (Wu 2011, 6). AT&T is a classic example, built by the great industrialist Theodore Vail into a vast telecoms monopoly by beating off powerful incumbents.[25] The 'Bell System' was more ideology than company, fusing technology, service, draconian usage restrictions and monopolistic economics. Similar patterns are discernible in the history of film, with its Vail equivalents like Adolph Zukor at Paramount ('the Napoleon of Motion Pictures') who invented the studio system, and radio, where David Sarnoff turned the Radio Corporation of America into a corporate behemoth smothering the once burgeoning field of amateur radio. At one stage just three networks dominated US television: NBC, CBS and ABC. In their heyday, like the BBC in Britain, they represented an extraordinary concentration of communication power. The process is not unidirectional and periods of openness follow extreme monopolies. We could, though, have reached a similar oligopolistic juncture for consumer digital technology. The Randian figures of Vail, Zukor and Sarnoff have their obvious counterparts in the likes of Jobs, Gates and Zuckerberg. All the major players focus on the 'master switch' of the Internet, aiming to be the superpower, the AT&T, of the digital age. History may not repeat itself. If Wu (2011) is right though, and the cycle keeps turning, we are looking at loss of openness and a further increase in centralisation.[26]

For those of us who like to believe in an open Internet encouraging diversity and offering new avenues for expression, this litany of technological and commercial binds makes depressing reading. Faults of old media are replicated and, worse, hugely concentrated as centralisation breeds centralisation. This is not to say one company

---

25 Ironically, of course, it was 'Ma Bell' that created the framework for the digital revolution that would up-end the entire industry.

26 Wu (2011, 273) is cautiously optimistic; the stakes are so huge, and the players so varied 'this time around, as compared to any other, the sides are far more evenly matched.'

will dominate, or to deny the enormous variances in culture, practices and aims between organisations as mutually incompatible as Apple and Google. New forces will emerge and become dominant themselves, before also succumbing to bad luck or bad management. Rather I merely note how one key aspect of communications networks is the tendency to centralise on a very limited number of platforms, whose owners accrue all the power and benefit of that centralisation. Luckily, this isn't the last word.

Fragmentation

Despite centripetal tendencies, the Internet and the web, thanks to the vision of its creators, remain open. Moreover, access is growing. Anyone with rudimentary skills and basic access can create websites. Even tethered services like Facebook are built with a high degree of openness compared with media outlets of the past. The profusion of websites and content is dizzying, a gushing fountain of data comprising trillions of web pages, hours of video footage uploaded to YouTube every minute, hundreds of billions of photos. Millions of blogs. A numberless blizzard of tweets, status updates and Foursquare check-ins. More content than ever before, far more, is now created and disseminated. Basic production and distribution are reduced to a fraction of their former costs. Understood from this angle, the centralisation of the web is actually a response to extreme fragmentation: Google indexes and organises what otherwise would be an impossible chaos of information. Many giants of modern technology are relatively young companies; Apple and Microsoft started in the 1970s; Amazon and Google in the 1990s; while Facebook began in 2004, reaching a valuation of above $100 billion dollars in just eight years, indicating the climate is not one of total ossification. Hope always remains for the agile start-up to make a difference.

Media once had a series of gatekeepers, whose blessing and permission controlled access to audiences. When everyone can communicate to everyone that breaks down. Compared to the media environment of the postwar years we live in an era of super-abundance. Overwhelming complexity and fragmentary content production are barely held together by the forces of centralisation. 'User generated content', now familiar to the point of banality, is part of the picture, as are new organisations and the still-expanding old media order keen to carve their place at the table of digital culture.

Yet another legal theorist, Yochai Benkler (2006), authored the canonical theory of fragmentation in his landmark study, *The Wealth of Networks*. Benkler (2006) looks at how the 'industrial information economy' evolves into a 'networked information economy' where non-market forms of 'social production' have a much greater role than when high capital constraints kept individuals and non-market actors from reaching large audiences. Benkler argues:

> the networked environment makes possible a new modality of organizing production: radically decentralized, collaborative, and nonproprietary; based on sharing resources and outputs among widely distributed, loosely connected individuals who cooperate with each other without relying on either market signals or managerial commands. (Benkler 2006, 60)

This works in an opposite move to centralisation, the effects of which Benkler (2006) regards as exaggerated. A hub-and-spoke system, with producers on the rim sending works to the centre, is replaced by a decentred architecture where everyone is a node, and power is distributed and the multiple connections are made in two-way communications channels. This is the essence of the networked information environment, a world of 'commons-based peer production' very much outside the mass-market, proprietary, professional and copyright-driven worlds of traditional media.

Michael Hart's Project Gutenberg is a classic example of social production. Relying on a huge army of volunteers to scan, proofread, error correct and convert to multiple formats its vast archive of titles, the labour is free, the results openly shared. Other examples of commons-based peer production are well publicised, especially open source software like the Linux operating system and, of course, Wikipedia. Information and communication are, Benkler (2006) argues, fundamental to humans and societies, so it is no surprise to see radical results when they shift. Where inputs were tightly controlled they are now open and widely accessible. Where outputs were high-cost restricted goods they are now, again, open and widely accessible. In such an innovation-friendly context, the problems engendered by fragmentation – information overload, polarisation of discourse, the splintering of content origination – will be solved. The very openness of the networked information economy generates answers without replicating the problems of big old media gatekeepers. No other communications mechanism has grown like the Internet. By working against the centralised capital structures of traditional media, it expanded and transformed the spread of culture and information. Far from centralisation fever, the Internet represents the greatest cultural democratisation in history.

Some implications for publishing have been teased out by fellow travellers in the movement against restrictive copyright, theorist Clay Shirky (2002) and novelist Cory Doctorow (2011). Writing about the growth of blogs in 2002, Shirky hit upon a particularly telling phrase to describe the then-recent activity: 'the mass amateurisation of publishing'. Suddenly barriers to entry, those choke points on supply in the physical world, were removed. Everyone, in theory, could be a publisher when steep entry costs were replaced with simple access. Cue hundreds of millions of blogs. This is 'a technological change whose ramifications are mainly cultural' (Shirky 2002). Doctorow made a similar point in the *Guardian* newspaper:

> The Internet has created a large number of new kinds of publishers who act to connect works and audiences. These essentially group into search engines, then bloggers, curators, and tweeters, and finally suggestion algorithms (such as Amazon's 'people who bought this also bought...' recommendations; Reddit's human voting system; Netflix's suggestion system). (Doctorow 2011)

The Internet means not just a 'mass amateurisation of publishing' but a mass amateurisation of all one-to-many communications and cultural practice in a global fission of media control.

In summary, digital environments have two seemingly opposed tendencies, powerful dynamics of centralisation and fragmentation. Seeing them as acting in conflict, however, is entirely wrong. They are part of the same pattern. Without key nodes the digital realm would be a maddening Borgesian labyrinth; without fragmentation it would be totalitarian, monopolistic and monolithic. The centre and the periphery evolve so drivers pushing towards centralisation complement and enable those moving towards fragmentation. Put simply, the network does both, and we can't see one without the other. Just as Google's indexing brings a measure of discoverability to the web's cacophony, so proprietary app stores offer discovery and delivery platforms to an ever-growing wave of software. This patterning has deep philosophical roots. Deleuze and Guattari, for example, saw the process as one with lineage stretching throughout the history of thought.[27] For Castells, 'networks have become the predominant organizational form for every domain of human activity' (Castells 1997, xliv), and certainly this problematic of centralisation and fragmentation vexes publishing. After all, no publisher can control these processes. The contours of this new networked environment, described as 'a possibility factory' (Kelly 1999, 46), are the real existential challenge for publishers.

The Digital Challenge

Disintermediation[28]

In conversation with publishers, one sometimes gets the sense disintermediation – a cutting out or unbundling of publishers from the literary value chain – isn't taken seriously. Publishers assume they'll always be wanted and needed and that their imprimatur means any attempt to disintermediate will be at worst equivocal, at best footnotes in the grand history of the written word.

Such thinking is mistaken. Papyrus workers, scribes, rubricators, hot metal typesetters and even map publishers probably all once thought themselves relatively secure, yet they have all been rendered irrelevant by new technology. For publishing, digital technology is an 'out-of-context' problem: like the Conquistadors in America being technologically more advanced and following imperatives incomprehensible to the indigenous population. Even recognising the true nature of the problem isn't obvious. It can't be couched in the usual terms.

The flow of centralisation and fragmentation clearly articulates a mode of disintermediation. Authors work as they usually do, alone, but centralisation enables the intermediating work of discovery and distribution. Fragmented practice and centralised discovery and distribution, the key movements of the digital network, require nothing more for the full functioning of a literary, even a print, economy.

---

27 Furthermore we might view the centralisation of the Internet as what Deleuze and Guattari (2004) called 'territorialization'. New 'lines of flight' create new 'segments' that are basically occupations. However, they also hold open the possibility of 'territorialization', which chimes with the counter-currents of digital culture.

28 The term 'disintermediation' originally applied to banking in the 1960s, when a bank's customers would invest directly rather than indirectly through depositing funds in savings accounts. It then enjoyed a renaissance in the first Internet wave of the late 1990s as incumbent media companies started to panic.

Disintermediation isn't an abstract or trivial possibility. It's a live threat to traditional publishers of all kinds. History is littered with resistance from antiquated technologies and their masters. Despite the fact that change often occurs at a slower pace than its more evangelical proponents predict, it eventually wins through efficiency savings and superior value extraction. On the Internet everyone is, or can be, a publisher. They might be bad publishers, unnoticed publishers and largely pointless publishers, but some of them will be good, lean and highly adapted publishers capable of winning market-share skirmishes. As traditional channels to market – bookshops – keep closing, the appeal of disintermediatory tactics grow. This is not to suggest publishers will overnight find themselves unemployed. It is to highlight how networks can bypass an industry adapted to a prior set of circumstances. Influential technology blog GigaOm has argued we live in the age of 'the artist as entrepreneur' with collapsing distribution channels, the growth of promotional and monetisation tools and a generation of creatives willing to run their own affairs.[29] We are in the age of disintermediation.

Doctorow (2011) and Shirky (2002) both make this point. They argue that publishers add value by accommodating the high fixed costs of distribution, marketing and generally producing content in a world of bricks, mortar, paper and print where scarcity is an economic constant and practical problem. In the context of digital media, scarcity is not a problem. Fixed costs to entry are nowhere to be seen. Coupled with network-enabled discoverability, publishers with their DRM, 'sustainable' pricing and recreation of atomistic sales models may actually be artificially manufacturing scarcity. In this scenario, it hardly helps that, as we saw in the last chapter, publishers are already highly ambiguous creatures that outsource work formerly seen as integral. Without a firmly delineated *raison d'être*, they might become more hindrance than help to the smooth circulation of content. If publishers cannot clearly define what they do and why, defending themselves will be difficult. Whereas previously no other options existed, now any talented writer can reach a potentially monetisable audience.

The music industry was, no surprise, first. Artists as diverse as the Arctic Monkeys, Enter Shikari and M.I.A. have used the web to virally grow their audience pre-label. While some like the Arctic Monkeys went on to work with traditional (albeit indie) labels, others like Enter Shikari and more famously Radiohead bypassed established companies to effectively become

---

29 See Wolf (2011).

their own record label. With strong branding, distribution through their websites and iTunes, and the growth of merchandising and touring as sources of income, they disintermediated swathes of the industry. Radiohead pioneered new pricing models with their album *In Rainbows* (2007) leaving fans to decide what they wanted to pay, if anything, for a download (a label subsequently released the album as a CD). They followed with *The King of Limbs* (2011) for which listeners were offered a menu of purchase options on the Radiohead website, from a cheap download to an elaborate, expensively priced vinyl special edition. Once again the band opted to release a CD through a conventional record label, but this time with a difference – they set up an imprint, Ticker Tape, under the aegis of indie star XL Recordings. This activity pointed to a new kind of collaboration where artists kept more power and had their own labels, but worked with existing players on logistical and financial control: not disintermediation *in toto* but a step in that direction.[30] MySpace may have launched as a social network but, out competed, found a niche as a music service that describes perfectly the centralisation/fragmentation pattern. MySpace itself is a large centralising platform open to a vast array of bands, allowing them to find audiences without large marketing budgets. Other services from Twitter to Soundcloud to Topspin create a further network for bands to cut out record company suits.

For acts big and small, the commercial landscape has changed, with entrenched players, notably record companies rather than music publishers, finding acts capable of marketing and distributing their work. TV has also seen the first signs of disintermediation. Comedian Louis CK's decision to ditch his usual network in favour of selling a show direct is a case in point. Book publishing is someway behind the hybrid ecosystem of disintermediation currently working through music, but looks set to follow. Given the early nature of disintermediation, all we have are examples pointing to underlying trends.

Three approaches to disintermediation follow from the publisher's lack of control in a centralising and fragmentary architecture, each of which will be considered in turn:

- Retailers and technology firms active in the book space;
- Authors and other intermediaries like literary agents;
- New actors altogether.

---

30 Rapper Dizzee Rascal and his label, Dirtee Stank Recordings, negotiated a similar arrangement with Universal's Island Records.

Each works on the principle you need both open fragmentation and central switching points for disintermediation to be viable. Not just low barriers of entry but platforms for successful exploitation and discovery of works are prerequisites.

One regularly mooted source of disintermediation is Amazon, the online book retailer *par excellence* (Brandt 2011). When Jeff Bezos founded the company he wasn't interested in retailing books as such, but wanted to find a product that worked well on the nascent Internet. Books ticked all his boxes: a highly diversified range meant traditional retailers had stock limitations, while standardisation and distribution tools like the ISBN meant books could be efficiently tracked. From beginning in the obligatory start-up garage (in Seattle not Silicon Valley), Amazon is now the colossus of web retail, dominant in online bookselling, ereading and a host of other product categories, with a string of high-profile acquisitions and new initiatives. Most observers now laud Amazon's aggressive yet patient strategy – it is willing, as Jeff Bezos publicly acknowledges, to be 'misunderstood' and lose money for long periods in order to win the wider war. This strategy has seen it grow into one of only a handful of web titans.

Amazon is another example of centralisation and fragmentation. Amazon is a hub, the most visible destination to buy goods on the web. It sells virtually everything, has millions upon millions of user accounts around the world and a highly developed brand presence. It has streamlined operations, centralised development of its platforms and owns a vast series of distribution centres. The Kindle is a closed system where only titles bought through the Kindle Store can be easily read. Anyone competing with Amazon is liable to find themselves outgunned on price, service and brand recognition by its deep pockets, hard-nosed business nous and alpha-league levels of traffic. Part of Amazon's power comes from its enormous scale, diversified revenues and the creation of the 'Amazon economy' (Jopson 2012). Retail, let alone book retail, is a small part of a system that includes immense cloud hosting services, the Mechanical Turk task outsourcing service, hardware manufacturing and distribution of the Kindle range, a proprietary app store, a string of high profile acquisitions from IMDB to Zappos.com, a film studio, and media streaming platforms in addition to Marketplace initiatives. However, at the same time, Amazon really does display an enormous range of writers and publishers. It's much easier to make a book available on Amazon than in a physical bookstore. What's more Amazon isn't a closed shop – its merchants system allows other vendors to plug into and sell through its infrastructure. An utterly obscure title has, in terms of its product page, a similar representation to a bestseller.

In this powerful mix, two avenues of disintermediation present themselves, first, through Amazon's self-publishing schemes for both print (known as CreateSpace) and the Kindle (Kindle Direct Publishing or KDP which includes White Glove, KDP targeted at agents), and second, through Amazon's publishing operations. Self-publishing ebooks is part of the Amazon economy, as well as a new kind of economy in its own right.

Many ebook bestsellers are self-published, spread through that old favourite, word of mouth, and helped by judicious promotion and the circular patterns of ebook buying.[31] On devices where discoverability is far from seamless, this matters. American author Amanda Hocking became synonymous with the self-publishing movement after her paranormal romances became breakaway hits.[32] Previously rejected by traditional houses, Hocking, along with other self-published writers like Kerry Wilkinson and Joe Konrath, is a highly visible instance of an author making decent money and selling over a million titles without a publisher. Amazon encourages 'direct publishing' by extending their lending scheme to self-published authors, complete with a monthly pot of money divided according to lending figures. While Hocking is an exemplar for disintermediation, she is also a check against it: after her success, offers from Manhattan publishers flooded in and she signed a hefty deal with Macmillan, indicating a music-style hybrid disintermediation. Compared to print, however, the ease, cost and potential effectiveness of self-publishing is high. There is a track record of writers beating the old boys by scoring No. 1s with appealing, low-priced, organically marketed works. Amazon's dominant position means it can afford to pay royalties far in excess of those offered by traditional publishers. Judged economically, the scales tip in one direction. As services develop the likelihood is more writers will, at least initially, take the disintermediatory path.

Amazon's proprietary publishing operations are recent and their strategy remains unclear. Whatever their motives, it seriously spooked publishers and competing retailers. In 2011, Amazon hired editor Larry Kirschbaum, described in a *Businessweek* profile as 'the ultimate industry

---

31 Ebooks in the charts are liable to sell well because the charts are obvious places to buy books, ensuring they stay in the charts and so on.

32 Hocking sold well over a million ebooks making $2.5 million in the process (Morrison 2012).

insider', to be publisher of its new content arm Amazon Publishing, a move that signalled its intent to rival the New York Big Six in content acquisition (Stone 2012). Amazon began building a series of imprints like Thomas & Mercer, 47North and AmazonCrossing. What worried publishers were Amazon's capital reserves and enormous dataset, almost certainly the world's most extensive and powerful information resource on reading habits and book buying, not to mention their decisive advantage in controlling the consumer relationship. The initiative points to the importance of new retailer or platform-driven publishing setups. Lulu is well established as a self-publishing medium, while print-on-demand systems like Lightning Source or the Espresso printer extend the potential for self-published works. Apple also opened its own platform; iBooks Author allows anyone to develop distinctive, multimedia ebooks for distribution through iBooks. Anyone wanting to compete in the ebook sphere needs to develop and push a self-publishing platform. Increasing options can only be a good thing from the vantage point of would-be authors.

When writers reach critical mass they transcend publishers. A signature case is J. K. Rowling. Rowling has by no means deserted publishers entirely, continuing to work with Bloomsbury on print editions of the Harry Potter books before signing with Little, Brown for a departure into adult fiction. However, with the website Pottermore she disintermediated her publishers. She uses her brand, the creative potential of digital technology and a devoted community to sell ebooks and new areas of entertainment somewhere between a game, a social network and a book. Rowling stole a march on publishers by abandoning unpopular DRM on her ebooks. Pottermore hints at a business model for writers of a type and scale, cult bestsellers like George R. R. Martin or Terry Pratchett.[33] Of course, such writers can work with publishers, but the Rowling case shows they may not, money not being a problem and the value-add of a publisher still hazy in the new field. A pattern of partial disintermediation is again reminiscent of the music industry.

When science fiction writers Neal Stephenson and Greg Bear embarked on a project called *The Mongoliad*, they set up a new company, the Subutai Corporation, to publish it. *The Mongoliad* was new on several levels: written in weekly instalments by a team of writers and guest writers working collaboratively; fully multimedia, incorporating video, audio

---

33 TV chef Jamie Oliver retains a highly successful relationship with Penguin for his cookbooks, but works on apps separately, effectively disintermediating his publisher on what could one day be the bigger business.

and images; purely web-based; with an annual subscriptions rather than unit sales; and community features built in from the start. In short, it was a product far from most publishers' output. So Stephenson and Bear created their own self-funded publisher.

Marketing guru Seth Godin took a similar approach with The Domino Project, a publisher he launched having 'no patience with obsolete institutions' as the website puts it (for 'obsolete institutions', read publishers). As he wrote announcing its launch: 'There is no middleman' (Godin 2010). Crucially however both *The Mongoliad* and The Domino Project shared one interesting feature: in different ways they both relied on Amazon. While originally a web only project, *The Mongoliad* was later revealed to have sold its print rights to none other than Amazon's 47North imprint.[34] The Domino Project was 'powered by Amazon' from the start; not so much Seth Godin alone, as Seth Godin plus the full weight of Amazon.com's fulfilment platform. Ultimately both are examples of partial disintermediation. Another example is how universities publish directly rather than using university presses. Universities here still offer institutional backing while disintermediating those formerly responsible for publishing.

In addition some literary agents started publishing their clients' work. The agent Ed Victor, for example, established Bedford Square Books as a publisher operating inside his agency. Aiming to make out-of-print work available to the public, Victor wasn't the only agent to spot an opportunity. Andrew Wylie launched an in-agency imprint Odyssey Editions, while PFD, Sheil Land and a host of other agencies have also experimented. Anecdotal evidence suggests some agency imprints are doing extremely well. It means authors have options like never before to follow non-traditional channels to market. As with retailers, other intermediaries in the literary supply chain are happy to route around publishers. Again, the pattern is not wholly one way, with publishers also setting up parallel digital imprints. Initiatives like Bloomsbury Reader and Pan Macmillan Bello in the UK show publishers are alive to the situation, creating once again a picture of partial disintermediation.

While the Internet opens new avenues for agents, they may not want to disrupt relationships with existing publishers. Media organisations with fewer qualms are realising that, even as they face disintermediatory

---

34 The team behind *The Mongoliad* project have now built a self-sufficient community publishing platform, LitHive, which they are running independently.

pressures in their own spheres, the Internet presents opportunities to disintermediate their peers. Take, for instance, newspapers, facing falling advertisement and subscription revenues and the problem of free content, now becoming ebook publishers. The Huffington Post, the *New York Times* and *Guardian* have all started ebook programmes where previously content would have been un-commissioned, published with a partner or used only once (Bosman 2011). Rather than work with existing publishers TED will do it themselves, while media network NBC is setting up a publishing imprint to make the most of its IP (Nawotka 2012). Digital technology alters the calculation to publish direct, barriers to entry being much lower and convergence creating more obvious synergies.

The last major route for disintermediation is through new entities in the content market. New digitally led publishers like Byliner and Open Road Media in the US, Touch Press and Unbound in the UK, 40k Books in Italy and Momentum in Australia, not to mention the highly successful web publishers in Japan and China, challenge incumbents. When looked at from the position of publishing as a whole though, they offer answers. Instead we should consider the deeper question of whether, in the context of 'the mass amateurisation of publishing'; our conception of publishers needs rethinking. In the network age who is the publisher but Google, aiding discovery, or Wordpress, the platform from which a writer speaks?

Even the microblogging service Twitter, then, is a form of publisher. The company has grown into one of the biggest Internet services in just a couple of years. Everyday millions of people (including this author) are glued to Twitter, to feed their addiction to a constant stream of news, information and idle gossip. A many-to-many communications platform, Twitter certainly fulfils the criteria of 'making something public'. Through following mechanisms and search indexing, tweeted comments have large potential audiences. Users are experimenting with their tweets – writing poems, retelling novels, reporting the news and building applications with interesting, useful and not-so-useful functionality.[35] Twitter might be conceived as a medium, like a book, but it might also be seen as a decentred web-native publisher. Like Blogger, Wordpress, Medium, Quora or even 4chan, Twitter provides a means of communicating with interested audiences, even if it doesn't offer a ready way of monetising those eyeballs.

If one were to invent a publisher for the web age it might look something like Tumblr, a social blogging service with an explosive growth curve

---

35 See, for example, 'Such Tweet Sorrow', a project that retold Shakespeare's *Romeo and Juliet* in real time using actors working through Twitter (@Such_Tweet).

similar to Twitter. Tumblr, now owned by Yahoo!, is even more content-centric than Twitter with an extraordinary ability to disseminate content at speed. According to Cheshire (2012), it generates a huge amount of sharing activity compared with other social and blogging networks. Its slick interface and emphasis on content make it the ideal platform for getting material shared and public quickly, easily and effectively.[36] With J-curve growth rates, an unfamiliar business plan typical of web start-ups and a service and user-oriented experience it would be simple to dismiss the suggestion Tumblr is a publisher. This misses the wider picture.

As digital technology reconfigures content, the possibility grows that new intermediary actors like Tumblr, Twitter or Medium may supersede the functionality of older publishers. This isn't to suggest these websites in particular will do so. Document sharing services like Scribd are more explicitly in publishing territory, and while not runaway successes like Tumblr they clearly challenge the rationale and operational strengths of book publishers. Historically publishers were the venture capitalists of textual production, advancing funds to authors and bearing the monetary risks of publication. Now services like Kickstarter offer an inversion of the funding model in a return to eighteenth century–style subscription publishing, whereby readers front money for unwritten books, thus removing the financing role of publishers. Subscription always had limited reach; online crowd financing, on the other hand, is eminently scalable, with one graphic novelist already raising over $1 million through Kickstarter (Charman-Anderson 2012).

Disintermediation comes in many flavours. The common ingredient is the enabling nature of the digital network's centralising and fragmentary traits. Traditional publishers find themselves on terrain they don't know, own or control. Disintermediation is a tendency, not an iron law. What we see is a heavily phased view of disintermediation; it's not a sudden and total shift, but an incremental, partial process with manifestations that are uneven, scattered and out of sync. Just because disintermediation can happen, doesn't mean it will happen. Powerful forces and behaviours stand in the way of disintermediation and the effects of technology, indeed technology itself, are always social products, subject to, or at least in a relationship with, the choices of its creators, curators and users: us. We shouldn't hail the inevitability of disintermediation just as we shouldn't reject it as fantasy. Bookshops may

---

36 By 2012, Tumblr was already generating a number of page views comparable to Twitter or Wikipedia, despite less traffic, which was still growing incredibly fast, suggesting extremely high levels of user engagement (Cheshire 2012).

well vanish long before publishers in what is likely to be an attritional process lasting decades and more.

Several things are clear. First, a growing body of evidence suggests the threat of disintermediation is increasing and will only intensify. Second, we are witnessing not just disintermediation but, to use a phrase from an OECD (2010) report, 're-intermediation'. Even when some players are cut out of the loop, 1) they are adept at resisting this and finding ways to reinsert themselves, and 2) new intermediary players are growing all the time, from international telecom giants to start-ups like Tumblr. Publishing activity isn't so much disappearing as shifting in locale. Disintermediation is complex and qualified, about comings together as much as breakings apart, forward and backward movements, creative and destructive forces. Self-publishing may dominate the headlines but in the network it doesn't matter whether it's self-publishing, Amazon publishing, Tumblr or anything else. The point is that publishers' structural positions can easily be made redundant. That array of options simply compounds the problem. *Fifty Shades of Grey* and Kindle Direct Publishing are only the most obvious tips of the iceberg. Growing markets for content and increased efficiency improving medium-term underlying profits belie this deeper and more intractable issue.

Even a hint of disintermediation should prompt serious reflection. Anyone can now publish in a way never before possible. Without a strong response publishers are inviting decline, irrelevance and, in extreme cases, annihilation.

Copyright

We have already seen that publishing is irreducible to copyright. This doesn't mean copyright isn't one of the foundations of modern publishing. Like all legal constructs copyright is a fiction, one with a particularly conflictual past and only relatively recent international acceptance, if indeed we can call the present regime acceptance. As Larry Lessig puts it: 'the property of copyright is an odd kind of property' (2004, 83)[37] – or in the words of pro-copyright Mark Twain: 'Only one thing is impossible to God: to find any sense in any copyright law on this planet' (1935, 381).

---

37 Lessig (2004) means, for example, that texts are non-rivalrous; which is to say, my consumption of a text, especially in digital forms, is not impacted by your consumption of the same text, whereas my consumption of a bottle of wine and your consumption of the same bottle of wine are rivalrous – one's consumption as an impact on other's consumption of the same good.

Only with the 1886 Berne Convention for the Protection of Literary and Artistic Works did we begin to have a truly international copyright agreement and even then major gaps existed in its application. Publishers invented copyright, with a history, as we saw in the case of Herringman, dating back to the internal workings of the Company of Stationers' Register and subsequent legal provisions like the Licensing Acts and the 1709–10 Statute of Anne, copyright's first legislative recognition. Piracy, though common, was constrained by the inherent difficulty of copying. After all, print piracy requires overcoming many of the obstacles to publishing in the first place. Bits, on the other hand, reveal copyright's fictionality – instantaneous, perfectly faithful copying is no longer difficult. Attempts to impose restrictions on copying run against the grain of the technology, a point eloquently put by Shirky (2002), Doctorow (2011), Benkler (2006) and Lessig (2004) among others (given the associations of many such thinkers with Harvard's Berkman Center for Internet and Society might we talk of a 'Berkman School'?).

While never free from controversy, copyright and intellectual property face a challenge not just over their desirability, as in eighteenth-century Britain or nineteenth-century America, but also over their enforceability and rationale. Notoriously damaging to the bottom lines of record companies, film studios and games publishers, file-sharing came of age in 1999 with Napster, a peer-to-peer (P2P) network for sharing music in the MP3 format. In a matter of months, millions used the service to freely download from a seemingly universal catalogue. Peaking in 2001 and eventually forced to change tack, Napster was followed by a series of clones using the powerful BitTorrent protocol.[38] Although the MP3 dates from 1995, it needed an easy download mechanism and commonly installed playing software for piracy to take off. Once it did the economic and legal superstructure of the creative industries would never be the same again.

Distribution was instantaneous and most importantly free. We've become used to the concept of free thanks to writers like Chris Anderson (2009), who argues 'free' is a potent business model when used creatively, for example, by giving away items to build demand for subsidiary goods. Back in the early 2000s, few people were thinking this way and the 'problem of free' became a full-blown cash-flow crisis.

---

38 BitTorrent and its clients are another excellent example of the hub-and-spoke model of centralisation and fragmentation.

Not much has changed however. Totally free is not, in the end, an option. Funding is always needed, whether through donations, taxes, revenue from goods or services sold or any other means of revenue generation. The introduction of free to any marketplace is at best immensely disruptive, in good and bad senses; at worst, it drives out parts of the value chain altogether. Laws of supply and demand inevitably impact content of almost all kinds. The real value of content is falling outside areas with price controls. Value itself is lost. A select band of web-savvy writers can make work free. They build careers in other niches and grow their profile, while, to use another Andersonism, a long tail of writers and publishers find money driven out of the ecosystem. Furthermore, free content comes with a major shift in commercial emphasis, from consumers buying the product to consumers becoming the product. This is how newspaper and magazine publishing works. For books, such ad-funded models supporting free or exceptionally low price points fail due to the highly diversified nature of the product set. Instead, the model plays into the hands of major content aggregators like Google, who can produce large audiences, despite significant audience segmentation, feeding the logic of centralisation and fragmentation.

No one's sure about the extent of copyright infringement. BitTorrent sites are beyond a standard analytic purview, and moreover, piracy in general is highly distributed and internally differentiated. A search for an author name followed by 'epub' or 'PDF' reveals the scale of infringing activity, indicating that with the growth of connectivity and ereading devices the problem has worsened. However, book publishing was able to learn from the music industry and moved immediately to closed retail-driven systems wherein purchasing is easier than pirating.

Piracy remains an emotive issue, with swathes of the IP industries predictably viewing it as a mortal threat to be stamped out at all costs, matched against a broad coalition of free-thinking lawyers, artists and content consumers that see copyright and, occasionally, remuneration, as out-dated constraints on the flow of artistic and intellectual goods. While print copyright infringement does occur, it causes nothing like the jitters of digital piracy whose possible totality is dynamite to publishers.

At root the problem is simple: content can be copied whether or not publishers like it. The economics of contemporary publishing work – rightly or wrongly – through limited title monopolies in given jurisdictions. Take this away and you remove the financial edifice upon which the current circulation of books is based. New laws may make piracy more difficult, but they will be contested and will never fully eradicate file-sharing of one description or another. The strong reaction against the proposed Stop Online Piracy Act (SOPA) from an effective coalition of grassroots activists and interested corporate parties like Google was only the latest in a series of tussles around copyright legislation. One persuasive argument from the revised licences side is that culture isn't produced in a vacuum, but involves remixing, drawing upon and remaking prior cultural forms. Creativity works via accretion not quasi-divine inspiration. In a world of copyright lock down, we destroy that process. What's needed, then, is a balance between protecting investments and ensuring a vibrant cultural sphere (Lessig 2004, 2006, 2009).[39]

English-language trade publishers have long used rights territorially. The world is carved into reserved blocs, that is, publishers monopolise the market for a title in certain territories, giving rise to features like the anachronistic legacy of empire in British publishers' retention of UK and Commonwealth rights. Generally regarded as advantageous to all parties, it ensures global competition doesn't threaten home markets. In places like Ireland, New Zealand or even Canada, publishers already struggle against larger foreign cousins from the UK, Australia and the US. Aided by accommodating ebook outlets, the digital enforcement of territorial rights and export markets has, so far, remained fairly consistent. The question is for how long. Just as copyright is threatened so this subsidiary area of publishing law is easily circumvented in the network. The territorially divided nature of English-language publishing looks vulnerable to globalised manoeuvres. Likewise the sale of translation rights could be blown open by sophisticated auto-translation software. Regional and linguistic federations designed to secure publisher revenues are vulnerable to new technology.

Copyright is not a binary of perfect enforcement/total infringement. New licences balance competing imperatives of openness and remixing on the one hand, control and remuneration, on the other. Richard Stallman was an MIT programmer in the 1980s frustrated with licensing arrangements for collaboratively produced software. He believed user freedom was the paramount benefit of software and attempts to restrict this were morally wrong. When working on the GNU operating system he started thinking about and popularising the idea of 'copyleft', or

39 Lessig's (2006) famous dictum 'Code is law' describes how there are no legal grey areas in digital culture. If something is law than it can be enforced with perfect and undesirable comprehensiveness that allows no nuance. See also Zittrain (2008).

more open alternatives to copyright for the GNU. Eventually, the GNU's General Public License (GPL) was introduced to ensure both recognition for its creators and maximum openness for users. The principle behind the GPL was that distributions could be made, subject to the terms of the GPL, thus ensuring no one could 'enclose' the IP generated therein as all developments, spin-offs and iterations would also be subject to the GPL. Open source software could come of age. Stallman is the patron saint of copyleft and since the launch of the GPL a raft of licences have been introduced, most prominently those of Creative Commons (CC) in 2001.[40]

CC licences come in several forms, the most permissive of which allow for commercial, copyrighted, derivative works with no attribution. More widespread are 'attribution non-commercial share alike' licences. Based around a series of rights waivers, Creative Commons opens IP to productive reuse and efficient sharing. It updates copyright for the disturbing possibility of perfect rights enforcement stopping all reuse. Such licences and policies don't challenge copyright outright; they are founded on copyright and form a subset of the rights pertaining to a work. Nonetheless publishers are wary of licences like the GPL or CC, unsure of a business model and how they work in contexts of growing piracy, downward price expectations and falling revenues.[41]

In academic and journal publishing, copyright has already played out as an all too real drama. Open Access[42] publishing is increasingly mandated by research funders and universities, tired of paying what they regard as exorbitant prices for content produced by people whose salaries they already fund. Like Creative Commons, Open Access is motivated by the idea that products of public research are inherent public property, part of a common resource for the greater good. Major businesses – so called 'toll-access publishers' – are facing policy hurdles and academic resistance. When Fields Medal–winning Cambridge mathematician Timothy Gowers announced he was boycotting journals giant Elsevier, a slew of academics joined him. A campaign began and the boycott quickly grew. Elsevier was faced with a public

---

40 Founded by none other than Larry Lessig.
41 Technical publishers O'Reilly Media, consistently at the forefront of publishing innovation, have dabbled, as have Bloomsbury Academic, but aside from these experiments progress has been tentative.
42 The term incorporates a number of different versions of Open Access (OA), for example, green OA, which means putting work in OA repositories or gold OA, where works are submitted to journals with a full OA policy (Suber 2012).

relations nightmare, and a major threat to their business model, which relies on bundling journals. Alternatives to established routes, with an open-access philosophy at their core, are simultaneously sprouting with increasing rapidity and, crucially, gaining kudos in the academy where reputation matters. Services like PubMed, a free database of medical research abstracts and references, and arXiv, a Cornell University–based physics publication platform in which a community of researchers share, critique and collaborate on research papers, are far from traditional business practices in academic publishing, yet dominate their respective fields.

Despite the many upsides to new licence arrangements, they still present a challenge. Without a significant overhaul their adoption is a powerful driver of disintermediation: as the Elsevier boycott shows, if publishers don't account for their authors and readers other options are now available. This is not a problem for publishing in the wider sense so much as a tactical headache for a category of information providers. As Peter Suber, one of the OA movement's leading advocates, puts it, 'OA doesn't threaten publishing; it only threatens existing publishers who do not adapt' (2012, 18).

If copyright no longer works properly, the present constitution of publishing doesn't either. Copyright questions are not separate from disintermediation but interact in a mutually supporting dynamic, exerting structural pressures on the future of publishing.

Taking up the Challenge?

Disintermediation and copyright are hardly the only issues on publisher's agendas. For the most part they aren't even near the top. The following are of more immediate concern: the evolving, multimedia nature of content already discussed and the risky investments therein; collapsing high street retail, and the associated problems of title visibility and falling sales; a corresponding increase in remaining retailer power; difficulties of selling digital products; reskilling and hiring new staff; falling print runs, rising print costs and price pressures on ebooks.

Every week brings a new set of issues to the forefront of beleaguered publishers. These are publishing challenges, not challenges to publishing. That is a key distinction. Throughout history, publishers, like any enterprise, have faced, overcome and been strengthened by any number of obstacles. What a move in copyright and the possibility of disintermediation, or at least re-intermediation, and to a lesser extent the changing formations of content present is an existential threat beyond the immediate concerns of publishing in a digital age. The digital network means, over the long term, that there can be no such thing as business as usual. It is the difference between digitisation and networked digitisation: a short-termist assessment of opportunities and threats and a deep understanding of media reordered. Bookshops going under are a problem in terms of sales and exposure. It is a longer-term problem as each closing shop creates conditions ever more conducive to disintermediatory actions. When conditions of scarcity break down extreme asset-price deflation is inevitable. Just as publisher safeguards like copyright are challenged there is an unprecedented rush of new entrants into the marketplace. This points at only one conclusion for publisher revenues.

The network age isn't short of champions. We've already come across Clay Shirky (2002), Yochai Benkler (2006) and Larry Lessig (2004), each of whom makes a powerful case that digital will unleash a renewed grassroots creativity and rejuvenated cultural landscape. Yet recently there has been a wave of well-publicised, broadly humanist critiques of digital technology from Jaron Lanier, Eli Pariser, Evgeny Morozov, Nicholas Carr, Cass Sunstein, Andrew Keen and Lee Siegel among others. Authors like Jonathan Franzen have questioned digital reading (see Singh 2012), while before his death John Updike (2006) gave a characteristically elegant appraisal of the ebook, seeing in its lack of 'edges' a loss of artistic integrity. For all the digital boosterism there are downsides beyond financial concerns. What kind of cultural marketplace, and indeed society, do we really want to build, and is digital helping us get there? Many of the critics suggest we should interrogate digital closely, remembering we are the engineers of its emerging reality.

My analysis of the digital challenge aims not to presuppose a theory of publishing. It outlines the challenge from a perspective familiar to established book publishers, without going further in talking about what they do.

Prior to digital, publishing had a conflicted identity requiring explanation. Now that theory is no longer abstractly needed. Without a deep account of how publishing, the original creative and copyright industry, operates, explaining its multiple identities, publishers will not be able to confidently face the digital age. A question mark will be hovering over their role and value. They cannot easily say 'this is what we do and this is how we are going to evolve to keep on doing it'. The problem for traditional publishing is twofold: it is assailed intellectually on one flank by lacunae and asymmetries of time, geography, definition, end product and work; and practically, on the other, by a technological maelstrom that undermines the precarious role of publishers in the content landscape. We need a depiction of publishing equal to the convergence age.

This chapter has set out the scholarly and practical problem and with it the need for a theory of publishing. It is to that we now turn. Having elaborated a theory of publishing, we can then return to the digital challenge.

So, what *does* make you a publisher?

Chapter 3

HOW CONTENT WORKS

We're surrounded by content. Inasmuch as we live in an Information Age, we live in a Content Age. Content has been king: challenged by context and social media in the battle for attention and rethroned. We talk of the content industries as major providers of jobs, playing an increasing role as technological and economic changes shift value to content. Once the positions of content strategist and content analyst were incongruous. Now they are routine. AOL, a digital infrastructure business fast pivoting towards content, even has a chief content officer. Content farms spew search engine friendly derivative material in vast quantities. Content was once a grubby, near disrespectful word in the corridors of book publishing. Not any more.

Having established the problems of publishing we need to address them. The precondition for publishing, one of those critical common factors, is content. There is no such thing as content-free publishing. The idea is nonsensical. Any comprehension of publishing must then be based on an understanding of how content works. Content, not communication, must be the foundation, as content only becomes communication with a further intervention; publishing itself, not content alone, creates the act of communication. Communication without content is unintelligible. Surprisingly, for a buzzword, the concept of 'content' remains relatively unexamined. Literature, communication and media groan under a weight of scholarly literature but content *qua* content is often marginalised as a focus of study. However, a theory of publishing requires a theory of content. If it doesn't state it explicitly, then it uses one tacitly nonetheless.

Drawing from a range of theoretical work in information, communication and media studies, I view content in combination with two supplementary concepts – the frame and the model. Content is an impoverished idea without them. The word content implies content of something. In other words, implied is an element not included in the word itself: that which content *fills*. This is the frame. Equally, content doesn't just appear. An interplay of causal factors, goals, motivations and ideological underpinnings shapes and provides the *raison d'être* for content: this is the model. Content always comes in specific frame–model couplings situating experienced, analogue and digital culture on a continuum while connecting that continuum to specific organisations.

We have here a context for publishing operations: to build a frame for content, according to a model. I will treat the frame and the model in turn.

From Containers to Frames

On 20 January 2012 at Christie's New York a book was sold for $7,922,500. It was, like any printed book, the end product of an industrial process, a copy, albeit heavily craft intensive. So what was the owner buying? Surely not the text? Then the physical matter itself? The book was John James Audubon's *The Birds of America* (published between 1827 and 1838), one of the most magnificent books ever printed. Bound in crimson morocco, heavily gilt, printed on exceptionally fine 'double elephant' paper, comprising four volumes of unique workmanship and 435 rich colour plates from three master engravers (William Lizars of Edinburgh and Robert Havell, Sr and Jr of London), the finished object is an undeniable masterpiece of book production. Failing to find orders or a publisher in Philadelphia and New York, Audubon had left America for Britain to secure publication. In order to finance such a task he needed advance subscribers and eventually found a reasonable 161, although more copies were printed. *The Birds of America* takes us into questions usually occupied by the philosophy of art – is its value in the content, in the specific instantiation of the content, that is the physical object, or is there something else? Are you buying the container for content, those superlative volumes, or are you buying content, those wonderful engravings? There aren't many copies of *The Birds of America* in existence, but scarcity today is a feature of many if not most printed works.

Prior to reproductive technologies content and media format were closely aligned. Copyability was a function of laborious like-for-like human effort, making the activity of reproducing content essentially the same as producing it in the first place. Any instantiation of the written word differed little from its initialisation and so there was a deep imbrication of copying and creating, content and media, content and form. We still talk of 'the book' both as the physical codex on our shelf but also as 'the text' or 'the work' in a more abstract sense; moreover we use these distinct terms interchangeably, shifting from one to the other without notice, suggesting we do not, in day-to-day circumstances, recognise a disjuncture between content and media. The publisher and commentator James Bridle gestures towards this when he sees the book as more complex than simply a physical object:

> Despite the growth of ebooks, the comments one mostly hears are appeals to a book's physicality. Rarely are the arguments to do with literature itself, but this is because we find it so hard to parse what is important about the book. Books are amenable to interaction analysis, yet those interactions are so complex, so embedded in our minds and our culture, that it seems impossible to separate them from the thing itself. Books are encoded experiences, they are repositories of the experiences we have with them, and they are ultimately souvenirs of themselves. The publishing industry has long profited from this unique assemblage of product and meaning. (Bridle 2012)

Bridle points out publishers are hardly neutral in conflating content and media, confusing book-as-medium with book-as-text. Yet publishers, too, are probably dupes. They see themselves as creators of books, the output of their work – the physical object – indistinguishable from the product – the text. Indeed to talk about a difference between output and product would have seemed strange to most publishers throughout history, despite the fact that of all people publishers are aware of the non-format-dependent nature of content. After all, they trade in content and manage it to fulfilment as a physical object *before* it is such.

The distinction between content and medium was evident in the printing press, when the means of reproducing texts differed from those of creating it, a disjuncture implying content and media were wholly distinct. With the printing press we see for the first time, to return to O'Leary's (2011b) phrase, the 'container' system of publishing, whereby publishers are curators of an entity 'content' which is then, to continue the metaphor, 'poured' into containers (in our case, books) amenable to distribution, sale and consumption.

Only with the rise of a new mode of content reproduction – digital technology – was the container model, not coincidentally, fully recognised and theorised. Print is an analogue technology, a smooth and corporeal phenomenon not obviously decoupled from itself. To contemporary eyes the container model of media may seem obvious; we live in a post-digital age saturated with media and content. But we shouldn't let our own digital savvy colour the analogue past. The godfathers of information and medium theory respectively give us a vocabulary for understanding the disjuncture of content and form. Claude Shannon was a mathematician working at the same Bell Labs instrumental in the early days of computing. He revolutionised knowledge of a slippery but fundamental concept: information. Shannon saw information as probabilistic, which is also to say mathematical,[1] and as capable of being understood syntactically. He used this breakthrough to provide a thorough account of information in which it was reconfigured as a 'message', originating from a 'source', proceeding via a 'transmitter' down a 'channel' to a 'receiver'. This vocabulary had a mathematical basis, allowing Shannon to completely divorce the message from the channel. To Shannon, message and channel were irrelevant to one another. The message went down the channel and no more. They were separate. Content, or information, had little other than coincidence to do with the media carrying it, the channel. Shannon's model was based on an idea of encoding and decoding in which the semantics of the message are irrelevant to understanding the communication structures at work. In book terms, the message is the content or the text; the channel is the book. Information theory cleaved a fruitful divide between the two, which is integral to the development and understanding of digital technology.

Just as content and media (a medium being the channel) were separate for Shannon, so they were for Marshall McLuhan (2001). There are important differences in how Shannon and McLuhan understand media, but they share the sense of content and media as fundamentally distinct. For McLuhan (2001), the content of a medium is simply another medium. The content of a book is writing, another medium altogether.[2]

---

1 For a loose definition I would follow that of Luciano Floridi (2010): semantic content.

2 This in itself raises questions of reflexivity about how we are to study media through other media. Studying media is therefore not separate from media, but like the study of consciousness, the object and the subject studying are not necessarily distinct.

The content of a CD is digital encoding the content of which is sound, of which the content is music. McLuhan shared the sense that this distinction was previously veiled:

> Before the electric speed and total field, it was not obvious that the medium is the message. The message, it seemed, was the 'content', as people used to ask what a painting was *about*. Yet they never thought to ask what a melody was about, nor what a house or a dress was about. In such matters, people retained some sense of the whole pattern, of form and function as a unity. (McLuhan 2001, 13–14)

McLuhan only uses content in inverted commas. For him it's a distraction from the big questions about media. 'Content' is a pointless sideshow.

Like Shannon, McLuhan (2001) has a sense of content and media as distinguishable, together in specific instantiations not by necessity but through chance and human agency. Content and media are different; media are just containers, channels, for content whatever those containers or channels should be. These thinkers operated in a shared context at the dawn of the Information Age, a time when media technology was evolving with unprecedented speed and scope. Media consumption ballooned. Both factors raised a new consciousness of the nature and effects of media. Where they differ is in their ascription of importance to media. To Shannon the channel was simply a vector or what is known in the telecoms industry as a 'dumb pipe'. To McLuhan (2001) media are everything. McLuhan's view of media famously posits media as key determinants of meaning; the nature of the dominant medium within a society informs the structures of that society. This is the essence of Toronto School medium theory – media are not neutral dumb pipes, but central actors with all too tangible consequences. Shannon and McLuhan are both concerned with the channel; they just disagree about its significance.

If we take from Shannon the basic tenets of a container system, we take from McLuhan the idea effect-neutral containers are chimerical. We can't just see containers as containers. We have to see how containers themselves shape content, how the contours of a container affect the contours of content (a point, it should be acknowledged, not without controversy). We also need an understanding for digital environments. O'Leary (2012) argues that containers break down in a digital context where talk of containers, with all their loaded analogue implications, no longer makes sense.[3] Geoffrey Nunberg (1996, 107) has noted that many see digital content as a wholly new and liberated version of its older counterpart: 'In the print world [content] was attached to things or contained in them, but now it can be liberated and manipulated as a kind of pure essence: we can break the bottles and have the wine.' However, he argues strongly against this proposition, suggesting that while digital may break old bottles, so to speak, it still needs bottles of some sort.

Our theory of content must then recognise how content is decoupled from its medium. An original Old Master painting, for example, is not content in this sense, as the content, the form and the media are interlaced. However, the image of that painting, separated from the painting, duly becomes content. It must account not only for how content is distinct from media but for how the two nonetheless have a formative relationship: how media have consequences and effects aside from content. It must also deal with the shift to a digital environment.

My term for content containers is frame. Frames are as much about presenting content as containing it. Frames in my language are distribution mechanisms, channels and media. They are contexts, modes of understanding as much as duplicative technologies. Frames are not just delivery systems or packages for content but content's experiential mode. They aren't dumb pipes. The book-as-container is a useful but flawed metaphor because it cannot encompass all forms of bibliographic, let alone cultural, experience. It fails to recognise containers are digital as well as physical. We never find pure, unmediated content as it's always framed in some way. There is always a system for distribution. Moreover we never come to content without certain preconceptions and expectations colouring our consumption. In other words we don't encounter content immanently – we encounter frame–content pairs. Typically the frame for long-form written content was the book. That is, a combination of paper, printing technology, ink, text, artwork, economic value and social status which collectively provide a frame for long-form writing.[4] But it needn't

---

3 O'Leary believes the discourse of containers has mislead us in understanding content: 'The way we think about book, magazine, and newspaper content is unduly governed by the physical containers we have used for centuries to transmit information. Those containers define content in two dimensions, necessarily ignoring context' (2012, 7). O'Leary calls the inability to conceive of content beyond containers 'container myopia'.

4 For N. Katherine Hayles (2008), terminology this might be the material 'body' of the text, without which the text cannot exist.

always be the book, which is now merely one frame among many. Looked at this way, the significance for publishing starts to become clear. Publishers are not just producers of books but constructors of frames.

To be clear, the language of frames and framing isn't new. The sociologist Erving Goffman speaks of frames, of which more later. The MIT artificial intelligence pioneer Marvin Minsky likewise developed a theory of frames, as have cognitive linguists. Book historians, cultural theorists and media analysts all discuss frames as a better means of conceiving of what books and indeed other media forms do and my analysis rests on the rich associative history of the term.

First, how do frames encompass the transition to digital? It's easy to imagine, as Nunberg (1996) implies many do, that ideas of containers are irrelevant in digital technology. However, digital technology itself comprises a delivery mechanism for content still subject to certain constraints – that is, forms of delivery – that comprise a large portion of its frame. Think of the screen. Digital content cannot be accessed 'directly', but is displayed on a screen. Whether E Ink, touchscreens, a projection on a wall or simply a PC monitor, just as books typically have pages so digital technology has the screen as the primary unit of delivery and display. Screens frame content.

Beyond this lay other sub-frames, notably specific encodings from basic HTML to high-level coding languages and the binary code on which all digital technologies rely. Adriaan van der Weel (2011) has argued that the nature of mark-up languages means that compared to the indistinguishability of content and form in analogue text, form and content always have greater separation when digital. Peter Brantley calls browsers an 'interaction container' (Brantley 2012, 192) for web content and standards; a very different container, to be sure, but a container nonetheless. Both screens and code rely on a physical infrastructure of fibre-optic cables, transistors, electricity, LEDs and so on. All of these frames condition digital content. It is no less mediated or framed than a book or broadsheet newspaper.

Far from being totally unbound, all digital content comes in a series of interlocking frames: hardware; screens and display mechanisms; mark-up languages; computer code. Screens and code don't contain or distribute content – they frame it, just as books frame content and in so doing enable distribution (in distributing the frame, you distribute the content).

Frames are not a static concept. They are malleable and pragmatic, crossing cultural and technological boundaries, as applicable to iPhone games as ancient sagas on fragile papyrus. Where we wouldn't speak of the iPhone as the container for a game, we could call it a frame. As an example of framing take one of the greatest feats in publishing, the *Oxford English Dictionary* (*OED*). First published in 1928 after seventy years of labour,[5] the first edition's statistics are staggering: 15,490 pages; 414,825 words; 1,827,306 illustrative examples selected from five million suggestions; 227,779,589 letters and numbers; 178 miles of type in 10 enormous morocco clad volumes (Winchester 2003). Clearly the *OED* wasn't just another book, another delivery system, but a scholarly monster in need of taming, a sprawling near unframeable enterprise. There are several levels of frame here. At the most basic, those 10 volumes act as a frame for the dictionary. At a somewhat meta-level, the goal of the *OED* is to be a definitive frame for the English language. Typically Victorian in its taxonomic ambition, it is a goal hitherto eluding the best lexicographers like Johnson and Webster.

Yet the history of the *OED*'s composition reveals further frames at work, up to the point where the chief executive of Oxford University Press (OUP) can state there may never again be a complete print edition, something previously unthinkable (Hui 2010). Originally growing out of the Philological Society, the project passed through the hands of several editors before a polymathic schoolteacher, James Murray, took it on. The *OED* needed special methodologies to achieve the comprehensiveness of its end goal, a total survey of English. Simon Winchester (2003) describes the system created by an earlier editor, Herbert Coleridge, who invented a standardised means of organising words through a system of quotation slips. This was the dictionary's basis. He also built a series of pigeon holes for holding the inchoate dictionary:

> The arrangement which he [Coleridge] designed was six square holes high, nine across – giving him a total of 54 pigeon-holes, with some 260 inches of linear space that were thought sufficient to hold comfortably between 60,000 and 100,000 of the slips. No greater number could Coleridge ever imagine having to deal with. (Winchester 2003, 57)

---

5 Long gestation periods are common for dictionaries – the Dutch *Woordenboek der Nederlandsche Taal* was started in 1851 and was only completed, inasmuch as dictionaries ever are, in 1998, some 147 years later.

A rebuilt set was 40 times larger and was still inadequate for the sprawling work in progress. James Murray called the room (initially in Mill Hill, London, from 1879 in Oxford) housing this vast assemblage of pigeon holes, slips and lexicographic effort 'the Scriptorium'. In a sense the Scriptorium embodied the *OED*, known as the New English Dictionary until 1895. If we can say a book is as much an 'information architecture' (Cope and Phillips 2006) as an object, then the sequence of stapled slips, scrawled definitions, folders and pigeon holes is such an information architecture, literally, for the dictionary.

Marshalling sufficient resources for such an organisational and scholarly endeavour wasn't easy. The Delegates of Oxford University Press, as its governing board is known, had originally budgeted £9,000 for completion. Relatively early it became evident the *OED* was intensely cash hungry and in the end it would consume some £300,000 of the press's money. One way of relieving the burden was to release small, lightly bound sections of the dictionary – fascicles – which could later be bound into a complete edition. The frame here is very different from the finished object; cheaper, smaller, bittier. However, through the fascicles the difficult process of typesetting and layout design was accomplished, all of which provides a sub-frame for the content or what you see on a page (incidentally setting the standard for dictionaries to come).

Slips, fascicles and finally august tomes are all alternative frames for the dictionary. A project as protracted and sprawling as the *OED* required framing in different ways for different times with different purposes. Those volumes published in 1928 were certainly designed to reflect the achievement of Murray, his team and their successors. However, even then different editions were on offer – you could get half volumes with different bindings, as well as the 'main' edition. But, of course, a living language is impossible to frame. English is fluid, rendering the dictionary immediately out-dated. The First Supplement to the *OED* appeared only five years after publication. What had once looked like a complete container suddenly had appendages. If we think in frames though, supplements are simply extensions of the original frame.

By the 1980s, it was clear a new breakthrough in managing lexicographic data was needed. With help from IBM, the Second Edition *OED* was revolutionised. Torn apart, rekeyed, converted into code, it was eventually printed and published to much fanfare in 1989. Again the scale is vast – 20 volumes, 615,100 entries, those definitions illustrated with some 2,436,600 quotations over 21,370 pages, using 59,000,000 words and no less than 63 kilograms of paper. Enabled by the digitisation of the *OED*'s production process, this was an order of magnitude bigger than before. This digitisation may have liberated it from print strictures, but simply provided a new (more flexible) frame for the book, which in 1989 was reframed back into print. Since 2000, however, the *OED* has been available online, updated every three months. If a Third Edition is released it will be a waypoint in an ever-expanding collection, not a fixed print landmark. The *OED* today is a database, not a book or set of books, or series of sheaves, or even mass of slips. That it is a database means it has simply been reframed by screens, code, database software, information management tools, server stacks, monitors – but not that it's unleashed from framing altogether.

In its monumental journey the *OED* has a constantly evolving set of distribution mechanisms, best understood as overlapping methods of framing the content. Each one articulates the *OED* in a subtly different way, emphasising a certain performative aspect of framing. Each acts as a 'container' for the dictionary, although the language of the container hardly helps us see the Scriptorium and the database on a continuum with each other and those handsome volumes gathering dust on library shelves.

Frames span digital and analogue, piles of loose paper and bound books, CDs and sheet music, postcards and Picassos, MySQL databases and physical storage, Shannon and McLuhan. Just as publishers choose frames in terms of demy hardbacks, B-format paperbacks, cover art, page design, typesetting and typography they might also chose frames in terms of iOS or Android builds, interface design and rendering quality. Frames allow us to view digital and analogue media on a spectrum rather than unbridgeable islands, to see how not only do highly divergent forms of published material all require delivery systems but how those systems present works in differing ways.

Frames as distribution systems – like books or MP3 files and players – gesture toward the ways in which frames and content are mutually involved yet also distinct. Frames condition content and vice versa. Miha Kovač (2008) and Clay Shirky (2002) have both discussed how traditional print runs shaped content. For example, novels and books in general have typically been a prescribed length because it was convenient for the codex, amenable to realistic print runs and hence economical, all of which is to say, the set of possible frames dictates what is possible for content (Kovač 2008). D. F. McKenzie (1999) and Roger Chartier (1995) both looked at the way non-verbal – framing – elements of texts produce meaning. Equally, content looks for new frames. Content creators don't passively wait for frames to evolve – they make it happen.

Frames have a presentational or performative aspect to them; they don't just deliver a work but deliver it in a certain way. The *OED*, finely bound, proudly embossed with the great golden crest of OUP, sporting huge page cuts, makes a statement about what the *OED* is and does. This presentational quality is part of why we can talk of frames as object nonspecific,[6] essentially a presentational mode as well as a medium, tying in with the notion media are never neutral but in themselves consequential. At the same time, this very feature is what allows us to maintain not just the separation of content and media but the force of content itself contra McLuhan (2011).

Not only are frames media, but they actively create the experience of media; frames have a subjective or phenomenological element, as well as a distributional or storage element. Frames may be presentational, but – because of this – they are also receptional. The way we experience a given work is a critical part of what we can say that work is. We cannot separate the delivery or framing of a work from the experience of it. Rather, experiential features are part of the frame. Moreover, such experiential features work both in terms of signals from the distribution mechanism itself and in terms of factors that are not at first sight 'built in'; namely, the penumbra of preconceptions, prejudices, expectations and complexes of personality and ideology subjectively brought to bear when cultural phenomena are encountered. The way we view a work is intrinsically part of that work.

To summarise, frames are the distributional and presentational mechanisms for content plus their attendant and subjectively experienced modes. 'Frame' is a convenient shorthand for grouping these interlinked concepts, the material and the immaterial aspects of presenting content.

How does this subjective aspect work?

A good starting point is the sociologist Erving Goffman, one of the originators of using the term frame in this context and a key influence on the practice of 'frame analysis' in media studies.[7] Goffman was an unusual sociologist keen to build an understanding not of social structure *per se*, but our individual, face-to-face interactions within it.

---

6 We could talk of a play at a theatre, an MP3 or the print edition of the *New York Times* as all being framed, for example.

7 Over the past forty years, there has been a pronounced shift to ideas of audience and reception in media studies generally.

He saw these 'co-presences' as highly evolved assemblages of
dramaturgy, rituals and games – productive metaphors for our daily
dealings. A large part of Goffman's (1997) study concerns the way
participants framed every encounter. Framing wasn't external to
an encounter between, say, a husband and wife, boss and employee
or customer and shopkeeper. Instead, the encounter was rendered
intelligible to the participants by dint of the frame itself. Frames
precede and therefore condition our interactions. Goffman (1997)
looks at the way frames put situations into certain 'keys' and how
frames transform and fabricate aspects of reality. At the nub of his
theory is the idea subjective preconceptions shape our experience in
predefined ways:

> I assume that definitions of a situation are built up in accordance
> with principles of organization which govern events – at least social
> ones – and subjective involvement in them; frame is the word I use
> to refer to such of these basic elements as I am able to identify.
> (Goffman 1997, 155)

Goffman brings a particularly social angle but was hardly the first to
think this way. The hermeneutic tradition of Hans-Georg Gadamer,
and to some extent a grand tradition of Western philosophy,
maintained versions of the idea. Goffman (1997) helpfully situates
it in our day-to-day experience and gave us a productive term in the
process. Gadamer's hermeneutics are interested in art or works of
cultural production, or rephrasing for our present purposes, books and
texts. Interpretation isn't an objective process, but one with a highly
subjective component in how we always already understand works
in certain ways. The school of literary theory known as reception
theory was founded on this argument. Writers like Hans-Robert
Jauss (1982) and Wolfgang Iser (1978) shift the burden of meaning
back to the reader and the interactions of text and reader. Texts
have no meaning in and of themselves but only in relation to their
being read.[8] Stanley Fish takes the position to its extremes, arguing
texts are entirely dependent upon the prior conceptions of readers.
Fish argues there is nothing about literature, or anything else for that
matter, that exists apart from the determining preconceptions of the

---

8 As Iser (1978, ix) wrote, 'the text represents a potential effect that is realized in
  the reading process'.

individual. As Robert C. Holub explains 'what we see or understand is always already determined by a prior perspective that enables the seeing and the understanding' (2003, 103).

Jauss and another theorist Tzvetan Todorov both use the Gadamerian phrase 'horizon of expectations', although with differing emphases. The latter sees 'horizon of expectations' as a function of genre, the former in terms of how we experience reading. The phrase is suggestive – the set of our possible expectations shapes experience of a work. My concern isn't with the theoretical minutiae, or with building a highly specific concept of frames. It is to follow the general argument. Not only do works have a subjective component but this component helps constitute works, telling us how to receive them; moreover these subjective components don't happen randomly but are purposefully created.

Pierre Bourdieu (1993) saw society enabling art. Only when external forces – society – tell us something is a work of art do we regard it as art: 'The work of art is an object which exists as such only by virtue of the (collective) belief which knows and acknowledges it as a work of art' (Bourdieu 1993, 35). Belief, discourse – for Bourdieu these are productive forces without which we cannot conceive of published matter. Bourdieu is saying the contexts of cultural products are what let us think of them as cultural products in the first place. Take away the context and you take away everything. Gérard Genette (1997) approaches the situation from a different angle, seeing all books as having what he calls paratexts. At one level these are internal – think of the epigraph and the title page – and so can be straightforwardly seen in terms of the frame-as-package. However, Genette also sees paratexts as external, so-called 'epitexts' like marketing materials also involved in the presentation of a work. Matters outside a book are still, for Genette, integral to a book's presentation and therefore reception. While the emphasis differs from reception theory, Bourdieu and Genette share with it and Goffman the sense cultural production is never experienced raw, directly, always involving prior and external constructions.

The publishing scholar Claire Squires (2007) ties many of these strands into a theory of book marketing as a productive force in contemporary literature. Developing the work of Fish, Bourdieu, Todorov, Genette and marketing theory, Squires sees marketing as part of the process by which readers' experiences of books are constructed, a process which has become ever more central as the industry consolidates into global media conglomerates.[9] Squires argues publishers don't just allow this mass of preconceptions to accumulate. Rather they constantly manufacture and influence the nimbus of preconceptions in a favourable way: 'Marketing is effectively the making of contemporary writing. In a very real sense [...] material conditions and acts of marketing profoundly determine the production, reception and interpretation of literature' (Squires 2007, 16). Numerous marketing avenues are available. Publishers are all too aware of how artwork, production, packaging, pricing, publisher and author branding, content signals, retail placements, market positioning, advertisements and other paid notices create impressions. Generic conventions are exploited to pre-position books in categories designed to guide readers. Before we encounter content, inflections, representations, thresholds, interpretive communities are produced; desire, opinion and purchase-decisions enmesh in the broad-shouldered work of 'marketing'.

Prizes like the Pulitzer or Prix Goncourt are good analogies of how lustre is imparted by a cultural equivalent of the 'halo effect'.[10] James English (2005) has examined prizes' 'economy of prestige'. Prizes are switching points between cultural, economic, social, political and media capital. Above all, prizes confer symbolic and media capital, radiating authority and esteem, which can then generate a monetary return. Publication itself works in an analogous, albeit weaker, fashion. English's analysis includes what he calls the 'rhetoric of scandal', the controversy and sniping surrounding prizes. This isn't antithetical to the economy of prestige but part of it. All the discourse around prizes otherwise known as gossip produces the symbolic capital attached to them. The more scandal the better. The point of prizes is to build a 'veil of magic, of collective make-believe' (English 2005, 245) skeined over victorious content. Publishers make and manipulate that same magic, that field of impressions. We shouldn't underestimate the value or efficacy the association with a specific publisher brings to content.

Brands work in the same way. Brands are built actively. They curl themselves around people's identities, symbols and behaviours, the uses

---

9 Walter Benjamin (2008) argues that a work of art's 'aura' is annulled in 'the age of mechanical reproduction'. If so, in the age of digital reproduction marketing and publicity departments exert enormous effort to recreate a kind of postmodern aura of controlled messages, hype, prestige and interest.

10 The halo effect is the psychological trait whereby we tend to judge a thing by one element of a thing, a 'halo' that rightly or wrong extends to the entire entity.

and imagined uses of products. Embodying immaterial elements like aspirations, tribal values and the (often idealised) context in which the item is consumed, brands produce a certain take on reality. They prefigure our experiences of products. For instance, we don't approach books from an austere academic press as we do imprints specialising in pulp romance.

Squires (2007) is mainly concerned with the contemporary experience of books. My argument extends such a condition to all content. Marketing is only our current term for how crucial parts of the subjective or experiential aspect of framing occur. Squires indicates how subjective components of frames dovetail with delivery mechanisms and how publishers produce impressions as well as objects. She talks of formats and packaging, suggesting content isn't divided between distributional and subjective aspects. The continuum on which they lie is the frame.

A concrete example ties these strands together. Alongside the *OED* as a landmark in British publishing (and *The Birds of America* as a favourite of elite auction houses) Shakespeare's First Folio has probably been studied more than any other single edition and can't be thought of in terms of twenty-first-century marketing dynamics. It's a good case study. Before the Folio, the scurrilous William Jaggard, a printer, publisher and initially bookseller working in St Paul's Churchyard, the traditional heartland of English books, produced cheap quarto editions of some Shakespeare plays. Jaggard didn't wait for approval before going to press; instead he printed all kinds of doggerel attributed to Shakespeare and corrupted versions of his plays in the late 1590s and 1600s.[11] Shakespeare saw theatre as his primary business, so the problem is likely to have been more vexing than ruinous.

When Shakespeare died in 1616, Jaggard had built a successful printing, publishing and bookselling operation, with two presses and around nine journeymen printers and apprentices. Shakespeare's former colleagues at the Globe Theatre and in the King's Men, John Heminge and Henry Condell, were instrumental in initiating the First Folio as a memorial to their friend and colleague. They formed a syndicate to secure rights already lodged in the Stationers' Company Register and bought Jaggard on board. The choice of a folio is revealing. Folios were large, imposing books traditionally reserved for only the most elevated

---

11 The first play of Shakespeare's to be printed, in quarto form, was *Titus Andronicus* by a printer named John Danter (Murphy 2003).

material and certainly not the cheap entertainments of the stage. Simply by printing as a folio, a theatrical honour previously accorded only to the playwright Ben Jonson, Heminge and Condell were making a statement about the aesthetic and moral worth of the content. They included a number of handy paratexts designed to supplement the message like Ben Jonson's famous dedication and the etching of Shakespeare (his only contemporary portrait). Heminge and Condell systematically compiled and edited the First Folio – there were few if any comprehensive drafts of Shakespeare's plays and they pieced together scripts, from memory if nothing else. Moreover in creating the First Folio they possibly invented acts as a dramatic structuring tool, the demands of framing shaping content (Collins 2009). Jaggard, Heminge and Condell were also keen to build an audience; so Jaggard, for example, announced the Folio in a catalogue at the Frankfurt Book Fair. Those paratexts like the portrait page also doubled as widely distributed promotional handbills publicising and shaping expectations about the coming product.

This audience-building work was reflected in the high initial print run in 1623 of an estimated 750 copies (Collins 2009), although given the expense of the First Folio it shut out many readers used to cheaper editions. It included 36 plays; 18 of which had never been published including *Julius Caesar*, *Twelfth Night*, *Macbeth*, *The Tempest* and *The Comedy of Errors* (for comparison, bear in mind most plays of the period have been lost forever). Binding was still mostly the buyer's responsibility; they could thus choose to further frame their edition.

From the moment of its printing, the content of the First Folio was in dialogue with the form of the medium. That format made huge statements about the content. Books were still enough of a rarity that the very act of printing the First Folio carried great cultural weight before anyone even read it. Shakespeare's name was reasonably well known, in its own way serving to *a priori* position the First Folio among the cognoscenti.

The subsequent publishing history of Shakespeare is well known. The Second Folio came in 1632, a third in 1663 and, after many of those were destroyed in the Great Fire of 1666, a fourth was printed in 1685. In the early eighteenth century, a vitriolic battle was waged between editors of Shakespeare, Alexander Pope and Lewis Theobald, as to the correct texts. Despite having backing from the great publishing magnate of his day (the superbly connected Jacob Tonson), Pope was on the wrong side of Shakespearean scholarship. The visibility of the debate indicates Shakespeare's growing stature in the canon of

English literature. However, up until the latter half of the eighteenth century, newer editions of Shakespeare were more valuable than old. Only when Shakespeare attained something approaching his present status did the First Folio become more valuable than more recent editions. In other words the value of the First Folio as an object was dependent on perceptual shifts about Shakespeare, literature and taste, whereby the First Folio was reconfigured as the original, thus more authentic and of more value. The First Folio as a container gradually became a symbol for the wider edifice of English Letters and in doing so became above all a cultural signifier; facsimile versions of the First Folio were available from 1866 rendering the informational – or channel – aspect of the Folio void.[12]

Copies of the Folio have unique characters. In the Folger Shakespeare Library in Washington DC, the so-called Folio #1 has a near-mythical status among Shakespeare scholars as being perfectly preserved. The Grenville Folio in the British Library was part of Thomas Grenville's incomparable bibliographic collection from the early nineteenth century and, again, is considered a peculiarly fine example. In the First Folio, we see a unique set of physical and cultural coordinates: Heminge and Condell's commemorative goals; the debates and machinations of journeymen printers in Jaggard's workshop; the limitations of existing copies of Shakespeare's work; conventions of book format; specific histories of folios over the years; evolving public tastes; and differing binding design. Literary icon it may be, but we shouldn't forget the First Folio is an information channel and an early example of an industrially produced content distribution mechanism. Each version of the First Folio is its own frame with its own resonances. Without the concept of frame we have a poorer understanding not only of individual folios, but the edition as a whole and by extension all editions of all books.

Returning to Audubon, if we view *The Birds of America* in terms of frame, with all the cultural and psychological baggage that brings, we begin to see how it can be worth so many millions despite disseminating widely available content. Frames take us beyond containers and beyond

---

12 There is another sense, of course, in which individual folios carry information: about their own histories. Studying the differences between folios has been a field of study in itself, revealing much about the business of printing in seventeenth-century London and Shakespeare's writing. They also contain information about their uses. For example, what better way to appreciate the gargantuan character of Dr Johnson than to witness the many food and wine stains littering his First Folio (Collins 2009)?

the language of media. They bring four things in addition. First, the subjective aspects of our media experience are built in from the start. Second, they are flexible. Discussions of different media parcels the world into neat segments, but as McLuhan (2001) notes, media contain media, or interact with different media. Digital doesn't do away with containers; it just changes them. Frames allow us to move flexibly between all these formats, appreciating points of continuity. Thirdly all frames come with a great deal of specificity. Media is an abstract idea ill-suited to analysing specific examples. Frames accommodate the abstract and concrete, the general and the particular – we can talk about 'The Book' or 'The Web' as frames, but also the Grenville Folio, a Wagner box set or a download of *The Wire* as specifically instantiated frames. Lastly and above all, content creators or intermediary actors carefully design frames to achieve precise results. Creators and intermediaries think carefully about frames, spending a great deal of time and energy getting them right. Frames allow us to unpick the decisions, reasoning and histories behind content creation.

It is to those reasons we now turn.

From Motivations to Models

Frames don't produce content. Generally, but in the age of content farms not exclusively, people produce – and disseminate – content. People don't behave randomly. Their actions reflect assemblages of motivations and expectations, conscious and unconscious, internally or externally conditioned, affecting their behaviour. Content is no exception. It therefore makes no sense to discuss content without some reference to how these motivational factors work, as the factors involved will have powerfully helped constitute the work in question. We have seen how creation and publication are distinct activities (even when happening simultaneously, as with self-publishing on the web, they remain conceptually distinct) and so each comes with its own set of reasons – writers don't necessarily write for the same reasons publishers publish.

The language in this fuzzy area of motivations and hidden causal parameters is difficult and loaded, and the concept, as with frame, has a catholic sense of inclusion. Talk of motivations is limiting for two reasons. First, because literary theorists regard the idea of reading back to authorial, or even publisher, motivation as impossible. Second, it is too narrow and personalised. It doesn't account for the social character of content origination. Instead I regard content as produced in line with models, which operate for the primary production of content but also for intermediaries like publishers. Furthermore, these models may be the same but they can also be directly opposed, and within either category there likely isn't one model at work but complex compounds of different models.

The concept of models will be discussed in greater detail later so my remarks here are confined to a general sketch and a few points of clarification. A model of some sort is a *sine qua non* for the production and framing of content. Models are abstract extrapolations, which we use to guide our actions, with both explanatory, predictive and, through those, causal efficacy. For publishers, the obvious model is the business model. From the earliest times printers and publishers were proto-capitalists, working in a capital-intensive, risk-laden environment to shift stock as quickly as possible. Publishing's business model has, in this sense, remained largely unchanged for hundreds of years. Whether in fifteenth-century Lyons or twenty-first-century Delhi, it relies on a careful costing of production and effective dissemination of works, with the expectation net profit remains after costs of goods sold and overheads. Typically publishers have a financial model that allows them to estimate return on investment for a title. However, the business model of publishing is by no means limited to selling books. Rights sales, contract publishing, editorial services and packaging are all distinct business models that often work in tandem with a basic unit sales model. Increasingly detailed financial modelling, as with many industries, is becoming an essential part of publishing.

A common mistake is to reduce all models to business models. It is assumed because publishing is predominantly a business, it can be understood solely in business terms. As I discuss later, political, aesthetic, religious and social as well as economic concerns shape models. Overtly political publishing takes many forms – whether national parliamentary records like *Hansard* in the UK or the Congressional Report in the US; output from bodies like the World Bank or the OECD; state-owned publishing enterprises like the People's Literature Publishing House in China; quasi-state connected, as with Mondadori in Berlusconi's Italy; or simply publishing out of political conviction, like Verso on the left or Regnery on the right. All of them operate according to various stated or unstated political models.

Communication models are also relevant. Communication studies has built a rich array of models for the understanding of communication and media. An in-depth analysis of such models is beyond the scope of this project, but each articulates a vision of content and communication. Communication models are not in themselves content models, insofar as they do not explain the actions behind content, but they do provide those actions with intelligibility. People expect content to have communicative force and communication models describe the mechanics of that force.

Models are always situated, intimately bound up with their contexts. There is no sense in which a model for content can ever be extracted from its milieu. It provides a link between social formations and cultural production, operating on both the creative and intermediary levels of a work. The selection of available models is bound by what is socially available; given that all content has a model, the nature of a society hence limits and structures the creation of cultural works by limiting and structuring the range of possible models. Moreover, models are actively constitutive of works and the publishing of works, which is to say they are intrinsically part of why the end product is the way it is. We cannot untangle content and model. Content aims to achieve things and is created and disseminated to achieve them; the content's model sets those aims. Diffusive, nuanced and partially determining, models connect publishing to society.

In short, content happens for a reason; although not a straightforward reason to be sure. Composed of differing, even oppositional parts, difficult to unravel and often greatly obscured, models are nonetheless at the heart of content. Just as content always has a frame, so it always has a model.

A Rounded View of Content

By introducing frames and models as metaphors for understanding content I don't mean to literalise them. They remain just that, metaphors, albeit productive ones that enable us to better perceive the workings of content and, by extension, the content industries, intermediaries, creators and, of course, consumers who sustain the entire ecosystem. While these processes undoubtedly occur in some form or another, their manifold complexity and endless variations are almost impossible to reduce to a single analysis. The language of framing and modelling are heuristics overcoming the limitations of alternative terminology.

A sustained example illustrates the value for a theory of publishing. To go with the *OED* and the First Folio, I will complete a remarkable troika of British publishing: the founding of Penguin Books in the 1930s.

This case is so instructive as at first glance, and certainly in the popular imagination, Penguin's signature breakthrough is one of format or container: the invention of the paperback. However, Penguin's rapid rise to the pinnacle of English-language publishing is more complex. For a start, Penguin certainly didn't invent the paperback or even the cheap edition. Editions like the Routledge Railway Library in the mid-nineteenth century or J. M. Dent's Everyman Library in the early twentieth pioneered popular, attractively priced publishing reliant on high print runs and sales.[13] Thinking of containers isn't enough to explain the founding of Penguin.

Lane was working in a heroic, clubbable age of British publishing, dominated by great characters and still-resonant names like Stanley Unwin, Victor Gollancz, Jonathan Cape, Fredric Warburg and Geoffrey Faber. Gollancz had already tried and failed with a cheap, paper-bound imprint by the 1930s. The real precedent for the 'paperback revolution' came from Europe where a German, Christian Bernard Tauchnitz, started publishing English-language paperbacks for Continental consumption in 1847. Tauchnitz Editions were distinctive and popular with Victorian tourists travelling the Continent. They were relished by British publishers, pleased their books were no longer pirated abroad but earning a royalty. However, by the 1930s, Tauchnitz books had started to look and feel tired, creating an opening for another German publisher, Kurt Enoch, who founded the Albatross Verlag in cooperation with the great Italian publisher Arnoldo Mondadori and a colourful Englishman, John Holroyd-Reece. In 1932, they launched a new series of well-designed, modern-looking paperbacks. If, Tauchnitz 'familiarised some British book buyers with the concept of the paperback book', then it was Albatross who 'directly influenced the format and design of the mid-twentieth-century British paperback' (Feather 2005, 172–3).

Albatross also made more up-to-date content selections than Tauchnitz, who were at the cutting edge in the nineteenth century but less so in the twentieth. Albatross published James Joyce, Aldous Huxley and Virginia Woolf. While Tauchnitz used coloured bands to indicate topic, Albatross went all out on the colour scheme as a way of identifying the theme or topic. At this time, the publishing world was generally conservative; it was against book tokens and new retail channels, and both ignorant and wary of the new media and tastes exploding into

---

13 There was also a wave of paperback publishing in the United States in the 1840s (Tebbel 1987).

public consciousness. Enter Lane, a young man with a controlling stake in a financially troubled publisher, The Bodley Head. Lane had already demonstrated a willingness to take risks and a head for business – both essential qualities for a publisher – but his plan for Penguin was far more ambitious than anything he had tried before. Lane would licence existing hardback titles and publish large quantities in a cheap paperback format, a model not too far from a Routledge or an Everyman. Established publishers were hostile, believing the concept vulgar or commercially doomed. Of the significant houses only Jonathan Cape offered serious support and even then in the expectation of failure.

Suffice to say, when the list launched in 1935 it was clear that the publishing world would never be the same again. Almost immediately, first Pocket in the United States and then Pan in the UK eagerly joined the paperback stampede to refashion the scale, economics and, eventually, the gentlemanly bubble of mid-twentieth-century publishing.

The question is if Penguin didn't *invent* the paperback, what did they do and why did it make them the period's great success story? Several factors are at play.

First, Penguin was, in part, about content selection. Lane was not especially literary. Rather he was entrepreneurial, with a great eye for publishing. He had a high-minded sense of what Penguin might achieve, comparable to that of Lord Reith at the nascent BBC. Lane wanted quality literature in his series, strong books, entire writer's *œuvres*. In later series, Penguin would display a distinctly left-leaning bias. The first ten titles blended the highbrow and populist, combining *Ariel* by André Maurois, a biography of the poet Shelley, and Ernest Hemingway's *A Farewell to Arms* with popular novelists like Dorothy L. Sayers and Mary Webb. During his career, Lane took principled stands in publishing *Ulysses* and *Lady Chatterley's Lover* to name only the most famous. Two points should be noted: 1) Lane was operating on a model not solely financial in its calculations – like Reith he entertained ideas about cultural value, which would ultimately become expressed through his publishing; 2) there was a subtle political inflection to parts of the list, particularly the non-fiction Pelicans and Specials.

Second, it was about design. From the start the series look was carefully crafted with still legendary Penguin designers like Jan Tschichold, Romek Marber and Hans Schmoller working on the books. Penguin was a major brand before the word was current, limning a lasting and powerful visual identity: contemporary but classic, iconic, fresh, different and clean, a considered exercise in recognisability when some publishers considered even dust jackets *outré*. Inside and out, the design standards were high, and the books immediately became collectable as a result.

Third, price was vital. Lane wanted books to sell at sixpence, significantly cheaper than hardbacks of the time and famously around the same price as a packet of cigarettes. Libraries were eroding the market for bought books and the Penguins needed to be in reach of impulse buying for a large segment of the population. This required enormous print runs to break even, shaping the format choice and making the venture a great gamble – but it also allowed the works to scale, reach wide audiences and have impact. Lane understood that shifting his customers' instinctive reaction towards price was imperative and so the container was secondary in importance to the perception of value in establishing the imprint.

Fourth, distribution was a crucial part of Penguin's success. At first business was not looking good for Penguin. With large fixed costs, high expectations and enormous print runs they were getting insufficient orders from sceptical bookshops. Despite printing 20,000 of each title, Lane initially received orders of only 7,000 per title. An enormous order of 63,500 copies from the general retailer Woolworth's saved the day (Lewis 2006). They flew off the shelves and Penguin never looked back. From the start, placing Penguins in non-bookshop channels like supermarkets and newsagents was critical to their success.[14]

Fifth, changing media consumption habits were happening in the 1930s, despite the retrograde desires of the publishing establishment. Radio and cinema were redefining popular entertainment. Meanwhile, the population was educated, enfranchised and politicised as never before. In other words, a newly constituted audience was waiting for what Penguin would deliver.

Lane was in the content game. But as should be clear, content was not the decisive factor for Penguin. After all, Penguin was about re-publishing works already available. It should also be clear reinventing the paperback was only part of the story. From the earliest chapbooks and handbills, print went beyond what became known as the hardback. What we see is a peculiarly successful coupling of model and frame. The format was driven by a need to produce low price points, as was the economy of scale in the huge print runs. Perception of value takes precedence over form in Penguin's strategy. Distribution was designed

---

14 This has echoes of the Routledge Railway Library, which grew symbiotically with W. H. Smith, which first opened its first railway newsstand at Euston Station in London in 1848.

to reformulate the elite activity of book buying into something as quotidian a purchase as cigarettes. Design, use of colour and even the name and logo of an Antarctic bird caught people's attention. It gave the series unity, class and distinction. The paperback is only part of this mix, simultaneously acting as driver and being driven by it. The point is not so much the paperback, but the *mass market* paperback. This is as much about constructing an audience (mass market) as a medium (the paperback).

When we look at Penguin's early years in terms of frames and models, this mix makes sense as an elaborate frame to recast content according to models of scalability, venture capital, flexible yet assured aesthetics and social democratic politics. We not only pick up the subtleties and intersubjective positioning of the frame, but we see how the models craft the frame, just as with the First Folio and the *OED*. Despite appearances, content comes in constellations rather than neat packages. In the twinned notion of frame and model, delivery systems seamlessly integrate with economics, consumers' cultural perception elides with systematic branding design and finely honed content selection meets media distribution platforms.

Without frames and models, or analogous concepts, we have an impoverished account of content. As Penguin demonstrates, frames and models aren't just useful for understanding content – they are essential to understanding publishing.

Chapter 4

THE SYSTEM OF PUBLISHING

Encompassing inky Nuremberg pressworks and MacBook-lined Lower East Side lofts, publishing is nothing if not diverse. Its definition is troubled and unclear. Frames and models are likewise multifarious – an incunable and a BitTorrented epub file are hardly alike. Yet the argument of this book is that despite these differences there is still something we understand as 'publishing'. Even though frames and models constantly evolve and change, what remains is a consistent understanding of frames and models in the abstract. We see a conceptual thread binding together the many-splendored edifice of content. In doing so, we find the conceptual thread binding together that of publishing.

Publishing is formed, as with frames and models, from components not obviously cohering. Historically and geographically publishing seems incompatible, unaligned. If we shift our gaze we see that there is a consistent practice, despite activities changing over time. Despite different contexts, conditions and operations, certain actions are part of a continuum performed repeatedly by those known as publishers across continents and over the centuries.[1]

At the heart of publishing are two mutable activities: filtering and amplification. Both resolve the question of what it means to make something public; the historical and product-based differentials within the use of the word publishing; the sense of publishing as simply an exercise in content management; and the new landscape of digital publishing and its attendant threats. Both are core because in some form they are always present. Other publisher operations fit the modular structure of publishing (they are optional elements in the publishing process like in-house proofreading, printing or rights selling). Filtering and amplification cannot be removed. They span time and space, as relevant

---

1 This point should not be taken literally. For much if not most of their history, in English at least, publishers were known not as publishers but as printers or booksellers.

in the imperial publishing houses of Song dynasty China or a student's Weibo feed in present-day Shanghai. They are at the centre of the ever-changing value chain.

Proposing these two concepts as the axes of publishing isn't new. Faced with the digital onslaught, publishers have started whittling their functions to a core, with ideas of curating, market making and audience building never far from the discussion. We still need an account of how these actions have constituted publishing historically, how they continue to do so and how the nature of their relationship with publishing shapes its future. This is not to claim some kind of Platonic 'form' of publishing, only to note and interpret a recurring pattern of behaviour.

Frames and models are integral to filtering and amplification: framing and modelling occurs at all stages of these processes and supplies us with, respectively, the how and the why of publishing. Filtering and amplification occur *through* frames *according* to models. This chapter describes what I call the system or network of publishing; it is an account that views frames, models, filtering and amplification in a network of actors, as they have been repeated, transformed and pushed through tectonic shifts in communications, economics and all the tumultuousness of history.

Publishing Theory and the Communications Circuit

Literary theory is a crowded field, spanning Aristotelian teleology to eco-criticism and queer theory. Books are the focus of a prodigious body of scholarship. As this argument has tried to establish, theories of publishing are rather more scarce. Robert Darnton's seminal essay 'What Is the History of Books?' (1982) is not about publishing, but his model for the processes around books has become standard for describing the function of publishing.

Darnton's programme was simple: to give 'a holistic view of books' in response to the expanding, fissiparous and nascent field of the history of the book by establishing

a communications circuit that runs from the author to the publisher (if the bookseller does not assume that role), the printer, the shipper, the bookseller and the reader. The reader completes the circuit because he influences the author both before and after the act of composition. (Darnton 2006, 11)

In the communications circuit, each segment on the circuit is understood as a function of the circulation of books. Publishing is thus positioned between author and printer on a book's journey. Darnton, it should be noted, is careful to specify that he isn't reducing book history to a connect-the-dots formula – something that applies equally to this study. The communications circuit is useful shorthand for the stages in a book's life, but it has come under criticism, for example, from Adams and Barker (2006). They argue that Darnton's scheme is oriented to people at the expense of the material book. In their view, the smooth finish of the communications circuit 'ignores the sheer randomness, the speculative uncertainty of the book trade' (Adams and Barker 2006, 51). They propose putting the book-as-material-object, not the roles or the social contexts, back at the circuit's centre.

The fact that Darnton discusses roles can be considered a strength when viewed from a publishing angle. As we have seen, publishing is not necessarily to be equated with books; if anything, it is some kind of activity, a role to be played. Yet Darnton's theory inadequately explains publishing and requires modification if we are to accept it as a feature of publishing studies. First, Darnton is dealing only with book publishing; hence, his theory will always miss vital parts of the concept. Second, as Adams and Barker indicate, Darnton's theory veils the messiness of publishing – there is no sense of financial risk, or risk of any kind.

More tellingly Darnton has created a flat structure that doesn't indicate the value, aims or primary function of the publisher. He demonstrates the circuit in a vivid reconstruction of how bookseller Isaac-Pierre Rigaud of Montpellier went about selling Voltaire's *Questions sur l'Encyclopédie*, by looking at the relations between Rigaud and other booksellers, the printers, the law in France at the time and the various distribution routes, via Lyons or Nice, needed to ship the books from Switzerland, where the book was printed, to Montpellier. This elucidates the circuit: 'For the printed sheets to reach Rigaud in Montpellier from the STN's [Société typographique de Neuchâtel, a Swiss printer who put out pirated editions of Voltaire among others] shop in Neuchâtel, they had to wind their way through one of the most complex stages in the book's circuit' (Darnton 2006, 15). Implied is a unitary circuit, with overtones of one circuit ('the book's'), despite the fact a multiplicity of copies must imply many different circuits. The circuit metaphor disguises the most important element of the printed book: there exist many copies going to many booksellers, thus ensuring the text is more widely distributed than otherwise. Publishers are almost by definition interested in multiple circuits for a given title, rather than a singular circuit for a book. The focus for Darnton is on the book more than Adams and Barker suggest.

Darnton and Adams and Barker do all acknowledge difficulties presented by publishers to any model of textual circulation, indicated by the inclusion of a double arrow in Darnton's original diagram, the only two-way relation in the circuit. As he admits, the understanding of publishing is far from certain: 'the evolution of the publisher as a distinct figure in contrast to the master bookseller and the printer still needs systematic study' (Darnton 2006, 18). Even as the circuit implies a fixed set of publishing functions, Darnton acknowledges the difficulty in making publishing's specificity clear.

While the communications circuit works as a device for grouping the flows and processes of books, it is less helpful for publishing. We still don't have a solid account of the relationship between making public and publishing. In Darnton's diagram social concerns are loosely sketched and left deliberately vague. Rather than abandoning the circuit, we need modifications. We need amplifiers and resistors, switching boards and power generators. As it stands, the circuit, in its linearity and focus on the singular, offers us a basis instead of a complete theory. A theory of publishing must work alongside a theory of the book, but it can't be contained by it. In other words, we must accommodate the circuit's publishing juncture with ideas of filtering and amplification.

Filtering

Issues of selection are prominent in media studies. While the means, methods and extents of selection are contentious, that selection itself must happen is generally taken for granted. The reason why is because we must distinguish between a medium, or media generally, and organisations and activities working within those broader umbrellas. If there is no element of filtering whatsoever, we have a medium. Whether we consider text, television or the Internet, the limitations are those only of the medium. In principle, anything that can be filmed and broadcast can be televised. In practice, unlike YouTube suggests, this isn't the case; only programmes that make it through the filter of television production companies, network executives, sponsors, scheduling boards and the like, actually appear on television. While the medium is filter neutral, the individuals and organisations behind the medium must make decisions about what, in the language of this study, to frame.

This split between an open medium and the more tightly controlled organisations collectively producing the content within that medium is reflected in the dual senses of the word 'media'. Denis McQuail registers this when he argues we must 'distinguish between a *process* of mass communication and the actual *media* that make it possible' (2010, 24), while Roger Parry notes how 'the word "medium" is both an adjective and a noun' (2011, 7). 'The media' in the sense of the organisations behind media, in this case publishers, bring an element of selection. This is no more than to point out that at some level publishing must be agentive; some decision must take place for a work to be published or excluded. Some kind of filtering oversight is needed to stop publishing segueing into the broader sense of media ('medium'). There are always filters, whether they are old-fashioned commissioners or ranking algorithms.

In most publishing houses, this element is uncontroversial. A regular acquisitions or commissioning meeting collectively decides what the firm will publish based on a variety of inputs and decision-making norms, what I call models. One can easily imagine applying this process to fifteenth-century publishers and printers as they grappled with recognisable problems of whether to publish a title according to house criteria. Filtering allows conceptual space between the printer and publisher, both now and in earlier times. Printers don't generally filter or select, they simply take jobs. In the eighteenth century, for example, printers were specifically banned from joining the Conger, a closed group that dominated British publishing. Printers were barred from becoming co-publishers. Publishing is where works are selected in the first instance, by agents, according to a model of some kind, or more correctly models. Filtering is thus structured by models; far from random, filtering is imbricated in the relevant models for a given publishing process. In the content flow, filtering is the pivotal moment after the decision to produce or write in the first place (although in digital environments they may happen simultaneously). Where financiers pay for a work to be printed, like the Conger, they are making the decisive choice to publish the content. They are the ultimate filtering agent.

Why filtering in particular and not, say, selection? The term filtering is more inclusive. Selection may be the dominant paradigm of the publishing industry; but historically, and especially with the advent of digital, the term doesn't give us enough space. Filtering implies a wider set of possible conditions of agency within publishing and more possible publishing methods. As publishing evolves and selection gives way to other intermediary forms in digital contexts, recognising the priority of filtering helps.

Take the difference between the Internet and Facebook. On the Internet anything goes. Its open architecture allows free dissemination of content. Much – perhaps most – of this content is created and disseminated purposively. However, the existence of bots, other automated programs, mirror sites and the lack of a primary filter means the idea of the web-as-publisher is nonsensical. Rather we shift the publishing role back onto those agents that choose and disseminate. On one level, Facebook resembles the web in its vastness and nominal openness. However, it is a far more curated space, owned, controlled and filtered by Facebook's various policies and user decisions. Facebook deliberately designs and filters its site to aid user self-publication. The primary publishers of material on Facebook are those deciding to publish; but we can start to think of Facebook as a collaborative co-publisher in a way we can't for the Internet. Whereas we might conceive the Internet as a 'printer', Facebook's editorialising means we can't think of it that way, even if its structure and openness take it beyond traditional ideas of a publisher.

Selection and filtering are hot topics among publishers. As the industry's ongoing value is questioned, they are seen as repositories of professional practice (hopefully) immune to disintermediation. Filtering of some kind cannot be replaced. In digital contexts there may be unlimited distributional capacity, but there is never enough attention. The corollary being filtering or selection are still necessary to highlight what readers should read, and, to that end, a mechanism is needed to control the apportion of resources. Scarcity doesn't go away in digital contexts; it just takes a new form. Scarcity now refers to a shortage of attention and the means to bring works to attention. Either way we need filtering given the impossibility of unlimited resources.

The idea of publishers and media as gatekeepers is an old one. Miha Kovač, Clay Shirky and Yochai Benkler among others argue the gatekeeper role grows with the unavoidably high capital costs of production and distribution in analogue environments. Throughout history, printing and distributing books was hard, based on small readerships and limited means, and so subject to arbitrary powers and periodic controversies. When even acquiring paper was expensive and difficult, the necessity of filtering, of choosing to publish this book and not that, was obvious. Printing the Bible in sixteenth-century Europe made good business sense. Nevertheless, you still needed to choose the 'right' bible or have the relevant papal or governmental licence. Despite publishable writing being comparatively rare, it still didn't impinge on the constant need for selection and filtering decisions from publishers operating with a huge range of models. This does not, for the reasons suggested above, change radically in the digital age. Gatekeeping hasn't gone away, it's just changed – much like publishing.

Filtering is heterogeneous. Self-publishers filter in the moment they decide to upload their ebook manuscript, but so do committees of suits in plush boardrooms. Filtering can be based on commerce or idealism; it could be massively inclusive or the pinnacle of exclusivity. A distant financier advancing funds to complete a project designed, written, produced and disseminated elsewhere filters, as does a writer, illustrator, printer, publisher and bookseller like William Blake doing everything themselves. In all instances, there is a common necessity for some form of filtering as part of publishing's modelling process, its calculation of a value proposition.

A growing body of work within media studies and publishing studies looks at filtering in practice. Communication scholars extensively debate the nature of selection and gatekeeping. Definite conclusions are, unsurprisingly, thin on the ground. Within publishing studies, Claire Squires (2007) talks about imprint circularity. That is, imprints become self-selecting replicators: literary agents only submit and editors only acquire works fitting the assumed ethos of their list. Filtering happens automatically, systemically, and so the extent of filtering is partially hidden to those doing the filtering.

In the 1980s, Walter W. Powell (1985) studied the decision-making processes of two academic presses in New York. Powell (1985) argues against a naive application of organisation and rational choice theory to describe the messy reality of selection. Decisions might be based on timing, commercial terms, accident, current inventory, the author, the state of the backlist or how the editor felt on a particular day. Moreover, editorial decisions are heavily conditioned by socialisation and subtle institutional norms. The 'premises' of the firm limit uncertainty and establish guidelines for decision making; these are set, tacitly, at the company level. External factors constantly impinge on the nominally autonomous activities of both editors and the house as whole. Chance and post-hoc justifications are common parts of a process entailing considerable ambiguity. There is rarely a simple input into a binary decision. Instead decision making occurs fluidly, evolving over time with many factors working on many levels. Yet it is not without strain. In surely one of the truest phrases about publishing Powell acknowledges 'conflict is endemic to the publishing process' (1985, 63). Filtering, choosing, is hard and leaves casualties.

For Powell's publishers, the filtering process is one of bewildering variety, detail and colour. It represents an extraordinary nexus of concerns and explanatory levels, from the idiosyncratic to the macro-historical. Detailing specifics of filtering across the history of publishing is therefore impossible. This doesn't mean we can't recognise a pattern, a consistent but changing action required to publish. Only by looking at filtering as one side of a coin, however, do we realise that *filtering precedes amplification*; the two together forming our idea of publishing not as a circuit but circuits. Here we find our theory of publishing.

Amplification I

Venice, circa 1500: Europe's entrepôt is a maritime power, mercantile hub, cultural centre and, not least, a publishing dynamo. Previously, Venice occupied a vital but occasionally secondary role in the long unfolding of the Renaissance against the munificent patronage of the Medici in Florence, the ecclesiastical might of Rome and the Holy See, the military pedigree of Milan and the scholarly backdrop of Bologna, Ferrara or Padua. Until, that is, the coming of a hitherto little-known scholar called Aldo Manuzio (or Teobaldo Mannucci) – Latinised as Aldus Manutius – in the 1490s. Within a few years around the turn of the sixteenth century he was to revolutionise classical scholarship, Hellenic studies, the form of the book, typography, reading and publishing. His achievements rippled across Europe and arguably still reverberate in the literary culture of the present. Venice was to become the centre of not only European publishing, but the intellectual engine and guarantor of the revival of classical learning initiated by Petrarch some 150 years earlier. How did he do it?

Aldus was born in Rome and later studied at Ferrara before arriving in Venice aged about forty. By the later fifteenth century, Latin authors were already common in Italy, with writers like Virgil, Horace, Livy and Cicero forming an emergent canon of the classics. While Greek had a growing stature throughout the *quattrocento*, it had fallen far behind Latin in terms of use, knowledge and influence. Experts were rare, Greek type rarer still. It was the mission to spread Greek learning that animated Aldus. Venice was the perfect location – it had aristocratic and mercantile capital, Greek refugees and texts fleeing the fall of Constantinople to the Ottomans in 1453 and, more significantly, expertise in print, having quickly become the major printing centre of the region.[2] The Frenchman Nicolas Jenson, once Master of the Royal Mint at Tours, had already made a mark with his well-regarded Venetian printing house opening in 1470. Jensen's breakthrough Roman type, a huge advance on the then-standard Gothic which simply aped manuscripts, was to have a lasting impact on both Aldus and the wider world of letters. Once Aldus had made the decision to turn publisher he quickly found the partners, connections and content to forge the most iconic house of the era.

From the beginning the Aldine press was a business making the most of what Venice could offer. Crucially, Aldus partnered with established printer Andrea Torresani, and the son and nephew of successive Doges, Pierfrancesco Barbarigo. They probably had controlling stakes, but Aldus wasn't in it for the money. Barbarigo brought serious investment and connections; Torresani had the printing background; Aldus the scholarly and editorial heft. In the early 1490s, Aldus worked to create a Greek type-font, unafraid to pursue new innovations and technical challenges working (often acrimoniously) with the talented punch cutter Francesco Griffo. Aldus also created an extraordinary environment at the press, where wandering scholars like the humanists Erasmus or Thomas Linacre mingled with hard-bitten pressmen, conditions memorably described by Martin Lowry as 'a now almost incredible mixture of the sweat-shop, the boarding house, and the research institute' (1979, 94). In this milieu he was to produce his most famous work.

The achievement of the Aldine Press rests on several planks. First, there was the content, for the first time introducing the world to 30 editions of Greek literature and philosophy. He published a hugely important five volume set of Aristotle in addition to other works from Greek antiquity by Hesiod, Aristophanes, Herodotus, Sophocles, Thucydides, Xenophon, Euripides and Pindar,[3] as well as major contemporary writing like Bembo's *Asolani* and Erasmus's *Adagia*, alongside grammars, primers and other workmanlike pedagogical volumes. In all he published

---

2 Brian Richardson (1999) quotes research suggesting not only that Italy dominated European printing at the time, but Venice dominated Italy producing 41 per cent of printed material printed before 1501.

3 Of major Greek dramatists only Aeschylus went unpublished by Aldus – for the simple reason his plays hadn't been rediscovered yet.

130 editions in 20 years, many of which had enormous influence on the spread of humanism and Hellenism in particular, not just in Italy but in England, France, Germany and the Low Countries.

Moreover, Aldus's influence lay in the form of what he published and how he chose to publish it. He reconceived what the book should be, and why. Before Aldus the smaller, lighter octavo format was mainly associated with practical or liturgical texts like breviaries, psalters and books of hours, whereas sturdy books of learning were in folio. By settling on a slim, portable octavo format, Aldus not only saved money on paper but also slanted his handy, portable books to a cosmopolitan new audience of courtiers, diplomats, merchants, soldiers, clergyman and bureaucrats in addition to their traditional readership of library-bound scholars.[4] He was targeting the stereotypical Renaissance men. This change in format went hand in hand with a revolutionary change in design and conception. With Griffo, Aldus perfected a new cursive italic script, allowing both clarity and density on the page. Whereas classical texts were usually stuffed with commentaries and a cluttered, unfriendly layout, Aldus, ever the grammatical and textual purist, stripped them out. He became known for the open space between and around lines, which left room for marginalia and for the words to breathe on the page. Around this time, the organisational principles of the book came into being – title pages, tables of contents, indexes, headings and running headings, numbering of pages – and Aldus played a part. Even if he didn't invent features (pagination started in 1470s Germany, for example) his editions cemented a modern-feeling architecture and aesthetic for the book. Lastly, Aldus pushed his print runs much higher than was usual for the time, often printing well above 1,000 copies of an edition, a feat made possible by saving on paper and the manufacturing capabilities of Torresani, Aldus and their employees. It meant they could sell in the competitive heart of Venice's book district and ship their titles around Europe.

Lowry summarises this incredible productivity, mainly in the years 1501–1504, as an

> exuberant fulfilment, producing most of the achievements for which Aldus is now remembered: the large octavo edition as a medium for literary texts; the italic type; a range of publication

---

4 The reader will note this is the reverse of the situation with Shakespeare – there his publishers wanted a folio not to gain a wider audience but to bestow distinction; here Aldus used octavos not to bestow distinction but to grow his audience.

which covers every contemporary field of interest in classical and Italian vernacular literature; and the apparent attempt to harness intellectual activity to the service of the press. (1979, 110)

In this extraordinary fusion of technology and design, learning and acumen, deal making and diplomacy, Aldus comes across as the Allen Lane or Steve Jobs of his era, a comparison particularly apt when one considers that like both men Aldus was the populariser of innovations rather than their inventor.

Elizabeth Eisenstein (1980) argues this constellation played a pivotal role in the Renaissance. Unlike previous flowerings of learning like the Carolingian renaissance of the ninth century CE or the Thomist and Aristotelian renaissance of the twelfth century CE, it survived largely because of the press (Eisenstein 1980). As with everything in Eisenstein's thesis, the argument is problematic and much critiqued. However, her contention that Aldus played a significant role in securing the place of Greek has to be taken seriously given his prestige then and now, the quantity and quality of what he produced, the people with whom he mixed and the role he played in the history of the book. Previous Greek revivals had been scattered, stalled and stymied; *belles lettres* were ignored. With the intervention of Aldine presses what had been an intermittent, dangerously fragile process was made permanent. Ultimately Aldus achieved something decisive. A self-sustaining break from the past, had, through his publishing, been cemented as a movement towards modernity:

> The Aldine editions drew on Greek aid. But they also emancipated Western scholars from their traditional reliance on this kind of aid. Not only Germans beyond the Alps but also Englishmen across the Channel – and, ultimately, Western colonists in the new world – could pursue Hellenic studies regardless of what happened to Greeks in Constantinople or Athens, in Crete, Venice, Florence, or Rome. (Eisenstein 1980, 223)

No mean feat for a humble Roman scholar without a background in publishing. How did he turn Venice into the publishing capital of the humanist world? One way of summarising all of the above would be to look at Aldus through the prism of amplification. When we consider the convergence of the choices of content and format, the innovations in design and layout, the judicious deployments of capital and connections, the large print runs and his clever use of branding, his international reach and solid production, the seriousness of his scholarship and the success of his sales, we can step away from the Eisensteinian fixation of content and view it as a mass process of amplifying humanism and Hellenism in particular. Aldus amplified Greek texts by printing more of them, printing them better and making them appeal to new audiences. He made them more accessible and desirable, distributed more widely, edited skilfully, designed cleanly. The unifying thread in Aldine practice, which governs and explains the innovations and distinction of this illustrious house, is amplification. However, this is a thread found not just with Aldus but in all publishing.

Amplification II

Defining publishing as 'to make texts public' is inadequate. As the thought experiment outlined earlier indicates,[5] limning a working definition of publishing within the boundaries between public and private is impossible. Confusion surrounds the concept of 'public', which can be viewed as less a feature of society and more a fiction of it. We need a better account of what making public means. Amplification fits the bill. By amplification, I mean something deceptively simple, getting to the heart of what all cultural intermediation – itself a nebulous notion – is about: acting so that more copies of a work or product are distributed or consumed, or are distributed and consumed by different people without the intermediating act.[6]

This understanding allows several things. It gives us something concrete. This isn't an abstract idea, but involves the solid process of having something encountered more widely, or by different people, than would otherwise have been the case. Thus, simply leaving a manuscript on a bench is not amplifying it in the way photocopying and posting it to all your neighbours is amplifying it. Equally, printing a work and

---

5 We have already considered whether leaving a manuscript on a park bench makes it 'public', but the question still stands. Does it mean it has been published? Equally, even if we print 10,000 copies of a book, none of which are read, in what sense is that a published book?

6 The nomenclature should also be seen to make use of its fuzzier edges, encompassing related concepts like augment, enhance, extend, develop, push, craft, position, pitch, spread, disseminate, expand and even, but not necessarily, improve.

letting copies fester in a warehouse isn't amplification; getting those copies out into shops and, more importantly, the hands of readers is amplifying it. Communication works in many patterns and directions – one to one, one to many, many to many, many to one – but amplification is unidirectional, by definition requiring a movement from lesser to greater exposure.

Amplification is a series of actions. In principle one could retrospectively unpick the steps that led to greater – or at least different – exposure. If 'making public' is intangible to the point of uselessness, amplification is a definite, traceable process with results that are all too tangible in the increased consumption or awareness of a given work. Looked at this way, it becomes clear how we can decouple publication from creation in self-publishing. Creation is writing, publication is amplifying the writing; that is, it is the process of ensuring people aside from the creator read it.

Ideas of cultural intermediation are similarly ill defined. What do we mean by something encompassing anything from upmarket art galleries to curating music videos on YouTube? Like making public, cultural intermediation seems a falsely applied construct imposed on the messiness of the real world. By looking at cultural intermediation in terms of amplification we give it coherence. As we shall see Bruno Latour's (2005) idea of mediation plays a part, as does amplification's ability to work across media. Unlike rigid views, when seen through the supple prism of amplification we can build a wider theory of the role, development and future of cultural intermediation.

Amplification keys into content, as it must given the importance of content to publishing. If filtering is governed by models, amplification occurs in and through frames and framing. Most of the time you don't simply frame content, but you frame in order to amplify.[7]

Frames, constellational nodes combining elements of a distribution system and a set of subjective preconceptions, use both elements to amplify. Delivery systems have, generally, evolved on a trajectory of ever-increasing copyability. In either the physical or binary framing of a work, we create the means for the work to be amplified; minus

---

7 Sometimes the apparent opposite to amplification is required in different cultural and economic formations like the art market. Framing still occurs, but with a view to limiting the work: there can only be one original. Publishers may also do something similar, as with a special edition. In both cases the apparent negation of amplification is being used as a strategy to amplify the appeal of the work in question.

the frame, amplification is impossible. This explains why, in fifteenth-century Europe, simply to print was to amplify. Prior to this copying a work was laborious; it replicated the act of creation in the first place. Fairly extreme textual scarcity was standard, with some notable exceptions like the Library of Alexandria. In times of rare reading matter, to copy a work was to amplify it. Conditions of scarcity created demand the press fulfilled. Once printing came along by virtue of printing a title you were, in comparison to the painstaking work of *scriptoria*, amplifying it. Given a general lack of textual matter, having more copies in existence was a *de facto* amplification. As time went on and books became more common, the context changed again, until a gradual process of print inflation produced our present situation wherein printing alone is no longer sufficient to constitute amplification. Amplification for Anton Koberger was not amplification for Allen Lane. Both, however, required and used the framing of texts to amplify them. By adapting his frame in the form of the cheap paperback, Lane increased his amplificatory potential; in contrast, by simply marshalling the resources to print Koberger was amplifying.

Enter the subjective component. Distribution systems always come preloaded with a set of assumptions, premises and preconceptions; even when the first books were printed, it was not just the physicality of their framing that amplified the text but also the enmeshed set of symbolically rich signifiers presented by the process, the object, its producers and by the text itself. Allen Lane created a specific complex of brand, content choice, design and aesthetic-political orientation for Penguin, all of which were woven over and into the books, feeding a mutually supporting dialectic as they became a landmark on the mid-century cultural scene. Further back, Koberger's careful, at times spectacular production, his fame and prestige, his extensive and robust distribution and sales network, also served to amplify his books via mechanisms not solely describable in terms of a delivery system or basic container. In our era of content surplus, this second part of framing and its amplificatory function becomes especially relevant. As framing technology is digitised, the amplificatory weight of frames shift from the distributional element, making it available, to the subjective, finding an audience.[8]

---

8 O'Leary, again, has a good take on this process: 'When there was only the Gutenberg Bible we didn't need Dewey. When booksellers were smaller and largely independent, we didn't have much need for BISAC codes. And before online sales made almost every book in print evident and available, ONIX was an unattended luxury' (2012, 16).

We can again modify our image of publishers as not just producers of books but filters for content and constructors of amplificatory frames.

Returning to Aldus Manutius, we get a sense of how this works, as well as a better appreciation of Aldus's pivotal position in the morphology of the book. In terms of filtering, we see how he created an effective screening process for the press by blending a variety of models. There is the animating mission of reviving ancient Greek. There are what a Boston Matrix of Aldine products would probably categorise as the 'cash cows': the practical grammars and primers. There are works published through friendship and association, like those of Erasmus. The weight of Aldus's partners and backers were felt in some publishing decisions. In Italy at the time there were publishers who, unlike Aldus, kept the printing element at arm's length, selecting, financing and distributing works, and hence the influence of financial backing on content selection cannot be discounted, as networks of Venetian power made themselves present in the publishing. With Aldus we see programmatic list building – far from publishing whatever came his way, or publishing under orders, Aldus was crafting a coherent, purposive set of texts that needed to hit quality benchmarks to be deemed worthwhile.

Amplification works on a number of levels. The large print runs, indeed print runs of any size, are only the most obvious manifestation of amplification, although their unusual scale gives Aldine texts a particular force. Alongside the editions' extended reach were their format, layout and typography, each of which represented state-of-the-art user experience design. Those merchant and courtier-friendly sizes and weights, that open readable style, all served to increase the possible audience, whereas the heavy, over-elaborate volumes of the period usually limited as well as created audiences. As well as being portable the smaller format saved paper, the principal production cost, and therefore allowed higher print runs. Then, there were the adverts and promotional activities deployed by publishers to bring a work to notice:

> Many of the devices which are still being used by press agents, were first tried out during the age of Erasmus. In the course of exploiting new publicity techniques, few authors failed to give high priority to publicising themselves. The art of puffery, the writing of blurbs and other familiar promotional devices were also exploited by early printers who worked aggressively to obtain

public recognition for the authors and artists whose products they hoped to sell. (Eisenstein 1980, 229)[9]

Renaissance publishers also thought about marketing. Lastly, the Aldine press evolved something of an aura. It's colophon or heraldic device, a dolphin entwined around an anchor, became famous (and is still used today as the colophon for Doubleday). It had humanist overtones, accompanied not only with proud name 'ALDVS' but also the Latin phrase *festina lente*, more haste, less speed, the motto of Roman emperors Augustus and Vespasian, among others. The dolphin and anchor were symbols not only of the Aldine Press, but by proxy markers of good quality books, classical learning, Roman grandeur and contemporary Venetian sophistication.

In all cases, the work of the press served to amplify, or rather to increase, consumption to a greater degree than would have otherwise been the case, according to a set of models, through highly adapted frames. Physical and symbolic forms of framing and amplification are exquisitely united, as are clearly delineated models and filters for content. Aldus and his collaborators took a series of steps that cumulatively took their texts to places they would have otherwise been unable to go. In short, they were framed and then 'made public' at the limits of what was possible in 1500.

The notion of amplification, like that of frame, has enough simultaneous flexibility and concreteness to bridge the physical/digital divide. If frames change in different environments but framing remains, this means methods of amplification change but amplification itself remains present. We can see this in the changing landscape of digital publishing. One of the most lucid theorists of this transition is the designer, publisher and writer Craig Mod. Mod (2011) perceptively views both books and publishing as systems, finding three interlinked systems in traditional publishing: the pre-artefact system, the system of the artefact (the book) and the post-artefact system (the book's dissemination and consumption). Each system is relatively static, linear and sequential, a world unto itself structured around a physical object. In the digital era the lines, clearly demarcated in these systems, between author/publisher/printer/distributor/reader

---

9 This focus on marketing spend seems fairly consistent. For example, Aileen Fyfe (2012) analyses a budget for the book *Our Coal and Our Coal-Pits* published by Longman in the early 1850s. Fully 21 per cent of the budget was for advertising, against 20 per cent for literary labour. Only paper and production costs, at 25 per cent of the budget each, consumed more resources on the title.

start to blur. We move towards a 'post-artifact publishing' where the old linearity of the creating–publishing–consuming process is collapsed. Now, with continuous development of texts and non-linear transmissions, they intertwine. Mod claims that publisher 'roles have shifted. Their value lies as community builders, curators and editorial advisors. Not just deep-pocketed gatekeepers and financiers to the mythical land of printed matter, national distribution systems and physical shopfronts' (Mod 2011). The systemic elision of digital publishing marks a moment when the way we think about publishing systems undergoes an irreversible transformation.

By switching from the isolation of each system to their interpenetration, Mod (2011) brilliantly analyses how digital transforms publishing. Without filtering and amplification as anchoring concepts, however, Mod's (2011) fundamental break works on an inadequate sense of publishing. When viewed through our lens of filtering, modelling, framing and amplifying, we see this transition as just that, a transition – nothing total or deracinating. For example, he heralds the move from 'gatekeeper' to 'curator'. Yet each role must still work with some kind of filtering mechanism, as curating still implies selection. Physical shop fronts and community building online are about finding or constructing audiences. Either way, publishing serves to foreground some works and not others. In the 'post-artifact system', the book goes away, but the necessity of amplification does not. Attention is never in unlimited supply and must be vigorously fought for by media suppliers. We need to change the way we think, yes, but that doesn't mean denying conceptual continuity, despite changing technology, practice and circumstance.

Filtering and amplification are designedly supple. Were it otherwise, they would have little explanatory force other than in the narrowest respects. For instance, around the turn of the twentieth century the publishing industry arguably shifted from being product led to market led, moving from an environment of product differentiation to market segmentation (Delany 2002). Essentially, publishing moved from being supply to demand driven. Likewise there is, as discussed in the first chapter, a vibrant debate as to whether publishing is, and historically has been, a product or a service industry (Anderson 2012). To what extent is publishing a service to academic or religious institutions, to pick just two examples? While such arguments seem rarefied compared to the daily grind of a publishing business, actually these questions provide a vitally important strategic framework for an uncertain digital world. The difference between product and service businesses may ultimately be the difference between those that survive and those that don't.

However we choose to view publishing it doesn't disrupt the core idea. Whether publishing is about product or service, filtering and amplification are present. They can be understood either as services to content producers and consumers, putting the two together effectively, or as a product-led process with the product having been filtered and amplified. In a practice with the history and diversity of publishing we should expect a range of depictions. Indeed amplification takes many forms: pre- and post-industrial, artisanal or corporate, mechanical or digital, publicity led or product led. Amplification is what allows us to talk about publishing in the first place whatever its composition.

Nor should amplification get us hung up on bestsellers. Bestsellers are commercially and academically fascinating.[10] The Sir Walter Scotts, Harriet Beecher Stowes and Agatha Christies, not to mention the bibles, qurans and government-mandated textbooks, are in many ways the backbone of the publishing world. Genre super-smashes from Edgar Rice Burroughs and Ian Fleming to Dan Brown and E. L. James are a big part of the trade and examples of amplification working at its purest, ramping up a text's dissemination to hitherto undreamt heights. The first novel recorded to sell over a million copies was Margaret Mitchell's 1936 *Gone with the Wind*. Nearly seventy years later a new Harry Potter would easily clear that in a day (Striphas 2009). Yet both the continuation of this inflation and its centrality to publishing are in doubt. 'Bestsellers' are a comparatively recent trend, a marketing tool from the competitive world of early twentieth-century American publishing. Most titles throughout history have not had sufficient amplification to make them a 'bestseller' but have been published nonetheless. Scale, while not irrelevant, neither constitutes nor invalidates amplification. Amplification has varying degrees and criteria for success, dependent on the model being used. At a conceptual extreme, the idea of amplification says that even if only one more copy is encountered than otherwise, then we have amplification; we have publishing.

---

10 It seems surprising to me that the question of why one book and not another, to all intents completely equal, should sell so many more copies. It is an intriguing academic puzzle and a potential goldmine for publishers given the economics of the industry work on a 'Pareto distribution' power law (Greco 2005). We may be waiting a long time before we have something like the humanities or business equivalent of the quantum uncertainty principle.

The idea of sales in general exists at a tangent to amplification. The two may sometimes be strongly correlated, tied together in an economic model, but amplification is a far richer, more unpredictable and intricate process. Amplification is an intermediation by the publisher, but by no means exhausts the potential reach of a title, which extends to the spreadability and durability of a frame and a feedback loop of demand and supply. As William St Clair has pointed out,

> If we wish to estimate the size of the total readership of any printed text, we need to take account of the fact that each book may have been read many times over, by being given or lent to friends, inherited, rented out commercially, sold to the second-hand market, or passed down from one class of school children to its successors. (St Clair 2004, 25)

By the same token plenty of purchased texts remain unread; famously a book like Stephen Hawking's astrophysics primer *A Brief History of Time* (1988) was more sold and displayed than actually 'consumed'. This ambiguity suggests publishers never absolutely control or dictate the amplificatory flow, they can only shape and influence it and are frequently surprised or disappointed by the results. Publishers are flying blind, using the bluntest of tools to spread their message, and we shouldn't pretend they do anything more. Everyone grappling with our vast and complex world has this problem, but few businesses are as subject to whim, taste, dictate and luck.

Filtering and amplification are concrete processes with seemingly irreconcilable historical, geographical and media modal embodiments. In order to remain both concrete and widely applicable they need to be flexible and open, with specific and transhistorical force. They emerge from the practices, habits, processes and norms of publishers. We find them by looking at what publishers do. When we find the pattern of filtering and amplification, we call it publishing, or, if we were minded to adapt Foucault (1980), the Publisher Function.

Amplification III

Publishing doesn't happen in isolation. Filtering and amplification cannot and do not function in a social and technological vacuum. They are dependent on the capabilities of their circumstances. In other words, separating publishing from technology is impossible, just as publishing is inseparable from legal, institutional, economic, political, personal and geographical factors. If amplification occurs through framing, framing is made possible by technology – the limits and nature of the amplificatory process is therefore dependent on the range of possible technologies at a publisher's disposal.[11] We can't talk about frames and amplification without also talking about what technology is deployed, how and why.

Technology is problematic. Whether it is a good thing, what effects it has, and above all, what it is are all open questions for philosophers of technology. I propose to follow the ecumenical and intelligent view of what Val Dusek (2006) calls the 'consensus definition' of technology. Instead of seeing technology as about tools or hardware, on the one hand, or rules and protocols, on the other, the consensus definition views technology as comprising systems. Moreover, these aren't closed systems. A technological system includes hardware, a category extending to people, and the knowledge embodied by roles from engineers to marketers, inventors to legislators, consumers to repair people. By looking at historical case studies, we get a sense of how this relationship with technology (and necessarily society) is both fundamental to framing, amplification and therefore publishing, while retaining flexibility. The hardware of tools and machines and the 'software' of knowledge and organisation have co-evolved to produce amplificatory channels. Rapid social and technological change soon translates into a transformation of framing and amplification. Because frames and amplification are social and technological, and because society and technology rarely stand still, publishing is involved in constant moments of change. Despite its sometimes throwback image, publishing has always been on the cutting edge.

As with so much, publishing started early in China, which has a publishing history dating back 3,000 years. When many Western societies were still basically illiterate, China had sophisticated media and information markets, distribution systems and technologies of transmission. The story of publishing in China is one of both amplificatory technology (paper, printing) and social trends (educated bureaucrats and monks, imperial projects, advanced culture). The legacy represents an extraordinary heritage of extant documents, despite the

---

11 As Adriaan van der Weel (2011) has pointed out, following rich seams of media theory, all mediums are inherently both social and technological.

upheavals of the twentieth century, amounting to some 2.3 million volumes from the Han to the Qing dynasty alone (202 BCE–1911). Some things have helped, like the relative stability of the language over time and the consistent guiding force of Confucianism.

Indeed, Confucius himself was a book collector and editor. At this time, roughly 500 BCE, books were comprised of a number of formats in China including bone, bronze, bamboo, wood, silk or stone tablets known as steles. Copying Confucian – and Buddhist and Taoist – texts like the *I Ching* or *The Analects of Confucius* onto these formats was an important driver of Chinese book production, as were the so-called *Jian Ce*, a bound collection of bamboo slips which formed a proto-book for works like *The Art of War*. However, China's amplificatory prowess really rests on the invention of two technologies, the importance of which can hardly be overstated: paper and printing.

Paper, made from plant fibre, was invented during the Western Han dynasty dating back as far as the second century BCE, although it was only commonly used later. It represented a step change in media capability – lighter, cheaper and more durable, allowing for a huge expansion of written matter and amplification. Papermaking techniques were further refined by the eunuch Cai Lun in 105 CE, ushering in the 'manuscript era' of Chinese writing when a government apparatus of scribes, libraries and publishing operations was developed. Throughout history official agencies like the Archival Bureau orchestrated book collection, storage, preservation and circulation. While the first bookshop was opened earlier in Chang'an in the second century BCE, paper led to a productivity explosion as *Jian Ce* were replaced by a 'scroll system' of writing which had taken over by the fifth century CE: 'Rough statistics suggest that about 11,754 works made up of 73,200 scrolls were produced from 25 CE to 618 CE, which included general encyclopedia, collected works, rhyme dictionaries, genealogies and other types of books' (Hu and Yang 2010, 35–6).

The second major breakthrough saw the emergence of the 'Manual Printing Period', an epic stretch of cultural production lasting from around 700 CE to 1840. The key advances were typography and printing. Block printing or xylography was invented during the Tang dynasty in the seventh century CE. It spread quickly, to the extent that in 835 CE the government banned private printing because of an oversupply of woodblock-printed calendars. The basics of the practice required ruled and marked paper, upon which the woodblock impression

would be carefully printed on one side. The next breakthrough –
ceramic moveable type – was discovered around the turn of the
second millennium by Bi Sheng in the Northern Song dynasty.
Using spinning wheels to organise the type and employing different
materials including wood, porcelain and, from the fifteenth century,
bronze,[12] moveable type printing was a further development in print
capacity, allowing not just larger print runs but gargantuan state-
sponsored research projects.[13] These were not always industrial-sized
enterprises (the literary equivalents of building the Grand Canal),
but, enabled by print technology, could be small scale. For example,
in 1298 one Wang Zhen used wooden moveable type printing to
print 100 copies of the 60,000-word *Records of Jingde County* in just
one month. Further advances in print involved registration or colour
(by printing successive layers of colour), embossing, new methods
of block printing almost like stereotyping and the development of
copper type, although xylographic printing remained widespread.

The highly trained bureaucracy was both source and market for
texts, as were Buddhist monks. Successive dynasties founded great
centres for publishing like the Imperial College of the Song dynasty or
the Central Inner Court of the Ming dynasty, which closely governed
official printing and publishing. Yet private bookshops, scholarship and
commerce continued to thrive and even pioneered block printing during
the Tang dynasty. Much like Aldus's printing centre, these bookshops
combined writing, editing, printmaking and bookselling in that
curious combination of high mindedness, collegiality and cut-throat
commerciality so characteristic of publishing. New forms of printing
gave rise not only to new competencies and markets but also new forms
of writing. Tang Poetry and Song *Ci*, a form of lyric poetry from the
earlier part of the 'Manual Printing Period', are still regarded as among
the finest art ever produced. From later dynasties like the Ming and the
Qing we have novels, such as the enduringly popular *Journey to the West* by
Wu Cheng'en from the Ming era, and the great encyclopaedic projects

12 'The most famous bronze moveable-type print was the inner court of *The Compendium of Works of Past and Present* in Qing dynasty. From the fourth to the sixth year of the Yongzheng Period, the Qing government printed 65 copies comprised of 5,200 volumes, each in large and small fonts. This was an unprecedented printing effort with exquisite typography' (Hu and Yang 2010, 55).
13 It was, however the Koreans, who were to achieve the most sophisticated breakthroughs in type before Gutenberg. For more, see Eliot and Rose (2009) and Suarez and Woudhuysen (2010).

which are discussed in the next chapter. As technology improved, civil and official channels worked in a sophisticated system of manufacturing, publishing centres, paper producers, libraries, distribution channels and retailers, in a context of literate elites, demand for content, new artistic and referential forms and even an early instance of copyright law. Eventually China adopted Western mechanical printing and today forms one of the largest markets for printed material in the world; its publishers must accommodate for the biggest domestic audience in history.

Behind the creation of this arrestingly modern publishing system are technical innovations that created viable forms of amplificatory media. Paper scrolls rather than bone carving, ramped up through multiple iterations of binding and then printing technology, culminated in sophisticated copper and colour printing techniques and eventually today's server farms and printing plants. Meanwhile, the extraordinary characteristics of Chinese society, including Confucian and Buddhist influences, bureaucratic elites and the enduring presence of a powerful imperial centre, created conditions receptive to these new technologies while providing the means and categories for filtering works. The history of publishing in China, as elsewhere, is one of increasing amplification predicated on evolving technology. The journey was never simple. Printed books, for example, often struggled for acceptance in a firmly scribal culture. Still, at no point is publishing separable from the technological potential of its position.

What was true of Song dynasty China was also true of Victorian Britain. Here, too, publishing and technology lived symbiotically, forming a systemic proposition. Aileen Fyfe (2012) has studied in detail how technology impacted the firm of one nineteenth-century publisher, the Edinburgh-based Chambers brothers, William and Robert. From humble origins they became one of the most successful firms of the period and they did it through clever exploitation of that most emblematic and transformative of industrial technologies: steam.

Their first breakthrough was publishing the *Chambers Journal* in 1832. Only four sheets long, it shared with other works of the time a moral pedagogical purpose and sold respectably well. More than the content, however, it is William Chambers' business nous that is of interest. The brothers' position in Edinburgh meant they had a good chance of a captive Scottish audience, but it put them at a remove from London, by far the largest market for print in the UK. Ensuring efficient production and distribution was essential. On the production side they were quick to adopt a series of new developments. First, they bought steam presses, much more prevalent at the time in the newspaper industries and more prevalent still in the US than the UK. Not only did they use them but they physically brought them in-house. Combined with machine-made paper it gave them decisive economies of scale and speed of production. Their presses produced 900 sheets an hour in the 1830s, far more than the hand presses still used by many publishers. By the 1840s, when circulation of the *Chambers Journal* was at its peak, they produced a weekly print run of 90,000. Moreover they kept investing in new, improved steam presses, spending nearly £10,000 or the entire year's profit on alterations or new presses in 1845. This new capacity led to a shift in publishing strategy as they moved into printing books, to ensure their powerful presses didn't lie idle. Foreshadowing Penguin's later strategy and a common motif in the economics of publishing, the high print runs permitted lower prices, which in turn allowed a higher volume of sale. Economies of scale and adroit technology application are never far apart.

In addition to the steam press the brothers were early adopters of stereotyping, at the time a difficult and expensive technology. Rather than recompositing works, this meant they stored copies to quickly reproduce popular back issues. Crucially, stereotyping solved a distributional conundrum: sending finished copies to London, usually by boat, was expensive and slow. Instead they split production between presses in Edinburgh and London; stereotypes could be made and sent overnight by post, beating the boats and ensuring absolute fidelity to the original edition, a key consideration in the brothers' drive for quality control. While the Chamberses were not the first to use such technologies, their case is instructive as they were among the first to apply them to book publishing, fully integrating them into the business and the market (producing cheap in-demand material of good quality). Change wasn't an easy or neutral process; it was a massive wrench from traditional ways of working with sweeping consequences:

> Publishers' decisions to use machine-made paper, stereotyping, and machine printing changed the structure and organization of the book trade. As in other industries, skilled craftsmen were replaced with semi-skilled machine attendants, though compositors retained their position, and stereotyping added a new craft process to the trade. (Fyfe 2012, 38)

New technologies created new skills, capabilities and liabilities even as they disordered and destroyed older practices. Throughout the upheaval the Chamberses' publishing thrived. By the mid-1840s their staff had grown to 150 and their large Old Town premises printed around a quarter of a million sheets a week. Steam wasn't done with publishing, however. In the form of the railway and the steamship a revolution in transport was underway – and with it a whole worldview. The railway had less impact on the distribution of Chambers material than might be supposed. Transporting goods on the railways was not initially cost effective, but it did provide a fast outlet if needed, expanded distribution to the provinces and lowered goods distribution prices by presenting serious competition to other channels (e.g. by boat). More interestingly for the history of publishing, it created a new market for readers as epitomised by the W. H. Smith railway bookstall and the Routledge Railway Library. Prior to the railways, bookstores would have been intimidating places for many. Placing them in the cosmopolitan space of a station, Smith's expanded the number of possible book buyers, and found a new audience whose tastes and budgets were ably catered for by the selection and pricing of George Routledge. Like the Chamberses, he matched a populist sensibility with a knack for using steam printing in high-volume low-cost print runs (although while the Chamberses retained their dignified sense of purpose, Routledge went for the purely popular). Even if they never came to dominate the railway reading market as Routledge did, regardless of the new competition the Chambers brothers were beneficiaries of the railway boom.

Meanwhile steamships were poised to disrupt the trade routes to North America, slashing a journey time of months to weeks. Export sales to colonies and the United States, the biggest foreign market of them all, were important for British publishers. However, as we saw in the first chapter, outside any international copyright agreement the pirate-driven reprint trade in the US meant selling works into the country was difficult. The Chambers brothers had originally wanted to partner with a US publisher by selling stereotype plates, which would allow the designated American publisher a marked time advantage against the pirates. For various reasons, not least format incompatibility problems between British plates and American presses (an oddly familiar nuisance to users of modern technology), trade was never easy and eventually it made sense to export pre-printed copies directly. Huge discounts helped the distributor to compete and steam-driven printing and shipping left the Chambers brothers with just enough of a profit margin to make it worthwhile. A helpful side effect was that it also stopped the bleed in pirated sales to Canada. Without steamships the Chamberses couldn't export finished copies.

Steam didn't just impact publishing, of course. Like the information and communications revolution of the late twentieth century it impacted everybody, in virtually every trade and walk of life. Here, we see how this one technology led to a revolution in publishing. True, the Chamberses were particularly adept at exploiting new advances, combining them with smart operational decision making and content acquisition. Nonetheless, the story of the nineteenth century is one of ever-increasing book consumption, powered in part by the amplificatory prowess of steam. Alexis Weedon (2003) estimates book production in the UK went from 8.72 million units in 1846 to a bullish 34.73 million by 1916, a fourfold increase. Throughout this period the costs of paper, typesetting, production and consequently the final product all consistently fell. Demand only caught up with supply in the 1880s as the population swelled and literacy increased thanks to the 1870 Education Act. The boom in exports was even greater: exports of books and stationery in 1898 were 22 times their 1828 level (£787,304 against £35, 841), with colonial markets in Australia and India alongside North America accounting for the bulk of the increase (Weedon 2003).

While the Chamberses were unusually astute with the adoption and leverage of steam-powered technology across the range of its applications, their increased print runs, expanded audience and supercharged distribution are microcosms of Victorian publishing. Starting with a few eighteenth-century experimentalists before spreading to cotton factories, steam technology up-ended publishing through its dramatic increase in amplification. This is not just about technology, however; it's also about a new kind of lower-middle-class reader looking for betterment, for the kind of evangelical writing published by the likes of the SPCK and the educational content of W. & R. Chambers. Equally, the use of technology is neither predictable nor inevitable:

> [A]s often happens in the history of technology, Chambers adopted the processes for one purpose and then experimented with applying them to other purposes: stereotyping helped with the production of back numbers, but it also speeded up production and simplified the problems of national distribution; steam-printing was originally intended for the high-circulation, high-frequency *Journal*, but was later applied to instructive tracts and entire books. (Fyfe 2012, 95)

As much as they navigated technology and managed machinery, the Chambers brothers navigated societal and economic change. Our definition of technology doesn't allow us to focus purely on the hardware without seeing this as embedded in a set of enabling relationships, knowledges, practices and distributions of power. Again, this is a quality of technology, and therefore framing and amplification, which all publishers must confront.

Operational know-how is just as much a technology as steam power. One legendary house gives a good example. If Koberger and Aldus were the greatest publishers of their day, then the greatest publisher of the latter half of the sixteenth century was the Frenchman Christophe Plantin. He settled in the then-capital of the book world, Antwerp, which prior to the Dutch Revolt of 1566 held around 70 per cent of Low Countries publishing (Pettegree 2010). Plantin was not necessarily a technical innovator along the lines of Gutenberg, or even particularly a stylistic innovator like Aldus. He, nonetheless, was undoubtedly successful, and even called the 'most famous printing establishment of all' (Febvre and Martin 2010, 125). This rested on two planks: a careful negotiation of a fraught geopolitical situation and the close management of labour and workflow.

Early in his career, Plantin was damaged by publishing a religious controversy. It taught him a lesson. From henceforth he would avoid taking sides. At the time Antwerp was caught between rival masters: the feisty Dutch burghers, Protestant merchants growing rich from trade, and the mighty Spanish, Catholic and colonial rulers of what were then known as the Spanish Netherlands. This conflict meant any publisher walked a tightrope between competing claims of loyalty. This problem was exacerbated as the battle for regional control intensified as the sixteenth century wore on. Antwerp was caught between the Protestant nationalist rebellion of William of Orange and the Spanish, whose army would once again take the city making life difficult for heretic Protestants. Eventually Plantin was to leave for Leiden; although he later returned, along the way he was forced into any number of reversals and conversions to survive and do business. Plantin would prove to be an adept printer for both Philip II of Habsburg Spain and the States-General fighting him for independence.

For the skilful publisher there was an upside as they now had access to two markets. In addition to the local burghers were Spain and her bullion-rich colonies in the New World. Financed by a syndicate of local merchants, Plantin was able to publish 260 books in 5 years. His most lucrative market was the court of El Escorial:

> [O]ver the course of several years Plantin supplied over 52,000 missals, breviaries and Books of Hours [to Spain]. It was a remarkable example of the extent to which the book market in one of Europe's proudest and most powerful nation states had been colonised by the more confident and economically sophisticated book markets of northern Europe. (Pettegree 2010, 263)[14]

He printed an immense polyglot bible for the Spanish monarchy, a huge undertaking in eight volumes and five languages – Greek, Latin, Hebrew, Aramaic and Syriac – over an initial print run of 1,100.[15] Yet, his Catholic publishing in no way stopped him from pragmatically publishing Hebrew texts for the Jewish community. Only royal patronage mixed with mercantile capital could produce such a lucrative balancing act; by juggling both, Plantin was able to publish more successfully than anyone else at the time.

His management skills didn't end at clever political manoeuvring and market exploitation. Plantin was about contacts and *organisation* (of money, men, markets and technology) and this extends to the proto-Fordist industrial organisation of his house.[16] His workshop was the largest since Koberger, operating 24 presses with 100 labourers, as well as shops and agents scattered around Europe. Those workers were organised into a rigid hierarchy of press pullers, compositors, journeymen printers and masters. Conditions were draconian. Each worker had a strictly demarcated set of repetitive tasks, performed over a long working day from 5 a.m. to 8 p.m. with an hour's break for lunch. Employee behaviour was monitored. Workers were expected to be among the most productive in Europe, pulling as many as 3,000 sheets per day. Plantin even had a formal relationship with a sort of

---

14 There was a downside to this arrangement. Like many monarchs, Philip II often thought invoices happened to other people. On the face of it, he looked like a good bet: a powerful ruler with a seemingly endless source of hard currency being shipped in from the New World. As with other creditors, notably Italian and German financiers, Plantin would learn about monarchical debt the hard way.

15 Plantin would have print runs of up to 5,000 copies, however, a vast number for the period.

16 The rigorous standardisation of industry and management based on the principles of Henry Ford.

nascent union among the workers and kept incredibly detailed accounts. Although technologically, in terms of hardware, Plantin did not have much of an advantage over his peers, his use of resources, his *modus operandi*, his manipulation of relationships and adaptations to the context were superior, enabling him to use that hardware more effectively, and so enabling his publishing – amplification – to spread further than any competitor. Effective management of people – what might be seen as a combination of good organisation and process design and effective lobbying and customer acquisition – was Plantin's technology of choice. Indeed, innovations in organisation design, distribution, workflow, process and business management are as important indicators of publishing development as the often-stationary progress of hardware.

We can begin to see how amplification is as much about strategy and tactics as conventional technology. Amplification need not just be product-facing, striving for greater levels of unit production, but can be reception-facing, as in our own era when the strategies and technologies of market making or audience building start to take precedence over duplication and distribution. If the simplified story of the nineteenth century is that of steam-driven supply, the twentieth century is surely that of marketing-driven demand, an unfolding narrative of new techniques aimed at manufacturing not so much books as interest. Understood this way, branding becomes part of the technology of promotion. Whether we are talking Mills and Boon, *Annals of Mathematics*, the *Lancet* or Lonely Planet, brands serve as sales propositions. Crucial to the subjective aspects of framing, brands are among the key determinants of successful amplification in situations of textual plenty.

Ted Striphas (2009) tells the story of how, in the 1920s and 1930s, US publishers hired the 'father of spin' Edward L. Bernays to promote books. The campaign he came up with revolved not around books themselves but focused instead on spurring builders and homeowners to install bookshelves in their houses. Bookshelves were not only aspirational, they combined elements of decorum and self-improvement with what Thorstein Veblen (1899) had already labelled 'conspicuous consumption'. Moreover, bookshelves were a problem in search of a solution – the solution being, of course, to buy books to fill them.[17]

---

17 Intriguingly this also led to a business of selling fake rows of books to fill bookshelves. This is the book as a cultural signifier rather than text, with a further remove. It is a signifier of a signifier; a typically twentieth-century gesture if ever there was one.

In certain respects the building of the bookshelves was less about the content of books than about the appearance of respectability and plenitude the presence of books could confer on homeowners. (Striphas 2009, 28)

This, of course, is something that didn't – and doesn't – matter to publisher bottom lines. These days, the retail of books has become more 'customer focused', to use the jargon. Book chain superstores are reactions to and anticipations of audience demands. Whereas bookshops previously conceived of their role as to tell readers what to read, as the chains grew this translated into simply making available what readers wanted to buy (Miller 2007). Aggressive discounts have made books cheaper in real terms, while bookshops, with their coffee bars and inviting table displays, have tried to overturn elite overtones (which as we saw started with the W. H. Smith railway bookstalls). Miller (2007) and Striphas (2009) both explore how methods of standardisation, in shop design or the creation of ISBNs for example, emphasise both the commodity-driven and demand-oriented nature of the business. Inventory management and speedy stock replenishment became operational norms. They are now just the basic entry point for selling, a task which is about building an audience as much as ensuring distribution. Strategies and technologies of amplification are still in place, whether supply or demand side.

Nothing in this equation of publishing and technology is meant reductively: not the definition of technology or amplification, nor their many connections and historical instantiations. Variations, oppositions, reversals and lulls should all be expected. Whether through frames as distribution mechanisms or in their more subjective aspects, amplification and technology allow us to spread and create frames in the first place. Technology furnishes our theory of publishing with a good deal of its praxis. Amplification isn't just an abstract idea of intermediating to secure exposure; it is a real process, founded on real technologies, operated by and through real individuals.

The System of Publishing

The word system has already made an entrance. Angus Phillips and Bill Cope (2006) describe books as systems. Val Dusek (2006) called technology a system, a label Mod (2011) applies to publishing. Indeed, publishing is a system. We have four primary elements to this system, each of which elaborately and inseparably intertwines in practice: models, filtering, frames and amplification. At every stage, the impact of technology and social context is co-present, enabling publication. Relationships are rarely if ever linear and straightforwardly causal. This is a system full of feedback loops, multiple lines of force and co-creation; it is a loose aggregate of thousands, millions, of small quotidian actions over time. The question becomes, what kind of system are we dealing with?

Before answering that question several things need clarification. We are dealing with cultural intermediation. Framing texts in order to amplify them or filtering them according to a mode are basic operations that are consistently encountered when discussing how the cultural industries work. Returning to the doubled sense of media as both the medium and those behind that medium, the system of publishing combines the two and shows how they are always distinguishable but nonetheless always related. There can be no theory of media without a strong account of how and why a medium is the way it is. That involves understanding how those within the medium function. But we cannot understand those working with media without first seeing how they are conditioned by available frames and amplificatory techniques, and by extension all the social and technological baggage they bring. The four elements of the theory of publishing let us see how the two processes are part of the same *system*. We are also dealing with an activity, 'creative labour' (Hesmondhalgh and Baker 2011). Publishing is about doing things; filtering and amplification don't just happen on their own.

While I have focused on book publishing, it is only part of the story. Whatever the form or context of publishing, interpreting this extraordinarily diverse range of cultural practice is relatively simple in these terms. Whether you are talking about *Halo 3* or Shakespeare's *Richard III* we find the same basic system. Seventeenth-century publishing doesn't resemble twenty-first-century publishing, but that doesn't mean they aren't grappling with the same underlying mechanisms.

This description of publishing can be distinguished from other processes by the unique nature of content as decouple-able from its medium; that is to say, it is distinct from the system of its delivery (unlike most goods or items) and composed of symbolic or informational forms. When filtering and amplification are applied to content in particular, with all their attendant characteristics, the specificity of publishing is clear. What distinguishes publishing from broadcast or 'flow logic' is more difficult. Previously one could claim the nature of amplification and framing in publishing created a clear, unit-based differential with broadcasting. Digital convergence complicates that view.

Convergence also renders Bernard Miège's (1989) description of 'publishing logic' incomplete. In his view, the publisher chooses the works to be published, assembles the production team and organises production and reproduction. It is an accurate workaday description of most book publishing today, but it doesn't explain much historical publishing or how publishing might change in the future. Equally, it only offers a surface reading of dominant characteristics and so loses deep explanatory value. Darnton's (2006) communication circuit has been a dominant idea in the still emergent area of publishing studies and theory. However, he describes the operation of a book or media artefact, rather than addressing the wider questions of cultural intermediation. Adams and Barker (2006) are right to refocus the communication circuit on the material object, as this is where it belongs. Publishing has multiple inputs and outputs and therefore cannot be easily described in terms of a single circuit. The metaphor doesn't fit and wasn't intended to fit. It remains an exemplary account of the book. Instead, what publishing resembles more, with those jumbled inputs and outputs, is something else: a network.

Bruno Latour (2005) has a useful vocabulary for describing how publishing operates as a network.[18] Following Latour, we should perhaps see publishing as not so much a point on a circuit but as a mediating actor-network.[19] Latour rejects grasping for abstracts and then slotting them in as explanations, for instance using the phrase 'social' as an adjective or a substance like wood or steel. He then argues that good explanations 'trace the associations' between actors. In a radical widening of the scope of agency, objects, not just humans, must be incorporated into actor-

---

18 Latour himself does not particularly like the term 'network'. He means it in a different manner to, for example, Manuel Castells (2010), but the word has become overlain with digital connotations not strictly relevant in this case. It should also be said Latour is against the 'application' of his theory – rather studies should practically embody his insights. In the most modest of ways that has been the aim here.

19 Latour is often regarded as the founder of actor-network theory (or ANT).

networks or the system of publishing.[20] We can start to see how dynamically connected are the technological and contextual elements of frames in the network; they are not passive but fundamental to its movement. In publishing, paper, presses, capital, accounting ledgers, associations, corporate bodies, wagons and steamships, buildings, colophons on book spines among many other possible actors all have efficacy in the network.[21] The image of publishing here stems from a careful tracing of associations between multiple actors producing networks of activity over time.

Furthermore Latour sees objects as either intermediaries, which are fundamentally passive, or mediators, which transform relationships in unpredictable ways. Mediators don't just pass things on; they change them. What could be more germane to publishing than this description of mediators: 'Mediators transform, translate, distort, and modify the meaning or the elements they are supposed to carry' (Latour 2005, 39). The products of publishing are what Latour might call 'hybrids' crossing different areas of knowledge and activity: symbolic, economic, technological, object based. In this network, change is the norm, and when things don't change there must be some serious work keeping them static. Publishing is about constant change, yet also in some respects a continuity born of repeated performance over the generations. The challenges faced by Aldus Manutius or William Chambers are striking in their immediate recognisability to a contemporary publisher.[22] They, too, worried about print runs and printing costs, stock control and distributional reliability, marketing messages and sales opportunities. From difficult editorial decisions to tough commercial negotiations, the skill set and the challenges are remarkably consistent over time.

---

20 So carbon atoms are ethical actors and viruses have political consequences.

21 A slightly expanded actor-network would encompass adverts, agents, artists, authors, balance sheets, banks, booksellers, book clubs, capital, cloth, coders, computers, contracts, corporations, designers, ebooks, editors, exporters, glue, ink, investors, Internet hosts, IT support, lawyers, libraries, lorries, mail, manufacturing firms and plants, manuscripts, marketers, newspapers and other media, OEMs, offices, owners, paper, photographers, presses, print, professional institutions, proofreaders, publicists, readers, remainder merchants, schools, shareholders, ships, software, translators, typesetters, typographers, universities, warehouses, wholesalers. The list could go on and on!

22 Indeed, their problems are not just relevant to modern publishers, but as Roger Parry argues to a wider group of media managers: 'The pioneer book publishers had to confront all the issues now so familiar to most media owners: the management of talent, copyright piracy, libel, spiralling marketing costs, and predicting public taste' (2011, 85).

Latour would probably disagree with the use of frame and model, filtering and amplification. These, he might argue, are too abstract, or that they tend toward oversimplifying rather than 'reassembling' the difficult realities of publishing. However, the pattern is too strong and too clear to ignore. The networks and the actors keep changing, yes, but there is something about those networks demanding explanation.

Chapter 5

MODELS

Filtering, framing and amplifying give us the 'how' of publishing, but they don't give us the why. Models do. They are the motivating factors behind any publication, they regulate intentions and in doing so affect outcomes. We must offer not only a description of what happens, but also account for why. In short, models require closer examination.

There is more to models than simple extrapolations used to initiate and guide the publishing process. In models we find an inescapably social element: if a model is not afforded by a society then publishing according to that model is impossible in that society. The range and nature of publishing must at some level be socially conditioned, just as it is conditioned by the range of possible technologies. 'Social' is here shorthand for many things such as ideologies, economics, politics, living and working arrangements, the availability and nature of resources, institutional factors, legal frameworks, cultural and intellectual milieus. As ever, contextual specificity should be taken as a given. Models change with time and place – ancient China had its models, as did ancient Rome and so do contemporary Sao Paulo and Stockholm.

Equally, and consequently, publishing often has many models operating at once, in or out of sync, consciously or unconsciously, harmoniously or even acrimoniously. What remains the case is that all models emerge from their societies and so ineluctably connect publishing and published material to those societies (after the initial, primary contact, the author). Models also introduce risk as part of publishing. Bearing risk in the supply chain is a vital part of publishing: a project risks failing under the terms of its models as the world behaves unpredictably. Hence risk is everywhere in publishing. Connected to risk is value. Insofar as a given work is a node of value, it accrues benefits under the terms of the models while the amplificatory function amplifies value.

This chapter, aside from offering a general profile of how models work, focuses on an intriguing question: to what extent are publishing models concerned with the pursuit of profit? While publishing is usually seen as a commercial activity, and in some definitions is explicitly equated with moneymaking, it need not be so. The Gideon Bible, one of the most widely distributed texts on the planet, isn't known for its cash-generating prowess. Yet publishing must be economic. Reading can take place with no resources other than a text, while writing requires, at a basic minimum, scarcely more. Publishing implies a greater marshalling of resources, however. To build amplificatory frames of any sort, especially beyond the manuscript age, necessitates resources, a means of production beyond the act of either reading or writing. Scarce resources are constants from which publishing, like most human activities, struggles to escape.

So publishing is always economic, if not profit oriented. How does this work in practice? What other kinds of model are there aside from profit? How do political, social or ideological factors come in? How fundamental is profit to publishing? These are live questions. Answering them we tread a delicate path between economics and more aesthetic or cultural theory approaches that see economics in cultural terms. As we will see over the next two chapters, more than anything else changing models are key to the future of publishing. If we cannot understand the delicate historical interplay of models, with their nuances of for and not for profit, we will struggle to understand the implications of and answers to the digital challenge.

Background

Before exploring models in more historical detail, it is worth clarifying a number of points about what is claimed by models.

First, what do we mean by 'models'? Generally, in an academic sense, models refer to representations of things; whether they are physical or intellectual, models are constructed to show us something nominally already there. Within science, and more pertinently in media and communication studies, models are used explain the world. We build a model of reality and then test it to see if the model works. This has become one of the dominant strands of comparative media studies. Daniel Hallin and Paolo Mancini (2004) for example, have created comparative models of local media systems as a way of better understanding the differences between national media. Such media models are more akin to this study as a whole, which in the terms of

Hallin and Mancini (2004) is about modelling publishing as an activity, rather than looking at publishing's models.

Publishers tend to use models not to understand the world, but to do things in it. They don't have models 'of' so much as models 'for'. This is a use in line with business models, models typically for making money (among other things). As with scientific or economic models, business models are based on assumptions about how the world works, with the success or failure of the model contingent on the validity of those assumptions. The difference lies in why these models, which equally apply to other areas from relationships to geopolitics, are created. Publishing models are premised on an interpretation of the world, but unlike academic models they primarily guide actions. They are motivations as much as explanations.

The central point about the use of models here is their inclusivity. Whereas most models have narrowly defined edges, these models are open, complex, containing internal contradictions, oppositions and apparently unreconciled elements. They are part consciously constructed, part unconsciously influenced, on micro and macro scales. They encompass many parts, ranging from the shape of a societal or company hierarchy to the design of a book's prelims. So whereas a business model is usually explicitly stated and narrowly defined, publishing models are often largely hidden or only partially understood by those using them.[1]

Like the concept of frame, the model is a productive metaphor; it is a meta-model, rather than an unbending description.

Bear in mind that nothing in this sketch should be viewed deterministically. There are two relationships here: 1) the relationship between a given society and the models it offers; and 2) between the model(s) used and the nature of the publishing (the filtering, amplification and the frame). In neither movement is there a naive sense of causality. Even the most ardent Marxist would, these days, be unlikely to support simplistic characterisations of a base/superstructure notion of culture, let alone the somewhat patronising ideas of a writer like Theodor Adorno. Many thinkers, from Antonio Gramsci and Stuart Hall to Terry Eagleton and Stephen Greenblatt, have introduced

---

1 There is no reason such a conception of models should only be applied to publishing; it could have a much wider application, in literary, media and communications studies and beyond. Indeed, all kinds of business or enterprise could be seen this way, although the peculiar features of publishing and content mean they are especially helpful here.

sophisticated modifiers to this position, reformulating views from ideology and hegemony, to 'mediation', 'homologous structures' and other ways of finessing the relationship between society and literature. It becomes about setting limits and establishing possibilities, inflecting, guiding, or permitting; not, in other words, mechanically causing. The same fuzziness applies to models. Moreover, in practice the messiness of the world frequently intervenes and interferes with models. Publishers, as with everyone else, don't have complete control of either the models they use or what happens when they use them.

This raises a question about society and literature. If one is to establish a full understanding of their relationship, publishing must be factored in. In the creation and dissemination of texts, publishing isn't just an afterthought. It co-constitutes texts and books. Hence a theory of publishing and a concept of how publishing relates to societal questions are utterly essential for a description of how context and text relate. Theorists like Fredric Jameson are quick to look at 'History' as the governing principle of textual communication, without examining exactly how history makes itself manifest in the second stage of a work's coming into being: the publishing. Literary theory needs publishing theory.[2]

For Profit?

The Rhenish origins of printing contain an instructive story for thinking about how far publishing models are about making profits. Johannes Gutenberg had spent a number of years in Mainz and Strasbourg working on a new technique for reproducing texts centred on type. He knew he was onto something big, but the costs kept mounting, eventually forcing him to take venture capital, first in Strasbourg, and then back in Mainz. While Gutenberg hardly came from a poor background, he needed the help of a local financier, Johann Fust, who leant him the large sum of 1,600 guilders in two instalments in 1450 and 1452.[3] While Fust was the money man, as investors are wont to do, he secured executive places for his own people, notably Peter Schöffer, who was tasked to assist Gutenberg and in whose shop Gutenberg was to work. It was

---

2 This is in no way to deny the enormous and invaluable body of scholarship that has grown up around publishing and the history of the book, nor indeed the general drift of literary studies in this direction. It is simply to restate the case.

3 As is often the way with venture capitalists, there is some evidence to suggest Fust leveraged himself to get the money to in turn lend to Gutenberg (Man 2009).

here, in the smithy-laboratory of the early 1450s, that printing emerged into the Western world. While Gutenberg made the decisive technical breakthrough trouble was, famously, looming; Fust was owed not only the principal but also quickly mounting interest, eventually resulting in a suit for reparations in 1455. On one side was the inventor, the man ultimately credited with sparking one of the greatest innovations in history; on the other was a merchant banker. There was only going to be one winner. Fust and Schöffer, newly in ownership of virtually the complete stock of materials and IP, went on to set up a successful printing house. Gutenberg had to start again. Ever since controversy has raged as to whether Gutenberg was set up by Fust and Schöffer, screwed into losing everything by canny operators quick to make as much as possible from his technology. Regardless, from the earliest days of printing one thing is clear: capital, and the interests of capital, held the trump cards.

In Mainz, the pursuit of profit was inscribed into the press from the start; it has stayed that way. If economics is often defined as the allocation of resources for competing ends under conditions of scarcity, then we should see nothing controversial about the suggestion that publishing is inherently 'economic', but this doesn't explain why publishing is so often profit oriented, or more bluntly, capitalist. Marx recognised the spinning jenny only became a capitalist tool thanks to the context and organisation of its use. Likewise, the printing press is not innately capitalist. Yes, resources are required to produce and maintain technologies like the spinning jenny or the press but they need not be mobilised through capitalist means. The relationship between duplicative technology and capitalism is historically contingent. Nonetheless throughout its history, publishing has been in the vanguard of capitalism, pioneering among other things industrial process and organisation, intellectual property, trade in intangible goods (the 'knowledge economy', 'creative industries'), the removal of censorship and government interference in business matters, free markets, luxury and consumer goods (books were among the first consumer Christmas presents), labour organisations, sponsorship and advertising, innovations in the retail experience from free browsing of goods on display, tracking and monitoring technologies (like the ISBN), the pioneering of web retail, product design, marketing, trade fairs and export markets. Such a list of innovations stretching to the present day is yet another rejoinder to those who think publishing a backward-looking industry.

This capitalist or profit-seeking base ultimately rests on the fact cultural and informational entities are, or can be viewed as, commodities or tradable assets. They have a value expressible in terms of the utility or worth markets assign to them. Moreover they often come with high fixed costs of production, creating conditions of risk, which in an open market require some level of return above investment. As the example of Gutenberg highlights this is why a good system of credit and strong liquidity have often been prerequisites for healthy publishing ecosystems. Undercapitalised publishers are chronically weak and cash hungry. Unpredictable demand, exacting creditors, sunk costs and thin margins mean various forms of (emergency) debt financing, like loans, convertible loan stock, equity injections, takeovers and fire sales are common on publisher ledgers.

There is also a dual sense in which books are assets. Both the frame and the text within the frame are tradable commodities. In publishing you are not just selling the book, but also a sequence of words. To those commodities come publishers, looking like the fabled rational actors of classical economics: they seek to maximise returns and minimise costs on their investment. This is the most basic model at work in profit-oriented publishing (as it is the most basic model of any profit-seeking activity).

Under this rubric the whole activity can be set in the language of capitalist economics – the marginal costs of adding consumers (readers) has tended to fall throughout history, and generally publishers will carry on publishing a title as long as the marginal costs don't exceed the marginal returns. Cultural economics is still economics. Publishing is a matter of investment, in intellectual property, paper, presses, etc. It is a matter of careful inventory management, balancing and manipulating supply and demand in the marketplace so that its products and activities will safely navigate elastic pricing structures to make a profit. Economists produce demand functions for cultural goods, which resemble those for any other commodity. The model behind publishing is the successful exploitation of that demand curve. Copyright is a part of these models that creates monopolies, which, in such a speculative practice, reduce risks, incentivise investment and protect returns, to a degree dictating price and availability (St Clair 2004).

Techniques of filtering, framing and amplification are used to create surplus capital from the potential of amplified products to create efficiencies based on decreasing marginal costs. Such surplus capital is required as an incentive to initially invest in the start-up costs of framing and amplifying. Pretty much wherever you look in publishing, some variant on this fundamental model is likely. This creates a unique corporate structure in which reproduction (framing, amplification) is tightly controlled to ensure profit, but primary production is left much looser, given a degree of 'creative autonomy' to adapt to market conditions (Ryan 1991; Hesmondhalgh 2002; Hesmondhalgh and Baker 2011).[4] It's striking how this pattern persists in places where the model, so pervasive today, was far from the norm. Fifteenth-century Mainz in the Holy Roman Empire, for example, with its strong guild and artisanal traditions was a utopia of enterprise compared to much of feudal Europe. Still, even here a rudimentary capitalism wasn't inevitable. Note, however, that this basic profit-seeking model doesn't necessarily imply a maximal amplification. On the contrary, it implies the use of models thought best at securing a surplus. Often, this is the near reverse of maximal amplification: publishers frequently see lower risk and cost premiums, and hence a greater likelihood of positive returns, in selling fewer copies at a higher price. A profit-oriented model uses amplification to secure profit, rather than as a goal in its own right.

In practice though my argument about models is that they are rarely monolithic. They are composites, blends, with multiple components and functions, working at once on a variety of levels. While profit models are the most significant, such models encompass a range of interesting externalities. A well-researched example is the difference in censorship structures between eighteenth-century Britain and France. Notionally Britain abandoned official censorship in 1695, when parliament allowed the Licensing of the Press Act (1662) to lapse (theatrical censorship remained, under the auspices of the Lord Chamberlain). In his monumental *The Reading Nation in the Romantic Period* (2004) William St Clair explores in detail how, a few years later, a new monopolistic system of organisation entrenched itself in British publishing. One consequence

---

4 Hesmondhalgh and Baker's (2011) argument is that the need for creative autonomy and its tension with the requirement for control in order to best make money are key structuring factors for the creative industries. The process by which the two are mediated is what they term 'creative management', which is a navigation, a 'balancing act' between what I would call profit and not-for-profit models: 'Managers need to reconcile artistic values with economics; novelty with familiarity; existing demand with the transformation of the market; vertical integration with outsourcing; and systems with individual inspiration' (Hesmondhalgh and Baker 2011, 82). Like models, creative management is historically and politically conditioned, not just a business problem to be solved. For Ryan (1991), it is part of the rationalisation attendant with corporatisation, both of which try and reduce the autonomy, or irrationality, of the creative process.

of this was the *de facto* imprimatur of the ruling classes on the period's publishing activity.

After the Statute of Anne and the introduction of copyright, texts became locked into a system designed for publishers' benefit. Publishing coalesced into what amounts to a cartel, the Conger, which collectively owned and traded in copyrights in a closed, quasi-masonic network of ownership and association. Copyright was meant to be time-limited but publishers, aided by the courts and their wealth, found ways around this.

> During the high monopoly period, the London book industry was as perfect a private monopoly as economic history can show. Examples of every restrictive trade practice known to modern regulators can be found, including cartel, conspiracy, price-fixing, predatory pricing, rent seeking, repetitive and baseless litigation, entry barriers, market division, credit-fixing, collective refusal to deal, exclusionary joint ventures, resale price restrictions, tying, and vertical non-price constraints. (St Clair 2004, 101)

Yet St Clair's argument is not simply that this restricted the supply of books by artificially inflating prices, but that it also had political implications. By means of this price function books would be kept from the masses; potentially 'dangerous' ideas would be neutered by their circulation only among those interested in avoiding their wider expression. A real-term fall in the number of books printed, high prices, exclusivity of purchasing and an extreme metropolitan concentration of ownership all added up to a mechanism of control ensuring undesirable works didn't spread too freely.

The situation in France partially resembled British censorship as it had been under the Company of Stationers. Then the ownership of works and state scrutiny neatly dovetailed in the form of the Register, into which all editions had to be entered so providing a monitoring facility for publications. Under the *ancien régime* and since the time of Richelieu and Colbert, France used an official state system of censorship. It consisted of two parts. First was a pre-publication submission-based censorship, which, like the Register, gave a monopoly to the submitting printer if approved. This was followed post-publication by the Inspector of the Book Trade, who would look for illicit or seditious materials and their producers. From 1723, packages coming into the country would be checked for illegal print matter. The first half of the eighteenth century, the Enlightenment, saw book consumption start to increase among the nascent *bourgeoisie*, while those pillars of the French state – God and the king – were increasingly questioned; against this censorship was designed to secure the interests of the Crown and church. To some extent it was a success: by 1789, the censors office in Paris had grown to some 160 people, proscribing between 10 and 30 per cent of books submitted. Between 1659 and 1789, they sent nearly a thousand offenders to the Bastille, 17 per cent of the total imprisoned there over the period (Darnton and Roche 1989).

Yet this paints only a partial picture. Anti-monarchists and atheists were never neatly ranged against the royalist establishment. In reality, the system had considerable forms of laxity, compromise and even consensus built in. Publishing was a commercial enterprise built on the foundation of public demand. If publishers couldn't print what people wanted to read then at some point they would go bust; the work simply transferred abroad. As the censors recognised the national significance and pliancy of a domestic publishing sector, this was something they wanted to avoid. Long-serving chief censor Malesherbes wanted a looser, more intelligent and negotiable arrangement, with deliberately blurred boundaries allowing a productive ambiguity. He tried to balance open markets, free expression and government policy.[5] Equally, thinkers and writers like Voltaire and Rousseau were not above working with censors to find compromises. At first glance, the emergent *laissez-faire*, copyright-driven, mercantile model of British publishing stands in contrast to the projection of state power in that archetypal absolutist monarchy. Yet when compared, the British profit-driven model – an apparently unprincipled enterprise revolving around money – isn't so different from the French. In practice, both models served a patrician consensus. A notionally profit-seeking model wasn't just about profit; it had a tacit political dimension and vice versa. Public and private concerns, proto–free market and dirigiste economic systems, censorship and free expression: none are so polarised as they appear.

Profit-centric models are a big part of publishing. Financial innovations (from subscriptions to joint-stock venture capital) and increasing commercial sophistication over the centuries, along with evolving technologies and audiences, powered publishing change and expansion. Entrepreneurialism and mercantilism are consistent leitmotifs. Operating margins, cash flow, growth: these are never far

---

5 Indeed recent scholarship on eighteenth-century censorship in France argues that the censors were not so much repressive influences as professional 'cultural intermediaries' in their own right; see Adkins (2012).

from most publishers' minds. In the words of Richard Nash, 'Books are not only part and parcel of consumer capitalism, they virtually began it' (2013). As this example makes clear, even at their most apparently straightforward models have complex compositions and implications. There are 'conceptual thickets surrounding creativity-commerce relations' (Hesmondhalgh and Baker 2011, 85). Profits aren't the end of the story.

Not for Profit?

Publishers are not only capitalists. They also need to be aesthetes and intellectuals, cultural mavens, trend watchers and astute critics. Without expert judgement, a publisher is liable to be found out. Moreover, it isn't simply a matter of 'good' writing pays, although it can do; some publishers build identities around commitments to writing seen as if not oppositional to financial concerns then somehow above them. Many publishers throughout history have prided themselves on publishing to make a difference not a quick buck. They feel it is their duty to bring out works of intrinsic merit regardless of remunerative incentives and disincentives. Nonfinancial considerations are powerfully present.

In his celebrated sketch of the 'cultural field' Pierre Bourdieu (1993) describes such publishers as working in the field of 'restricted production', as opposed to the field of 'large-scale production'. The former operates not via financial incentives but through the accrual of symbolic capital. Indeed, it defines itself against the field of large-scale capital, where cultural production is merely another form of industrial production looking for scale and a decent return on investment. For Bourdieu (1983) the logic of the field of restricted production creates works of ever more extreme difficulty and self-referentiality in a spiral of artistic inwardness unconstrained by the mass market. 'Cultural legitimacy' or 'consecration', not profit, are the goals of the small, educated coteries usually found behind these loss leaders.

Bourdieu claims cultural production is polarised between restricted and large-scale cultural production, structured into a series of oppositions: '"pure art"/"commercial art", "bohemian"/"bourgeois", "left bank"/"right bank" etc.' (Bourdieu 1993, 64). Yet in his perceptive portrait of the publisher there is a more nuanced picture:

The latter [publishers and gallery owners] are equivocal figures, through whom the logic of the economy is bought into the

heart of the sub-field of production-for-fellow producers; they
need to possess, simultaneously, economic dispositions which, in
some sectors of the field, are totally alien to the producers and
also properties close to those of the producers whose work they
valorize and exploit. The logic of the structural homologies
between the field of publishers or gallery owners and the field
of corresponding artists or writers does indeed mean that the
former present properties close to those of the latter, and this
favours the relationship of trust and belief which is the basis of
exploitation presupposing a high degree of misrecognition on
each side. These 'merchants in the temple' make their living
by tricking the artist or writer into taking the consequences of
his or her statutory professions of disinterestedness. (Bourdieu
1993, 39)

Here Bourdieu describes the familiar figure of the publisher caught
between aesthetic and market imperatives. To succeed publishers must
be both economic and cultural agents. In the necessary 'misrecognition'
between the two sides, he acknowledges this tension can translate into
difficulties with writers. However, although Bourdieu here talks about
the field of restricted production ('the sub-field of production-for-fellow
producers') he has in fact created an image of both fields: separating
commercial from non-commercial publishing may at least accurately
describe the practice in twentieth-century Paris, but broadly speaking
creating two camps, one about profit, the other about, say, aesthetics, is
far too neat a depiction. In fact, profit and not-for-profit models often,
indeed usually, blend to form hybrids.

Models are likely about making money and gaining cultural
legitimacy *at the same time*. Bourdieu's (1993) portrait actually works
for both major sub-fields. In reality they both mix profit and non-
profit models. Models are made of numerous components, which may
have institutional founding, as in Powell's (1985) record of publisher
decision making, or may be specifically formulated for a given project;
either way, they are likely to combine financial and nonfinancial
considerations.

Neither models nor the filtering process can be simplistically described.
The normal situation is for numerous apparently incompatible models
to work in unison. Non-capitalist publishing has a long history and
just as profit-seeking publishing has consequences beyond monetary
considerations, not-for-profit models aren't so straightforward either.

David Throsby (2001) uses a suggestive word to unite the cleavage between culture and economics – both are about ideas of 'value'.

For much of history one nominally not-for-profit, or non-capitalist, model dominated: patronage. Patronage was still an economy to be sure, if not a capitalist then a more Maussian 'gift-exchange' economy. Books still had to be produced and the relationship between patron and client was clearly transactional. Typically, it involved a dedication to the patron – this would often insinuate patronal ownership of the work both on the level of owning the text in some way, but also a deeper sense of having inspired or caused the work to come about. We associate patronage with writers, who, in return for their dedications, Literature and Learning's dusting of fame and glory, became the patron's gun-for-hire,[6] reaping benefits including hard cash, prestigious posts (like the Poet Laureate or Historiographer Royal in England) and sinecures as bureaucrats, diplomats or clergy. Among other things, 'hospitality',[7] 'favour', various forms of protection, the authority of aristocracy in political, social or artistic cover, credibility, sales and introductions were all part of the compensation package (Griffin 1996). Social and financial capital were fungible.

Dedications and patronage were used strategically. Roger Chartier (1995) discusses the case of Galileo. In 1610, the great astronomer was teaching mathematics at the University of Padua, but, like many since, wanted more time to research. He needed a patron to finance a research position. His solution was to dedicate his book, *Sidereus nuncius* (Starry Messenger), to Grand Duke Cosimo II de' Medici's favour, a standard gesture. Galileo's masterstroke was to also dedicate the 'stars' or moons of Jupiter he had discovered to the Grand Duke, which in the classically influenced cosmology and astrology of the time was particularly fortuitous and flattering.[8] It worked. The Medici granted him a research post allowing him to pursue his studies unsullied by the distraction of students; everyone was a winner. These patronage-seeking manoeuvres were by no means confined to writers; publishers were similarly implicated in the economy of patronage, and would often

---

6 William III, for instance, opened up the Civil List of government positions and benefits for friendly writers, who effectively became propaganda agents as he raised unprecedented taxes on the population to finance a series of wars.

7 Chaucer, for example, received the benefit of a gallon of wine a day for life from King Edward III. While he may have preferred hard cash, who would refuse a lifetime supply of wine from the king?

8 Galileo even offered a telescope in which to view them.

delay publication to ensure patrons received advanced copies. Indeed, publishers fought for patronage:

> Authors and translators were not the only persons who presented books to princes. The booksellers often did so as well, which meant there were times when a dedication put the author of the text and the producer of the book in competition with each other. (Chartier 1995, 34)

Thus, we can't say that while writers sought patronage publishers inhabited a world of balance sheets and conventional profit. Patronage seeped through literary production, organised according to models not entirely describable in terms of monetary profit and loss.

The trick was maintaining the fiction of patronage's disinterestedness. The enlightened patron was always candid and beneficent; likewise was the client in recognising their betters. Nonetheless we can be sure that in most cases a sophisticated calculus of benefits was in play. The first modern British prime minister, Robert Walpole, exemplified this duality being one of the largest patrons of his day and an exceptionally shrewd operator. Patronage has never really gone away and neither has this tension.[9] The modernists had their patrons,[10] as we do today: gallerists like Charles Saatchi or Larry Gagosian fulfil a role neatly poised between speculative investor and grand Medici-esque patron, while multinationals like BP or Deutsche Bank are major sponsors of the arts. Nor has the state lost its patronal role, with ministries of culture and publicly funded arts bodies sustaining the cultural economy. Universities and research funders act as academic patrons freeing up the ability to research like latter-day Grand Dukes. So the tension persists: everyone knows the relationship is about mutual benefits even when couched in different terms.

Patronage may not be about profit, but it is about interests and exchanges. It often merges with profit-seeking models. A writer may operate under patronage, their publisher capitalism. No one is accusing Charles Saatchi, or for that matter Robert Walpole, of investing in art purely for altruistic reasons, even if it provides some explanation.

---

9 Dustin Griffin (1996) argues a particularly Whiggish interpretation of eighteenth-century letters has obscured the degree to which throughout the century patronal forms were prevalent in literary production.

10 Think of James Joyce and Sylvia Beach. Without her support we might never have had some of the crowning achievements of literary modernism.

Patronage has never really been about disinterested *noblesse oblige.* It has always been about trading mutual benefits. At the same time it has also always been political. Patronage is about upholding a political system, stating political beliefs, creating factions and support, and disseminating propaganda. Patronage in itself represented a certain kind of political constitution. In the minds of patrons, writers or publishers, politics, aesthetics, literature and economics weren't separable. There was no false choice between serving one's wallet, one's interests and the cause of high art. To understand models we can't unbundle the aesthetic from the political, the scientific from the economic, or the religious from the profane. In any model there is likely to be a mixture.

University presses are another illustration of this knot. Today they have a complicated role, mandated to support scholarship while not becoming a cost centre for the university. With luck, they might financially contribute to their parent institution. This is their model in a nutshell. In most cases, the primary measure of a university press is the dissemination of knowledge, which is why academic publishing has developed a strict and expensive system of quality control in the peer-review system. As with patronage, as with publishing generally, the underlying picture is rarely so straightforward.

By some accounts, Cambridge University Press (CUP) is the oldest extant publisher in the world. Founded by Royal Charter in 1534, it is certainly the oldest university press (although it didn't print anything until 1584, a year before Oxford University Press (OUP)). Despite this longevity, its relationship with the university was only formalised by statute in 1981, having only been granted tax exemption on the grounds of charitable mission in 1976. Contrast the language of the press in the statutes with its original 1534 charter. The 1984 mandate is as follows:

> There shall be in the University a University Press which shall be devoted to printing and publishing in the furtherance of the acquisition, advancement, conservation and dissemination of knowledge in all subjects; to the advancement of education, religion, learning and research; and to the advancement of literature and good letters. (Black 2000b, 77)

While the sixteenth-century Letters Patent include the lines:

> These Stationers or Bookprinters, assigned in the aforesaid manner, and any of them, shall have lawful and incontestable power to print

there all manner of books approved, or hereafter to be approved, by the aforesaid Chancellor or his deputy and three doctors there; and also to exhibit for sale, as well in the same University as elsewhere in our realm, wherever they please, all such books and all other books wherever printed. (Black 2000b, 75)

In the 1981 text, there is no mention of profit, or indeed of any motive or model other than the university's goals, here officially echoed in the mission of the press. As with the university itself, if the press is not about 'knowledge' or 'research' it is about nothing. In 1534, there was far more ambiguity; nowhere is knowledge invoked as a reason for being licensed to print. In contrast to the markedly non-commercial wording of 1981, the 1534 document explicitly mentions books should be made for sale. Making money, not furthering knowledge, appears to have been the animating principle. For contemporary publishers, well used to the financialisation of publishing, it is curious to see these models almost the 'wrong' way round.

For many years the press printed mainly bibles, a lucrative trade given the tight control of the London-based Stationers' Company, out of whose clutches the historically autonomous university had extricated itself, and not without considerable acrimony from the metropolitan fraternity. Bibles were important as the press needed profit, not least as it had guaranteed to pay the university every year for the privilege of printing under its aegis (Black 2000b). Far from being subsidised, all costs would be met by the press. Books were hence often less scholarly than might be expected from an academic institution or in comparison to the output of many university presses today. Simply to cover costs, the press needed to print commercially secure titles sure to sell and reprint quickly. Throughout the seventeenth century CUP increasingly took jobs as a subcontractor for the major London printers or booksellers, which provided a good stream of work with a solid contribution to overheads. The bibles printed by one Thomas Thomas, in 1590 and 1591, are perfect examples. They had predictable demand, good margins, were safe (aside from the legal sniping from London) and, given he was basically working as a printer, profitable.

Painting the story of CUP solely in terms of commercial considerations would be wrong however. Its birth was about religion and religious control. Puritanism had deep roots in Cambridge and many college fellows were writing theology of a distinctly Puritan bent, something the urbane, controversy-avoiding publishers of the company and court churchmen wanted to avoid. Having technically secured the right to print in 1534, the university was moved to start printing in 1584 as a generation of dons started producing troublesome writing about church governance that they believed deserved an audience. Despite the press's smallness (it was a fraction of the size of Plantin's contemporaneous firm, for example), with only one press and a handful of apprentices, it fitted the corporate identity of the University of Cambridge as beyond the purview of the local bishop and London authorities alike, answerable only to the monarch.

As time went on, the scholarly dimension came more clearly into view. At the close of the seventeenth century the scholar Richard Bentley, later a master of Trinity College, became publisher, along with a talented printer, a Dutchmen Cornelius Groeneveldt. The press had expanded to four presses and was governed by a body of scholars called the Curators (today known as the Syndics) who would oversee the business of the press. Bentley saw himself and the press as intellectual pioneers, putting out a second edition of Newton's *Principia Mathematica* in 1713, one of the most important titles in the history of science, which had fallen out of print. Happily, and unlike other books the press was publishing, it was also a great commercial success. Only in 1755 was a 'public benefit' explicitly part of the charter, and even then what this meant was still left unclear. If today CUP is about scholarship, we can at least say its journey has been neither totally for nor not-for-profit, but always hovering in a space I believe is the norm for publishing. Note, too, the discrepancy between the reality and sentiment of the 1981 statutes; reading it, it is easy to forget that CUP is an efficient multinational company with turnover approaching £250 million, employing 2,000 people, milking considerable margins from an enormous stack of IP accumulated over the years. The mistake is to believe the two are necessarily out of sync.

Systems of patronage and university publishing are not obviously about making profits. A closer examination reveals several things. Even if they are not about making profits as such, they are still working under models trying to achieve goals, whether allowing students to learn the laws of thermodynamics or persuading a writer to politically inflect their work. In this 'targeting' sense they resemble profit-seeking models: they are all publishing in order to achieve something. To this end, we almost never find pure models. What is apparently not-for-profit nonetheless lets profits seep in; the most commercial of projects reveal other standards and considerations beyond the financial. Because publishing must be economic, because it must gather and deploy resources in changeable circumstances, among motley groups with competing means and agendas, it would be a surprise to find many models that weren't mixed.

Even in societies with alternative economic bases we find composite models. Take the East German house, Aufbau. Founded in the ruins of war in 1945 Berlin, Aufbau at first made the most of cultural leniency in the early days of Eastern European communism. Along with its Western cousins S. Fischer in Frankfurt and Rowohlt in Hamburg, it was one of the largest postwar literary publishers in Germany. As time wore on and the impact of Soviet dominance became more pronounced, it started publishing the pseudoscientist Lysenko and other Soviet works, the liberal publisher was removed, replaced by a Party man, Walter Janka, and print runs came under more centralised control, as they were in the USSR. Party ideology became a major part of publishing decisions as a national censor's office was established.[11] Yet even here, in that most controlling of environments, Aufbau maintained a commitment to serious literary publishing in spite of the consequences. Under Janka, and with talented editors like Wolfgang Harich, Günter Caspar and Max Schroeder, Aufbau managed to navigate the twin demands of the communist state and the calling of a high-classic aesthetic in writing and thought. They published major editions of Thomas Mann, Johann Gottfried Herder and Heinrich Heine. Even when, in 1956, many senior figures were arrested or removed from the house, this tradition continued. On the back of popularity and valuable exports to West Germany, Aufbau found a niche in East German publishing. It wasn't easy but even in the most seriously constrained of situations models resist an ascription to just this or that.

Models might depend on an editor's mood or an epoch-spanning socio-economic formation. More likely it is a combination of both, encompassing a host of other factors. Models are about assemblages of value: prestige and religious conviction, cultural authority and aesthetic judgement, covering basic resource issues and generating large returns. Even if we grant primacy to profit models in publishing, we cannot ignore their complexity, nor those features beyond the narrow command of money.

---

11 We could also say ideology is a major part of decision making across all publishing, only it is not explicitly acknowledged as such.

Four Encyclopaedias: Four Composite Models

Encyclopaedias are a good example for several reasons. They have a long pedigree, dating at least back to Roman times and the *Naturalis Historia* of Pliny the Elder. The word itself comes from a misreading of Greek roughly translating as 'complete knowledge'. Together with their long history, they have a totemic societal importance and geographic spread. In addition to Rome, encyclopaedias have been found in East Asia, Byzantium, Charlemagne's Frankish empire and across the caliphate Middle East. They are repositories of the limits of knowledge, statements of development and intellectual capacity, and so present major publishing and research challenges with significant resource implications regardless of where we find them.[12]

Two of the largest publishing projects in history originated in China, respectively in the Ming and Qing dynasties. Both were encyclopaedias attempting to capture an entire civilisational *Weltanschauung*. Even by today's standards, they are huge. The earlier Ming encyclopaedia, the *Yongle Encyclopedia*, named after the Ming emperor Chengzu, was commissioned in 1403 but has numbers familiar to the digital age: 370 million Chinese characters, 22,937 block-printed rolls in 11,095 volumes (Hu and Yang 2010). It covers virtually everything, from agriculture to religion, encompassing a vast corpus of texts from the official archives. It was never widely circulated, but packaged more as a kind of library in and of itself. Its scale was only surpassed by the *Siku Quanshu*. The Qing's vast attempt to outdo the *Yongle* extended to some 800 million Chinese characters (44 times larger than the *Encyclopédie* of Diderot). It was so large the chief editor, Jiyun (or Xiaolan), had to write a book about how the project was organised.[13] As with the *Yongle* it was published in only a limited sense, with seven copies housed

12 Robert Darnton writes of the *Encyclopédie*: 'A whole world had to be set in motion to bring the book into being. Ragpickers, chestnut gatherers, financiers, and philosophers all played a part in the making of a work whose corporeal existence corresponded to its intellectual message. As a physical object and a vehicle for ideas, the Encyclopédie synthesized a thousand arts and sciences' (1979, 522).

13 To give a sense of the scale: 'The book [The General Catalogue of Siku Quanshus] records 3,461 kinds of ancient works in 79,309 volumes in Siku Quanshu, and 6,793 kinds in 93,550 volumes not included in Siku Quanshu, which basically includes ancient Chinese works before the Period of Emperor Qianlong of the Qing Dynasty. With 200 volumes, the book can be divided into 4 classifications, 44 categories and 66 minor-catalogues' (Hu and Yang 2009, 48).

in specially constructed buildings between 1772 and its completion in 1782, including one in the Forbidden City.

What prompted work on such an enormous scale? We are clearly dealing with models of great power and size. These works were the pinnacle and expression of a culture, only possible in the context of an absolute power for which massive resource deployments without tangible return presented no problem. They keyed into ancient traditions of scholarship and wisdom dating back to the first Chinese encyclopaedia, the *Imperial Reader* of 220 CE. Moreover, we see a historical or sequential element to the models in play: the *Siku Quanshu* is conceived, its model conditioned, in reaction to what had already been created. The *Siku Quanshu*'s model is in part about establishing dynastic legitimacy for the Manchu Qing, as well as capturing knowledge. While these great monuments were not about a capitalist return on investment, they still had multifaceted models of immense power working on many levels. There was a subtler way it buttressed imperial power. A handy side effect of measuring the total sum of Chinese letters was to let the Qianlong emperor and his officials know which books they should ban.

Europe has a similar succession of models, working in braided historical sequences. Perhaps the most famous encyclopaedia of them all is Diderot and d'Alembert's *Encyclopédie*. Often seen as the paragon of the Enlightenment, it was made in reaction to earlier encyclopaedias like Ephraim Chamber's *Cyclopedia* of 1728. It was to be more comprehensive, accurate and in tune with the currents of rationality and science then coming to prevalence. As with the Chinese encyclopaedias, the numbers alone are an impressive indication of the challenges and goals of the work: 17 volumes of articles were published 1751–65, 11 volumes of illustrations in 1762–72, with further supplementary material following, over an initial 28 folio volumes, comprising 71,818 articles and 2,885 plates. The motivating model was originally Diderot and d'Alembert's emancipatory theory of knowledge, although this was only partially shared by the original publisher Le Breton and his business associates. For such a large project to get off the ground it needed both a profit and a not-for-profit motive to bring together all the parties required.

In *The Business of Enlightenment*, Robert Darnton (1979) recreates the 'what happened next' of the *Encyclopédie* in astonishing detail. Diderot eventually came to realise the impossibility of his task: one project alone would never be a summation of knowledge. Publishers were not so circumspect approaching such a juicy proposition.

After Diderot was done with the work in 1777, the publishing model drastically shifted from large expensive folio editions to cheaper quarto and octavo editions with larger print runs and distribution. Darnton (1979) weaves a 'Baroque' narrative involving Parisian, Lyonnais and Swiss publishers in a tangle of contracts, mixed models and a general desire to profit from the Enlightenment. He calls two of the major players – the Paris-based Charles-Joseph Panckouke and the Lyons publisher Joseph Duplain – 'Balzacian' in their epic machinations and drive to make money at all costs:

> As the history of the *Encyclopédie* shows, the most prominent publishers of the Enlightenment operated by bribery and extortion, by falsifying accounts and stealing subscription lists, by spying on each other and manipulating Machiavellian alliances that gave full play to treachery and intrigue. (Darnton 1979, 531)

What started as a bold and worthy attempt to free minds with the light of reason had descended into a squalid battle for printing rights displaying the kind of unprincipled business acumen that has been a hallmark of publishing over the centuries. Paradoxically, this most commercial of battles broadened the scope and audience for this controversial work: larger print runs meant cheaper editions meaning the *Encyclopédie* spread to more people.[14] From one perspective, the models of capital and scholarship were opposed; yet they can also be seen as not only compatible but complementary. Even so, the picture is richer still, not a just matter of profit-ravening publishers and sage authors. Panckouke in particular had a many-sided relationship with the project of the *Encyclopédie*, a curious mixture of intellectual commitment, desire for profit and sheer compulsion:

> Panckouke felt sympathy for the ideas in those books [those of the *philosophes*]. He developed close ties with the philosophes and wrote some philosophic works himself. But ultimately he seems to have been inspired by something akin to the spirit of the robber barons

---

14 Interestingly Darnton (1979) shows how it was the traditional centres and classes of power, rather than the thrusting mercantile bourgeoisie so often associated with the French Enlightenment and Revolution who formed the major audience for the *Encyclopédie*. It is a good reminder that whatever a publisher's models they ultimately do not control either who has access to their books or, above all, the success of their model.

in the nineteenth century. He speculated because speculation had become an end in itself, a way of life, for him. (Darnton 1979, 393)

Huge resources were expended over a long time on publishing the *Encyclopédie*, as they would be on a famous response. The *Encyclopædia Britannica* was started as a Scottish riposte to Diderot and co. (two centres of thought and book culture in a dialogue between the Scottish and French Enlightenments) but following the form of the German *Conversations-Lexikon* and aiming for popular rather than scholarly use. Over its history the *Encyclopædia Britannica* has gone through 15 editions revealing subtle changes to models in play. The ninth edition (1875–89) bursts with Victorian taxonomic confidence. Edited by the philosopher Thomas Spencer Baynes and assisted by theologian and orientalist William Robertson Smith, it's known as the 'Scholar's edition'. After this high watermark of scholarship in the *Encyclopædia Britannica*, emphasis was thereafter tilted back to the general readership of the original 1768–71 edition. Changing ownership in the twentieth century – the *EB* became American as well as British – again nudged the focus towards populism, becoming a household must-have, an essential part of middle-class Anglo-American consumer culture. Over the years, changing ownership led to an evolving pattern of models, which in turn translated to shifts in content. Throughout, the accuracy of the *EB* has reflected not only a commitment to truth but a business proposition: its readership was built on trust in the brand. Failures in accuracy were commercial risks.

Today we lean toward something no one saw coming, a model and an encyclopaedia as radical and vast in its own right as the Chinese projects of earlier centuries. By now we are all used to Wikipedia. If you time travelled back to the mid-1990s and presented the idea everyone would assume you were mad. Nowadays Wikipedia is a project of neo-Enlightenment, a capacious, ever-mutating knowledge bank (which one hopes would have delighted the early Diderot) and poster child *par excellence* for the open license movement propagated by Stallman, Lessig et al. (initiated in the 1980s and ongoing).Wikipedia isn't based on venture capital, doesn't want to turn a profit and relies on volunteers donating millions of man hours purely for the sake of increasing access to the sum total of human knowledge. For the first time in history, the mind-boggling size of the *Siku Quanshu* has been overcome: as of August 2012 there were 285 editions (languages) of Wikipedia with over 22 million entries, 4 million of which are in English. According to Alexa (2013) it is the sixth most visited website in the world. In comparison the *Encyclopædia Britannica* went from 400,000 entries in 1989 to 700,000 by 2007. No profit-seeking interest could finance such an enormous project. Only a power comparable to the Chinese imperial bureaucracy could harness such energies, and yet no single such power exists in the world today. Wikipedia at one level represents a whole new model for encyclopaedia publishing: utterly decentralised, 'pure' in mission, more akin to forms, say, of religious publishing than the business focus of the *Encyclopædia Britannica* or even the *Encyclopédie.* This portrait would not be quite accurate, however, as the story of Wikipedia is more nuanced. Far from starting with its present mission, the origins of Wikipedia were almost wholly commercial.

It was founded by a young market analyst called Jimmy Wales. Wales had a web-hosting company, Bomis, a web directory making money in the time-honoured Internet fashion from advertising. The idea for a free online encyclopaedia was, ultimately, to generate ad dollars, as well as opening up knowledge. This already marks it as a different model from that of the *Encyclopædia Britannica*, which had for some time relied on direct sales to consumers and institutions. The project, run by Wales and his collaborator Larry Sanger, was originally called Nupedia: while it would be free, online and voluntary, the content generation was to be closely policed, with each entry rigorously sourced and peer reviewed before going on the site. Launched in 2000, it quickly became evident people weren't interested in going through the whole rigmarole. It was too unwieldy. Using wiki software created by the developer Ward Cunningham, Wikipedia was at first conceived as a daring feeder project to Nupedia, an experiment to see if content could be created fast and at scale with a view to filtering it onto the main platform. Wikis were part of a new crowd-sourced culture coming into bloom and the results were dramatic. In comparison to the tepid growth of Nupedia, Wikipedia had 22,000 articles only a year after launching in 2001.

At first Wikipedia had a commercial slant. Badly hit in the dotcom crash the year Nupedia launched, Bomis needed money. The servers, bandwidth and other costs quickly climbed along with the traffic. The burden of supporting Wikipedia was born by Bomis, which owned the encyclopaedia. When, in 2002, Wales suggested putting ads on the site there was uproar in the community,[15] who wanted formal acknowledgement of

---

15 The reaction against this initial move was such that almost the entire Spanish community on the site simply left, leaving a legacy of lower than expected engagement on Spanish pages, although this eventually was overturned (Lih 2009).

the openness of Wikipedia, the success of which was dependent on their voluntary contributions. The mass editorial resources needed to monitor the site and ensure a decent level of quality relied on a small army of dedicated volunteers. In effect, the value of the site was predicated on their vigilance. The shift of ownership to the Wikimedia Foundation in 2003, a charitable organisation whose mission statement explicitly commits them to the free dissemination of knowledge in the public domain, was therefore a later revision of the Wikipedia project, not something built in. It reflects the reality of what had been almost inadvertently created. Now with an institutional structure formalising Wikipedia's model of openness and donations amounting to $27.5 million in 2011 (enough to cover basic running costs), its hacker ethos, distributed model of peer production and open licences appears secure. It need not have been so. Without the original financial interest of Bomis we arguably wouldn't have Wikipedia.

These four episodes from the history of encyclopaedias provide four sets of composite models. Encyclopaedias come in many forms. Correspondingly they have many models. In each case we see mixtures of models uniquely combined, matching end product and circumstance. The sketches here are, of course, simplifications. In fact, the number of actors involved in the incredible work of compiling these giants of book history is such that the mix is likely to be even more blended when examined at granular levels. The point is we can't really understand what encyclopaedias are doing until we understand the models under and for which they were published.

Risk, Rationality, Diversity

Models are searching for a multitude of possible effects, as various and many sided as there are publishers. The fluid notion of value offers us a way of tying these strands together. Value is integral to one of the most useful ideas in recent discussions of publishing and other media industries; namely, the value chain or the way each part of the publishing process aims to add value above costs, so producing surplus value. It also has obvious economic connotations. A given sum of money or profit has a given market value, exchangeable for a certain quantity of goods and services. Yet value can also tie into other categories.[16] The accrual of

---

16 As David Throsby describes it: 'In the economic domain, value has to do with utility, price and the worth that individuals or markets assign to commodities. In the case of culture, value subsists in certain properties of cultural phenomena, expressible either in specific terms, such as the tone value of a musical note, or

cultural or symbolic capital, prestige or influence, for example, also has value; we may or may not be able to reduce this to an economic scale, but either way the value is real enough, even if only because people believe it to be real. We can take some insights from the old Frankfurt School 'culture industry' thesis but also the revisions and criticisms from more nuanced work on culture, society and economics following in its wake. We can consider how credit arrangements need not be based solely on self-interested calculation but also trust, reputation and friendship. We don't need to specify the make-up or governance of models, we simply need to sketch rules for how they work in practice. Aside from detailed studies, we can do no more.

Models aim to extract value from content by framing and amplifying. Filtering and amplification are both about adding value to content through framing. Economic value is *primus inter pares* because publishing requires resources and resources are not free. We must always be attendant to how value – whether aesthetic, political, religious, etc. – saturates publishing, coexisting in complex assemblages of motivation and opportunity. What we might call 'mono-models' are the exception.[17]

With value comes risk. In today's publishing, bearing risk is part of what a publisher does. They advance funds to the author, create the product, pay for it to be produced, hold the stock, invest in the marketing and promotion of the book. Everything a publisher does requires investment without certainty of return. Publishing without cash is impossible. In many countries, this risk-bearing role is exemplified in the returns system whereby retailers don't hold inventory on a firm sale basis. If a book doesn't sell they can return it to the publisher, often with disastrous consequences for the publisher's budget. The risk of retailing is pushed back from retailer to publisher.

Time and again publishing echoes over the centuries and this situation was to some degree always the case. Gutenberg held all the risk in the work of the press, using the IP he created as security for the loans he took from Fust. He needed to finance the project's immense

---

the value of a colour in a painting, or in general terms as an indication of the merit or worth of a work, an object, an experience or some other cultural thing' (2001, 19).

17 Mono-models being, for example, a model that is solely devoted to making money with no other concerns whatsoever, or solely about supporting a certain cause with zero ancillary goals. Both would produce fairly strange, not to mention bad, end products.

research and development (R&D), the costs of labour, the expensive stock of paper and other materials required, the capital costs of equipment and in doing so he took on the risk himself. The Conger, realising this, went to great lengths to remove risk from the equation, engineering as benign and risk-free a publishing environment as they possibly could, until, in another familiar pattern, government intervened. Stumping venture capital for publication of works with no guaranteed audience remains a central feature of publishing to this day.

It may be possible to think of a risk-free model for publishing – something along the lines of contract publishing, where a third party bears all costs including a built-in profit margin. Unsurprisingly most publishers like this model. The world, however, is still unpredictable and unruly. Things can and do go wrong even in the surest bet. Models need to be tested against reality for their validity and reality is frequently an uncompromising partner. This is why, when trying to accrue value, it is almost impossible to remove risk from publishing: you always might fail under the terms of your model given the inherent unpredictability of the world. Someone must take on the risk and publishers are, historically and structurally, the ones to have done it.

To see how the system works overall, let's return to our early example of the Aldine Press. In the case of Aldus we can see from the beginning a many-aspected model was in play. Aldus's partners and investors were after a return, stable employment and perhaps influence, all of which was to be achieved through publishing. Aldus himself sought a chance to cement Greek on the syllabus and in the contemporary mind. The main goal of either party was to remain financially secure. A huge amount was staked on the project. Various outlays of capital were calculated to return themselves, but it was their combination that drove their success and delivered value back to the stakeholders. Aldus's model was unique. It came at a critical juncture in the Renaissance, in one of Europe's wealthiest, most open and eastward-looking locales, at a time when the future of the book really was up for grabs. Outside the Most Serene Republic c.1500,[18] the Aldine model might never have worked. Filtering and amplification are tied into this modelling process; they grow from it. All that amplificatory finesse expresses a complex, specific set of models. Those small handsome volumes were products of precisely audited models.

---

18 As the Republic of Venice was known until its dissolution by Napoleon in 1797.

In summary, because models are ultimately about value so they create risk as a by-product. Risk and value are two parts of the same story. Whatever the model, publisher strategies will usually seek to maximise value and minimise risk. The *Yongle Encyclopedia* still could have failed, leaving out chunks of knowledge, displeasing the emperor or closing access to the wrong people. Although we can't fully recreate the detailed modelling process involved, we can see despite the weight of its models and surety of its funding there were still risks the project could fail, probably with unpleasant consequences. Likewise Wikipedia has risks; it may not secure enough donations to cover its considerable hosting expenses or it may succumb to pressures to close or restrict the open editing process. Wikipedia is often filled with graffiti and misinformation and there is always the risk this will overwhelm the sterling work of those policing the site. As with value, risk need not be financial and for this reason we cannot escape it. Cultural, symbolic and intellectual capital is, in publishing, ventured, lost and accrued. If value is now widely used in the study of culture and communication, with multiple uses and modes, risk is less visible: we talk less of aesthetic or religious risk in cultural production, perhaps because it is harder to see, more difficult to identify unless things go wrong. Jeopardy is always more present to actors themselves than to commentators after or outside the event.

Before moving on, there are three points I would like to address. They relate to publishing and rational choice, the relation of publishing to the public sphere and what a theory of models implies about the constitution of our publishing.

First, rational choice theory is the idea economics can be described in rational terms, with actors behaving rationally, calculatingly, given their circumstances. Publishers in this view will act rationally to maximise value – which even here need not be economic – and minimise risk in their models and the execution of their models. While I believe rational choice theory (RCT) is helpful, it by no means offers a complete description of what is going on here. It doesn't give due weight to how much publishing works on subconscious or non-rational grounds. Equally, while the language of RCT can encompass emotional or aesthetic payoffs, it underestimates how integral they really are. Models are not just pragmatic constructs used for an academic analysis, as many models are in RCT. Publishers really are using them. Here is where it gets difficult: much of what publishers do with models is extremely self-conscious, yet there are other elements that may be blind spots.

In short, we can look at models partly through the prism of RCT, but we need a more internally nuanced account that takes in many of the criticisms of RCT while also tying it more closely into the specific societal formations in which a model operates.

Second, models provide a social nexus for publishing. The whole process of publishing is inescapably, if not obviously, social, economic and technological. Models are where the first burden of this wider context is felt. Those encyclopaedias can only work under models socially possible for their time and place. Sometimes we invent new models or even technologies and knowledges, yet this must be pushing to some extent against an open door. Models only inhabit the possible. As power is distributed through a society so power is distributed through publishing. Yet this does not necessarily occur in the same proportions or pattern, as publishing is too varied for lazy classifications and blunt functionalism. I leave it an open question to what extent publishing is embedded in and reflects dominant interests of society.

This societal nexus also points to a further aspect of publishing: growing from a society is only one part of a loop, which also includes how publishing helps produce societies. Publishing changes minds. Publishing has large consequences on the public sphere as the littoral between private thoughts and the public realm. When Winston Churchill said, 'There is no such thing as public opinion. There is only published opinion', one imagines he was pursuing a similar line of thought. There is insufficient space to explore this idea in detail. Providing an explanation of the public sphere is itself a book-length project or more. It should be noted however that there must be a relationship of some sort. Alexandra Halasz (1997) uses the phrase 'commensuration' to relate the marketplace of print and the public sphere,[19] and in this relationship lies the efficacy of publishing and one of the pivotal factors in understanding how texts and societies relate.

Finally, to adapt Karl Marx (1846), the point isn't just to interpret publishing but to change it. To that end I would venture a modest normative conclusion. Having a greater number of available models is

---

19 She writes 'the marketplace and the public sphere are mutually constitutive but not coextensive' (Halasz 1997, 167). They are non-identical but related. The marketplace creates the public sphere, but it then cannot control the public sphere: '[T]he question of commensuration becomes susceptible to a reading that allows for a constitutive ambivalence in the public sphere without thereby reducing the discursive field to the operations of capital' (Halasz 1997, 171).

desirable. Societies that limit the number of workable models, whatever those models may be, have more limited publishing sectors and hence a more limited public sphere than those allowing a greater variety of publishing models. More models allow more points of views, more ways of thinking and more ways of existing. This freedom creates a better chance of innovative and different work coming through, as well as greater opportunities to have real debates and make progress through the process of sifting through ideas that compete and coexist in equal measure. Diversity of models is hence always to be encouraged. Think of the ossification of societies with limited models like dictatorships: they have fixed views, progress only slowly, if at all, and eventually become vulnerable to more nimble and advanced societies. One could hardly pretend model diversity is a major factor in this, but surely it is a factor.

We should ensure the sector has a variety of possible models. In Anglo-American publishing in particular, even before the digital challenge, there was evidence that the general range of models was becoming more limited, and narrowly profit-centric, resulting in a contraction of content range. André Schiffrin's (2001 and 2010) angry accounts of the corporatisation of publishing (Adorno's worst nightmares come to pass) have been seen as overly partial; however, the picture they paint will be easily recognisable to those working for major publishers either side of the Atlantic, even if other reactions are not as averse.[20] Retail and publisher conglomeration, the rise of super-agents and super-advances and the accelerated logic of capital running throughout the cultural industries have consequences. Independent bookshops have withered. While there is a boom of small independent publishers in terms of numbers, they struggle to find a readership and stay afloat. In many countries tacit or overt state support is a major component of the book world. Extreme risk and tight margins, especially in open markets, mean publishing is heavily exposed to policy decisions. Countries with retail price maintenance for books like France and Germany have arguably enjoyed more success in supporting a diversity of publishers, booksellers and models. Arguments for media pluralism are prey to the charge of papering over cracks.

---

20 There is another view of corporatisation, that it transformed sleepy and unproductive publishers into modern, efficient organisations, with not only higher turnover and profits but an improved responsiveness to consumer demand, more marketing clout, better output and a greater capacity to take and absorb risks. If they hadn't adapted in this way, the argument runs, they probably wouldn't have survived.

Against such a view, we need a dose of realism and to recognise that open, public and rational discourse is still possible and desirable. The case shouldn't be overstated; the UK and US still have an incredible range of models and there is always a diversity of models in any publishing environment. It is rather a question of degree and trajectory. If we care about writing and the public sphere, we should care about cultivating conditions for a genuine efflorescence of models.

Chapter 6

ADDRESSING PROBLEMS, MEETING CHALLENGES

Twisting through the byways of publishing history and theory we have created a sketch of how publishing works. The below diagram is not to be taken literally; it simply clarifies how publishing slots together and how the flows interact to comprise the system of publishing. Models undergird the process and introduce risk and value into the equation. Filtering precedes framing and amplification; amplification happens through the framing process, which collectively form the idea of cultural intermediation.

Nowhere is the word 'book' mentioned or necessary in the chart. Publishing covers all manner of materials, in fact anything focused on content. When it comes to meeting the digital challenge this feature is utterly central. The wrongful description of identity in publishing, as makers of books rather than amplifiers of content, is at the root of the challenge; consequently, a shift in identity provides the key to its resolution. Once publishers recognise both the accidental nature of their content-framing standards and the continuity of publishing wherever content is to be found, they can start building robust strategies for the future.

Nowhere in the diagram is a 'publisher'. Being a publisher is a function of the activity of publishing. Anyone can be and increasingly is a publisher. Publishing is a structural, functional feature; what people call themselves within it is ultimately irrelevant. If it quacks like a publisher, it probably is a publisher, despite what it might call itself. The relationship with content is once again key.

Returning to the problems outlined in the Introduction we can see how the modelling–filtering–framing–amplifying view of publishing tries to resolve them. Any working, high-level view of publishing, we recall, must account for the following.

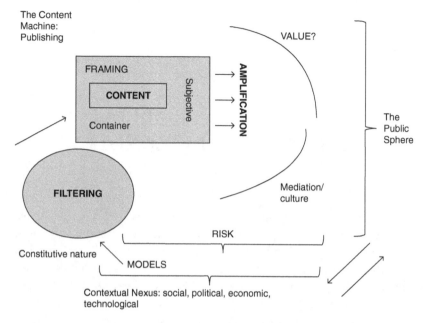

It must *account for the public and institutional character of publishing,
explaining what makes something public.* Early uses of the word publishing
often meant either to make something public or, most commonly, to do
so within an institutional context like the church. Most contemporary
definitions of publishing, in both the dictionary and operational senses
revolve around the idea publishing is about 'making public'. The
weakness of such a view lies in the lack of clarity about making public.
At what point does something become public? Replacing 'making
public' with amplification puts us on more solid ground. Amplification
is any intermediation through framing designed, according to a model,
to increase the consumption or exposure or value of content. The
institutional context slots into this. Institutions both enable and require
the work of amplification to function. Hence, old institutions had
more need of publishing than other areas of society. Amplification is a
simple concept. Were it otherwise it wouldn't help us. 'Making public'
has sufficient generality to cover the many forms of content and work
done over the years, but without the specificity of describing something
tangible. Amplification gives us both.

Like 'making public' cultural or informational mediation is
easily invoked, less easily spelled out. Thus a working view of
publishing must also *account for the role of publishing as an act of mediation.*
Leaving it as a shady area is potentially productive but clearly doesn't

give us real answers. The outline of content and the nature of filtering and amplification provide us with a helpfully open idea of mediation. Moreover, publishing is active; it is not a passive matrix through which content passes but a force partially shaping and inflecting content. This is why anyone interested in literature or the history of information more broadly should pay attention to publishing studies and theory.

This requires us to *account for divergent historical understandings*. From the first time written communication was disseminated, probably in Mesopotamia around 3200 BCE, publishing, of a rudimentary sort, was taking place. All the ingredients of publishing were present: the content itself, the clay tablets and sharp stylus used to etch what became cuneiform script (the frame) and then the work of spreading the message, passing the tablets, teaching others to read and write. The earliest writing systems were appropriately enough accounting systems and balance sheets; what could be more important to record than one's debtors? Fast-forward 5,000 years and the technological and economic base has changed. Hugely. Our capacity for filtering, framing and amplification is immeasurably greater. Yet our need to do those activities has remained consistent. Throughout this study examples have been deliberately cherry-picked from all over the historical record: fourteenth-century China, fifteenth-century Nuremberg, sixteenth-century Venice, seventeenth-century London, eighteenth-century Paris, nineteenth-century New York and twentieth-century Seattle among others. The fact that we can look at publishing in all these contexts demonstrates that publishing is at once about unceasing change and also a relatively stable set of goals, needs and functional features, analogous to a concept like the law. It is always disputed and evolving, but remains a recognisable feature on the historical landscape nonetheless. Only by outlining a theory of publishing through history can we create a conception of publishing that encompasses that history. This means we can't simply describe publishers today. We must pay attention to forms of historical publishing, finding their commonalities and patterns. The system described *comes from* a reading of history, not the other way round.

If we are to contextualise this view of publishing history, we must also *account for divergent media forms published.* Journal publishing, for instance, is very different from publishing novels; publishing computer games shares little with newspaper publishing. They are different businesses, attracting different people with different cultures. Yet they share at least one feature: content. While my focus has been book publishing, the book is simply a frame for content and it is not hard to replace the book in the analysis with any other format. For example, music publishing is a specialist part of the music industry; yet in my argument, the whole music business becomes part of music 'publishing'. Music publishing itself becomes a subset, a particular model in the context of the music industry. Using different models and frames, publishing hardly seems like one thing. The commonality is the underlying structure of modelling, framing and amplifying. Differences between publishing industries are large and more work is needed in understanding them. However, if we fail to see common areas we fail to see what makes publishing important and distinctive.

Finally, a view of publishing must *account for facets such as (financial) risk, the relationship to content and market making*. Risk results from the ineradicable possibility of failure under the terms of any model. Risk is tied up with another foundational concept: value. The framing of content is a necessary ingredient of publication. Setting aside reductive notions of media as containers, delivery systems present content in certain ways. This ductile presentational/subjective aspect of framing is basic to the work of publishing. Lastly, market making takes us tidily back to amplification.

All of the points made here aren't particularly controversial. Many of these ideas are built in to discussions of publishing, media or the history of the book and are alive in industry debates. The theory is a modest one, making sense of difficulties inherent in a long-lived and complex activity. Theories have value in advancing debates and describing underlying patterns, tendencies or even producing helpful simplifications. Problems are addressed, not solved; these arguments are far from the last word. Indeed, I hope they stoke further debate in the inchoate area of publishing theory. Five thousand years of history is a long time and counter-examples and problematic instances are sure to be found. They will have an important role in further developing a theory of publishing.

Meeting the Challenge

Publishing grapples with digital networks on several fronts. The open architecture and tendency towards convergence is altering content and frames. In turn, this opens possibilities for disintermediation as new and old players cut publishers out of the value chain in which they were once central. Lastly, digital technology has troubling implications for the model of intellectual property underpinning publishing for 250 years. Taking a long and deep view allows us to reconsider and recalibrate this challenge. We can better separate the value chain as it exists today from the underlying value chain of publishing. All the ideas presented below are familiar parts of the conversation about digital publishing. The language of content, frames and models, filtering and amplification simply gives us a new perspective.

My goal is not to set out what publishers should do. That is up to publishers themselves; and in my experience they are intensely focusing on this area anyway. It is rather to outline a way of thinking away from industry bromides. One problem with commentary on digital publishing is its short time horizon, driven by budgets, publishing schedules, initiative launches and consumer tech releases. Two, five or even ten years are all much too short for thinking about the real implications of digital publishing, which like other new media will take decades and centuries to fully manifest itself, and even then will not stop changing. I should also stress publishing's response has been generally surefooted. Revenue streams and businesses have not collapsed. Publishers haven't shirked innovation, forward planning and hard questions. None of this is grounds for complacency, however.

Changing content and the imposition of new media forms and formats is the least of publishing's worries. New skills, working methods and cost structures are needed. Yet there are two closely related reasons why it's not a critical problem. First, new media are the norm. Media history, in spite of periods of near stasis, forms an ever-quickening rush of graphic, oral, written, printed, aural, visual and now digital media coming thicker and faster than ever. Guglielmo Marconi's experiments with radio transmission in the late 1890s occurred only thirty years before John Logie Baird's first public demonstration of television. From Betamax to Blu-Ray, a procession of formats come and go. What's more new media developments are always denounced until attention moves elsewhere. Although well established by Plato's lifetime (around 400 BCE), he still felt the need to denounce writing in the *Phaedrus*. According to Plato writing makes us lazy at remembering. Written records are static, doomed to repeat themselves, addressed to only one audience, unlike speech unable to adapt or clarify on the spot. Ultimately writing is but a 'phantom' of living speech and cannot find truth. As with much else, Plato stands at the beginning of a long argument. From the church's initial denunciation of the press through to the moral panics around television, including more nuanced critiques like that of Neil Postman (2005), and fears over violent computer games, new media attracts criticism, fear and uncertainty. It creates problems for established media. Convergence represents a step change in the interaction of media, but these changes are part of a long tradition. Even if we are going beyond the specific information architecture Adriaan van der Weel (2011) calls the 'order of the book' we are not moving beyond an 'order of publishing'.

Second, bearing this in mind, we should return to the idea of disintermediation in historical perspective. Earlier, it was suggested the present pattern of disintermediation is one of 'partial disintermediation'; greater complexity instead of hard and fast breaks, a thickening of the value web as new players interact with old. This has been predicted by a number of media theorists and takes its simplest formulation as Riepl's Law. Wolfgang Riepl was the editor of Nuremberg's largest newspaper in the early twentieth century. In 1913, he formulated his law of media: new media don't displace old media, but accrete on top of and converge with them (Küng, Picard and Towse 2008; Parry 2011). New media has a big impact, absolutely – old media usage, creation and dissemination all become utterly transformed by the arrival of things like radio, cinema, television and the Internet, but that doesn't mean they simply disappear. Riepl's Law seems to hold even today. Although widespread adoption of television was supposed to destroy the radio, radio altered its output. It first catered for a new audience of rock 'n' roll listeners before mutating into shock-jocks and talk radio. Likewise videos, DVDs and movie streaming have not killed cinema; instead they've changed the tenor (and value) of the experience. One of the implications of Riepl's view bears underscoring. While some digital enthusiasts speak as if they're already gone, printed books aren't going away. We should remember to never underestimate the resilience of media formats in general and the book in particular.

All the questions around book publishing are really about comparative relevance. Are publishers comfortable occupying a hugely diminished place in media as a recondite craft like calligraphy, or will they reassemble to stay competitive? Paul Saffo's (1998) awkward neologism 'disintermediation' is useful here. Saffo argues new technology opens niches best exploited by new entrants adapted to those niches. They pioneer innovation giving them an advantage. Soon, however, that innovation becomes standard. Although digital lowers the transaction costs for entrants this doesn't mean incumbents cannot play the game. Whether we call it 'remediation' or 'disinteremediation' the general, somewhat Hegelian movement of media posited by Riepl's

Law is not one of redundancy in the sense of buggy whip makers going bust with the coming of automobiles.[1] Published products are resilient, changeable and well used to adaptation. As a result, book publishing in some form is also secure. Whatever technological or economic revolutions we undergo, so long as there is demand for content then publishing will play a necessary structural role in meeting that demand.

Put another way, frames change. This is normal. As frames change so do amplificatory methods. Filtering is still needed, in the blogosphere as much if not more than the monastic library. We are witnessing a periodic but nonetheless epochal occurrence: a radical shift in models as their techno-socio-economic base starts to crumble. *Pace* Riepl publishing and publishers in the broadest sense are not going away but the models they are predicated on, the weakest element in the present-day edifice of publishing, may be.

This isn't a technocentric problem. If anything it's a problem of markets and the logic of digital markets in particular. Digital economics put pride of place on scale and traffic flow as the marginal cost of adding users in digital is even less – much less – than that of adding them in traditional publishing. This goes back to the process of centralisation, with its power law dynamics, device lock-ins and oligopolistic drives. In this world, value shifts from ownership of content to aggregation of both content and audience, completely altering the economic fundamentals, the models, of traditional filtering and amplification. So it comes back to the giant platforms and their ability to harness value at a tangent to traditional media owners. New models have started to appear and we don't yet know whether they can coexist with or must supplant the older unit and IP models characterising Miège's (1989) 'publishing logic'.

On the levels of centralisation, fragmentation and the resulting challenge to IP, old publishing models are under assault. Centralisation favours the models of big and web-native companies and organisations. Publishers are unable to compete, too late to the game, now comparatively too small to make up the technological, financial and market-share deficit.[2]

---

1 The much used buggy whip analogy for disintermediation is not without problems: see Stross (2012).

2 Not that they aren't trying. Both vertical and horizontal integration are being pursued to create scale and synergies capable of taking on large digital businesses. The merger of Penguin and Random House and Universal's acquisition of EMI are two examples. However digital is not the only driver of this merging and acquisition activity – newly favourable regulators, globalisation and the general power of retail also all play a part.

Google, Apple, Amazon and the rest have a business model, which, if not oppositional to the industrialised model of publishing, is not symbiotic like a bookshop's basic business model. Content sales are probably regarded as small parts of their future business. In fact, they derive considerable value from the free flow of content in direct opposition to the models of most contemporary publishers. In addition to editorial and marketing, a huge part of the model in current publishing is the coordination of production, distribution, logistics and accounting: the detailed nuts and bolts of getting content into the hands of readers requiring know-how, money and established operations. Large platforms can do all this. If publishers no longer have an advantage in these basic areas, their model looks fragile.

Fragmentation favours writers and newer, better-adapted publishers without the legacies of sunk costs, overheads and debts marring their balance sheets. Publishers rely on adding value through framing, filtering and amplification, but the availability of low-barrier-to-entry methods for doing all of the above, for both creators and consumers, calls into question their ability to keep adding that value. If in the minds of some being an author still requires a literary imprint, being a writer certainly doesn't. The question has similarly long been moot for musicians, who easily move back and forth between mediational methods. So closely tied are the identity of a publisher and the value chain they have worked under – in other words, publishers and their existing models – this pattern gravely threatens them unless they adapt their value chain and model. Presented with other options, established brand names and new entrants alike may go to destinations where the value added/value extracted arithmetic (such as the new models) works more in their favour.

A symptom of the above movement is the debate around intellectual property. This is no trivial matter; by some estimates, IP is the biggest export of countries like the US and UK (Howkins 2001). Time-limited monopolies, it is argued, are the guarantor of investments made by publishing; they are also antiquated eighteenth-century devices produced and subsequently maintained by a self-serving rentier gentry, damaging the potential of the networked world. Virtually no one disputes the need for creators and facilitators to be fairly remunerated (defining 'fair remuneration' is another matter). The question around copyright laws are really about who benefits from them: creators or companies, which either productively invest in or shamelessly milk copyrights depending on your perspective. Many of the questions around extreme discounting and second-hand file services like ReDigi are subsets of questions around intellectual property frameworks. They are about who has access on what terms and at what cost. Even as both sides throw lobbying money at the question, it can't now be unasked. The genie is out of the bottle and publishers are only just beginning to sketch new models predicated on something other than traditional intellectual property rights.

In the network age, publishers' basic business model is their Achilles' heel. While it is deeply tied into the digital evolution of framing and amplification, the impact is felt most in the model. Their reliance on powerful external networks leaves them vulnerable. Publishers are facing, to use the term of Harvard Business School guru Clayton Christensen (1997), 'disruptive innovation'. Christensen has a Schumpeterian vision of companies innovating, thriving and dying as disruptive innovations wreak havoc with established businesses models.[3] Most companies focus on 'sustainable innovation', which represents a continuation of their present model. Disruptive innovation is ignored as an unattractive investment with lower profit margins or existing in small niches and, crucially, is not, at first, wanted by a company's prime customer base. This is why such innovation is so dangerous, as standard management practice heavily counsels against any involvement. And yet it repeatedly reorders entire industries, even societies. Characteristics previously making an organisation strong suddenly render them weak. The 'value networks' into which businesses have been built fall apart. Typically, incumbent businesses can't support their weighty cost structures on the reduced margins of disruptive innovation and only rescaled companies, usually new ones, can survive. Cue creative destruction. Christensen's (1997) argument is surprisingly radical: this is about not letting customer demands, accountants and perfectly sensible managerial principles dictate resource allocation and strategy formation within firms. Christensen (1997) and Saffo (1998) may look opposed at a glance, with Christensen warning about disintermediation, while Saffo argues that disintermediation is never simple – but in practice they are probably closer than that would suggest. Both would argue disintermediation and disinteremediation are not inevitable and rely on decisions made by companies.

The drama of disruptive innovation is playing out in publishing models. While publishers have built an uneasy accommodation with digital, they have ceded huge ground in the provision of content to

---

3 Referring to the Austrian-American economist who popularised the phrase 'creative destruction' in his book *Capitalism, Socialism and Democracy* (1942).

new actors, partly because of a failure to invest in digital growth when no one read ebooks, the Internet was for geeks and monetising digital was a distant fantasy. Fear of cannibalising existing sales governed a conservative and, from one perspective, entirely rational approach.

On one side, publishers can take comfort in Riepl's Law and the long layering of media. Most content forms don't go away, but find new places in a reshuffled pack. On the other, they should be keenly aware of the 'Schumpeter–Christensen' argument: business history is littered with organisations that doomed themselves to, if not bankruptcy, mainstream irrelevance and decline.[4] While publishing goes on, publishing as it is now faces continued market-share loss in the total media market (a trend from the early twentieth century) – at best. This is the problem when, in Clay Shirky's words, 'that one word [publishing] comes to stand in for a business, a production method, a product, a cultural signifier – the whole range of it compacted into a single thing' (Keen 2010).

This analysis suggests that for publishers to thrive in the face of the digital challenge they need to find models working with the new grain of framing and amplification. What might they be?

Provisos: of course, there is no magic bullet and this is a book of theory not strategy, still less future gazing. The mantra remains that of screenwriter William Goldman's dictum on Hollywood: nobody knows anything (even if it never stopped them pretending). My interest is underlying movements and trends and the below are arguments, directions and thoughts which, in the context outlined, seem most fruitful to explore.

Market Making

Digital technology is part of a transition in our societies and economies dating back to the sociologist Daniel Bell's formulation of the 'post-industrial society' and before that the business writer Peter Drucker's concept of the 'knowledge worker'. Whether we call it 'informational capitalism' (Arvidsson 2006), 'the economics of attention' (Lanham 2006), the 'networked information economy' (Benkler 2006) or the 'age of access' (Rifkin 2000), there is a profound set of changes occurring in how the world operates, largely stemming from the trend towards post-industrial or non-material production and a confluence of new technologies. The shift has often been overstated; we don't live in a free-

---

4 Randall Stross (2012), again, suggests that half of the biggest American industrial companies between 1912 and 1995 disappeared.

floating society composed of emails and graphic design software. We still need goods and they still need to get from A to B. There is still much hardship and the actual impact of digital technology on companies, businesses and society is often less than its most ardent proponents think. Nor is the shift reliant on information technologies; in fact, the general shift to market making can be traced back to the Second Industrial Revolution of the mid-to-late nineteenth century, with its step change in productivity and the subsequent growth of a consumer economy. This is not to say there hasn't been a change, however.

Explaining framing and amplification I suggested they don't disappear in digital, but change formation. Framing goes from being about physical distribution mechanisms to digital presentation and signalling processes. Amplification goes from producing and distributing units to harnessing attention. Both changes are part of this shift, although again, the roots go back much further to increasing print supply. Print productivity, digital technology and relatively high disposable incomes between them change which part of framing matters most in the work of amplification.

Let's zero in on Richard Lanham's (2006) argument around the economics of attention. For Lanham attention has become a new kind of currency as content is now found easily, and in abundance at a cost approaching free. An attention deficit is the major problem faced by content owners, not a content scarcity. Consequently, he argues, those who can gather and create attention are the new bankers of an attention economy, citing artists who manufacture attention from arrestingly basic materials like Marcel Duchamp or Andy Warhol as exemplars. This isn't a niche argument. Businesses from blue chips to start-ups are increasingly based on their ability to attract the attention of customers not as a means to an end but as an end in itself.[5]

For publishers this means amplification has moved on. It now means drawing people towards a work, through publicity, marketing and the correct deployment of metadata. Amplification has gone from a supply-side to a demand-side problem. Amplification is attention. Just a few years ago metadata was the province of a handful of specialists on the fringes of the publishing industry mainly concerned with the recondite technology of warehousing and inventory. Now at the heart of most workflows, publishers recognise its importance as a work's first online sales pitch. Good metadata doesn't sell books on their own, but bad metadata leads to invisibility, the cardinal problematic of digital

---

5 Is this sustainable? The jury is still out.

publishing. Marketing has consistently grown in importance, from the small notices in chapbooks and at early book fairs to expensive transmedia campaigns spanning multiple territories. Struggling high-street bookshops accelerate the trend as their role as discoverability channel *par excellence* diminishes. It would be quite wrong to present this market shift as a turn away from content, however. Good content is far easier to market; indeed, it markets itself far, far better than bad. Quality filtering is as important, perhaps more, in a market-making context.

Business-to-consumer selling is already here. One consequence, and again a common part of the wider shifts we are seeing, is the growing value of brand equity. Design, slick production, customer-facing initiatives, ownership of the retail channel and the discipline of customer relationship management (CRM) are all brand-cultivating processes that aim to harness the value of communities formed around brands. Websites are retooled to facilitate this, oriented around reader subsets. Another possible future for publishing is as a species of specialist book marketers, working with writers to build author brands.

Publishing has never been about simply making content available. There have been times when it has been close, sure, but amplification always requires something extra. However, the gap between making a book available and establishing a market has never been wider, and not just in digital contexts. In the informational economy, demands on consumers' attention, time and money are more prevalent than ever. Convergence means publishers compete across the entire spectrum of media production. On a tablet you can browse Facebook, watch *The Killing* or play *Angry Birds* as easily as you can read a book. Some book publishers deny the direct competition of other media (I have argued with many of them). If people want to read they want to read, runs the argument. Unfortunately, this fails to grasp the nature of convergence and the informational, attentional economy. In essence, framing and amplification of other media are now often the same as for books and with books they share an increased emphasis on market making rather than making available. To withstand multimedia competition publishing needs to keep turning towards the new reality of framing and amplifying, not clinging to the old.

'Open' Revisited

Almost anything can be 'open' and often is. Despite creeping 'open' fatigue and the end of early utopian excitement around the concept – big business tends to do that – we shouldn't ignore how significant the term may be for publishing. If the pivot to 'market making' constitutes a new set of business practices then 'open publishing' suggests a whole new model.

At the heart of the question around Open Access (OA) and open publishing in general is a simple question: is free a viable business model? We have already seen how publishing has usually had capitalist overtones. Resources are needed and there is no reason to think this will change, albeit in reduced quantities in the context of web and open publishing. Journalist Robert Levine writes eloquently about one problem of free: 'It's the new-media catch-22: you have to give away content to attract an audience that turns out to be worth less than you thought because they're attracted to free content' (2011, 78).

Yet academic publishers are finding a way. So called 'author pays' models, where 'author' usually means 'research funder', are now a major part of the scholarly publication process. While scientific, technical and medical publishing pioneered the model, there is some evidence of transfer to the humanities and social sciences. Low-cost or free tools like the open peer-review system or Open Monograph Press are changing the resource implications of academic publishing. New currents of research, notably the digital humanities, threaten not just to reassemble the entire epistemic edifice of humanities research but also its dissemination: it is hard to see how, in their present incarnations, most monograph publishers will deal with research, the outputs of which are data sets, software, interactive renderings and the like.[6]

Momentum from the academy is propelling a revolution. New services are sprouting with an extraordinary fecundity, driven by low barriers to entry and an entrepreneurial spirit. The Public Library of Science (PLOS) has a basket of high-quality journals and a non-profit commitment to OA. Even more radical is PeerJ, which abandons the author pays model in favour of a membership scheme. Users pay a fee, starting at $99, for a lifetime's access not to publications, but to publishing through the platform. All papers are then freely available and a proud ticker on the homepage lists how much research funding the service saves every year. PeerJ's ultra-low article processing charges

---

6   The main barrier to research like the digital humanities and the widespread acceptance of Open Access is probably not publishing but the institution of academia itself. Unless it can professionally give equal weight to less established journals, publication methods and research outputs, it is hard to see how they will truly thrive. Currently a conservative bias towards all three is still in evidence, although challenges are becoming more obvious.

(APCs) create an awkward challenge for industry leaders like Springer and Elsevier used to fat margins.

The humanities and social sciences are also riding the wave, buoyed in the UK by a government stance strongly backing OA. An ambitious journal project, the Open Library of the Humanities, aims to be an arXiv, PubMed or PLOS for the humanities – a highly regarded and discipline crafting centre of research. Knowledge Unlatched aims to build coalitions between publishers and libraries, allowing income for the former and a better deal for the latter, freeing up works to become OA. One problem with Open Access has been a splintering of access to a string of university repositories and publisher platforms. Without some degree of centralisation, the space was too fractured for end users to derive maximum benefit. This is being addressed with projects such as the Directory of Open Access Books. The entire higher education and research sector is going after free information in a big way.

Free content is becoming the norm in academic communications; academics, at least, want information to be free. It won't eradicate prestigious names like Harvard and Chicago. However, it's already forcing publishers with serious overheads to re-examine their business and content models. When a host of new entrants can survive on tiny or non-existent APCs then most players with financial drag face a stark choice: either adapt to OA or become uncompetitive and unappealing to authors.

The model is spreading beyond academia and technology. The UK *Guardian* newspaper is pioneering what its editor, Alan Rusbridger, calls 'Open Journalism', a means of working with technology to reformulate the whole journalistic enterprise as collaborative, networked and in real time. The paper aims to become a digitally native organisation that embraces free content, crowdsourcing and other pioneering journalistic practices, new techniques of data display, full social media integration and commitments to editorial transparency. With web traffic to the *Guardian* website regularly exceeding 80 million unique users per month in 2013, the third highest total for a newspaper in the world, on one level the strategy is a success. Only a third of readers are from the paper's home country, something inconceivable in the pre-digital era. Yet arguably it has also been catastrophic: the organisation runs at a substantial loss and has only survived thanks to its unusual and deep-pocketed ownership. So the policy may fail in the long term, but the *status quo* was hardly an option. If, and it's a big if, 'Open Journalism' works then it could save the beleaguered newspaper industry's business models from digitally induced collapse.

Open publishing is not product but service driven. This analysis explains why education publisher Pearson would, presciently in my view, buy a business like the self-publishing platform Author Solutions, moving the company towards services at the expense of products. In spite of serious criticisms in the self-publishing community, the centrality of Author Solutions as a key diversification of revenue and a hedge against disintermediation was underscored by senior executive placement in the hierarchy of Penguin Random House. In an opposite move a services and advertising company like Google bought the publishers Zagat and Frommers, not for the intellectual property as a revenue-generating category in its own right but as a way of buttressing the services and advertiser proposition it already offers. Publishers are starting to view content in a different light, with Pearson and HarperCollins, for example, creating (admittedly restrictive) application-programming interfaces (APIs) for portions of their content. Productive, intelligent and legal reuse of content in a digitally natural fashion is possible. Whether on the consumer or educational side, it's a step towards a reconceived approach.

Moving to services reflects the evolving nature of framing in a digital world. In an analogue world, the work of packaging content for distribution was essential. While part of the change involves market making, another change is the shift in value to the tools and services to package content, rather than the act of packaging itself. The creation of the means of production is the new means of production. This isn't necessarily publishing as such. However, it is a recognition that publishing has become more open, varied and competitive, and a way of guarding against that is to behave with the grain of the trend. The principle is: don't dig for gold in a gold rush; sell shovels. New models are evolving where frames are not only used for publishing but franchised as services to make good losses of sales income. Examples abound. O'Reilly Media, for example, are releasing Atlas file creation and management software. Start-up The Atavist has created a SaaS-based (software-as-a-service) digital publishing platform called the Creatavist, while Penguin has built a collaborative authorship and peer feedback site, Book Country. Many such services were developed for use in-house before being spun out. One issue here is that publishers have traditionally underinvested in proprietary systems and IT generally.

Educational publishing offers a good case study of services, as it has always been one of the most service-driven parts of publishing. Educational publishers provide a service to schools, supplying them with the books and course materials they need to teach. Textbooks were an incidental means of fulfilment. Digital courses, either blends of print and digital or digital only, are adaptable, multimedia, more in tune with the ebb and flow of a term and a classroom, more customisable and potentially better value for all parties. New services like CourseSmart are creating an ever-purer service environment for educational publishing. However, even here another model may supersede older publishers. Massive open online courses, known as MOOCs, are shaking up the entire educational sector. Either from commercial providers like Coursera and Udacity or from top tier universities like Berkeley or Yale, MOOCs offer not only the basic functionality of textbooks but of education itself; they replicate the course and teaching methods of schools and universities and offer qualifications. If one wants to learn to code, Codeacademy seems a far more effective choice than a learn-to-code textbook.

If Udacity is a publisher, its content is framed and modelled explicitly as a service. It's as much college as educational publisher; at some point there may be little difference between the two. Content-as-a-service (CaaS) is a real part of publishing balance sheets, whether it's selling access to business titles to Fortune 500 companies or putting books on aeroplanes as part of an entertainment package. Content is framed, amplified and predicated not as a thing but as doing something. You aren't buying a book; you are buying something to help you. While this has always been an element of book publishing, it becomes ever more important as a node of value.

Writing, content in general, will always need improving, editing and finessing. Writers need training. Conferences, gatherings, speeches and events grow in popularity, as the value of live experience inversely mirrors that of content. Likewise content always needs discovering, marketing and publicising. Brands will want content published to professional standards. There will always be individuals and organisations with sufficient funds to pay someone else to do the work of publishing. Opportunities for service-based publishing businesses are not in short supply. Going 'open' or pivoting to services is partly a commercial challenge to develop a viable business model but also a conceptual challenge in reconceiving the publishing dynamic as not about selling units, rights or audiences.

The writer Steven Johnson (2010) argues the value of writing increases in open systems. By this he means that when text freely and easily combines, unexpected connections, new ideas, productive dissonances and creative associations are liable to appear. In the free-form notational writing of Enlightenment era 'commonplace books', kept by thinkers from John Locke to Thomas Jefferson, quotes, ideas and thoughts would be randomly jotted down to productively mix and brew. Johnson (2010) argues we harm the entire literary ecosystem by keeping text locked down in what are now artificial silos. We've gone backwards. This, in essence, is the position of the entire 'Berkman School': we are damaging our creative and knowledge economies with restrictive practices when open approaches would be generative of far more value. While distributing content is now incredibly easy, the problem is getting paid for it has correspondingly become more difficult; open publishing needs to find ways of harnessing the increased value conjectured by the Berkmanites.

Connected as it is with market making, the shift from product to service industry predates digital technology, which exacerbates, rather than conjures, the lineaments of the challenge. Open publishing is not the only direction for meeting the digital challenge. When seen as part of a move to service-side propositions rather than a missed revenue opportunity it looks interesting. After all, as newspapers prove you can find more readers, more possible customers, than ever, even if you can't readily monetise them. The future of copyright and IP more widely hangs in the legislative balance, on the one hand, beefed up, on the other, radically loosened. Aside from stronger lobbying, publishers should at least explore options for what happens if the foundation of their basic model falls apart.

Forging the New Publisher

The CEO of Faber & Faber Stephen Page (2012) published a newspaper article asking what good publishing looks like in a networked age. His article, prompted by a panel at the FutureBook conference, has many intelligent suggestions for publishers, including seeing copyright in 'three dimensions', focusing on the consumer and recognising that value must be created and shared by the publishing system in new ways. All moves endorsed by this analysis. The original panel was about the 'New Publisher'. What is the New Publisher? Do we need one? As with anything in publishing there was a lively debate; naturally, no consensus emerged other than agreement the New Publisher, whatever it was, would play a larger role. The idea is worth unpacking, as the *status quo* is unequal to the promise and threat of the future. Inventing the New Publisher is at the core of responding to the digital network.

On one level, inventing the New Publisher isn't new at all. William Caxton in London and Johann Heynlin in Paris were New Publishers when they introduced the printing press to those cities; throughout the long eighteenth century, as the modern position of a publisher was more firmly limned, figures from Jacob Tonson to John Murray II were New Publishers, brokers of the cultural world; in the nineteenth century, those publishers responding to the deep implications of steam technology were New Publishers; and more recently, the string of mergers and acquisitions since the 1960s and 1970s creating global, highly professionalised, MBA-festooned corporations were New Publishers as well. Bound, printed paper creates more commonality than is really deserved; each has fundamentally reinvented the role of publisher. This is not to deny the epochal challenge of once again reconfiguring the role, only to place it in due historical context and take heart – it has been done before and in all likelihood will be done again.

Page's (2012) analysis picks up on two shifts discussed here already: a different approach to intellectual property and the turn to the consumer or market making. Dealing with the industry, it is suggested, will be a waste of time when all the tools to reach consumers directly are now readily available. If market making is about a shift in amplification, and Open Access is a change to the models used by publishing, what of filtering? The Internet has increased not lessened the need for filtering. If content exists in ever-increasing abundance at ever-lower cost, then the consequent value in finding the right content is actually greater than ever. Already a host of algorithmic tools suggest content to users online. To date, their flaws have been an inability to launch new products and, most damagingly, the tendency to produce what Eli Pariser (2011) calls a 'filter bubble': self-referential circles of taste antithetical to newness, originality and the unexpected. Our cultural experience is locked in a cycle dependent on our previous choices. The magical serendipity of finding something completely new, outside our usual tastes, disappears.

So, on the one hand, writers and content producers no longer need the 'permission' of intermediaries to produce; ergo the basic online scenario of unprecedented content deluge. On the other hand, the tools to filter this environment are effective only to a point and have in no way eradicated the need for human interaction. The middle way is another of those jejune but unfortunately useful buzzwords:

curation. Filtering is slowly shifting from a selection emphasis to a curation emphasis. Large technology firms put growing resources into solving the problems of curation, making acquisitions and building large teams to ensure an appealing curatorial balance is maintained on their properties.[7] The digital media world from teenage bedrooms to VC boardrooms view the problem of curation with an obsessive focus publishers would do well to note, recognising curation as one of the fundamental puzzles of the Internet. Curation differs from selection in that it is a looser framework. It is less about commissioning, more about combining; less about origination and binary choice deliberations, more about arrangement and patterning. Curation also implies an element of development, of bringing out the best in a work also present in editorial development. There aren't any cut-and-dried rules or definitions here, which is why it is about emphasis and nothing firmer. When publishers were gatekeepers they selected. Now that anyone can publish, they can still create audiences through skilful curation. In their filtering element publishers have always been content curators; the question now is how they can build on this role and use it to intermediate in digital contexts.

Part of why curation is so valuable to the future of publishing is that almost by definition it cannot be totally mechanised. Curatorial algorithms, of which the Google search algorithm(s) is only the most famous, will surely play a large part in sifting the expanding data cloud for human consumption. Where processes of any kind can become automated, they probably will, be it curation, typesetting, translation or sales ordering. Yet curation isn't just about efficiency; it's also about personal taste, an individual's style and judgement. Curation has value precisely because of its fuzziness, its ability to surprise with a flash of insight. As we increasingly drown in a torrent of content, much of it low quality, curation becomes genuinely important and irreplaceable. New Publishers and old can, with sufficient chutzpah and talent, carve curatorial niches. What's more curation competencies lie within the ambit of publishing speciality; this is one area where a computer science degree from Stanford is less helpful than one in the arts and humanities. My hunch is that curation will be one of the big ideas of the twenty-first

---

7 For example, Twitter bought a start-up called Summify to increase its ability to curate and Apple bought Chomp. Google now has large teams focused on content. A plethora of start-ups are working to aid self-curation, from original web 2.0 poster boys like Delicious to newer entrants like Flipboard, Summly and Pocket. Curatorial websites like Brain Pickings have also grown in popularity.

century, reaching into and transforming huge swathes of the economy with publishing foremost among them. More work is needed to map this change. Watch this space.

A loose collection of start-ups and incubated units offer some examples of the New Publisher. Random House Canada, for example, has a blog, Hazlitt, designed less as a traditional publishing exercise and more in the spirit of a Salon.com. Indeed most publishers have blogs or Tumblrs and only the most amateurish would use them as a crude marketing channel. Instead they cultivate community, linking out to other books, products and writers. Unbound has taken the Kickstarter subscription model and applied it to publishing – here the community becomes gatekeeper, the publisher simply hosts and curates the possible range of works which may be published. New directions in tie-ins with television producers to create a publishing path adaptive to multimedia environments are emerging. Publishing becomes part of a transmedia blend: editors become producers, content becomes marketing and marketing becomes content in an unproblematic way. The kinds of New Publisher are as diverse as publishing: Touch Press builds sumptuous iOS apps around reference topics; Frisch & Co. opens new digital translation opportunities for European publishers; Byliner specialises in a new kind of content somewhere between book-length writing and long-form journalism; OR Books focuses on direct sales of radical content; The Written World turns novel writing into a game; Open Book Publishers and Amherst College Press are pioneering Open Access and digital monograph publishing. And so on. These are only the publishers; the wider system of new entrants, with new models, mechanisms and foci is flourishing, bewildering and exhilarating.[8] In highlighting these publishers, I am not trying to pick winners, only to illustrate the diversity of New Publishers.

Existing publishers must find ways of leveraging their assets from brands to relationships, while building new ones. In these circumstances, a revision of the product set is likely. They have to rethink standard operating practices, for example, moving from outright competition with other members of their sector to a position of 'coopetition', partnering, sharing and building networks with former rivals as a means of withstanding novel pressures (Küng, Picard and Towse 2008). It is hard, for example, to see any single publisher building a retail channel

---

8 For and longer and updated list see Bhaskar (2011).

of sufficient scale to rival Amazon or one of the major chains without cooperation of an order of magnitude greater than has been typical. They need to work across media, both in synergistic partnerships and also internally, to reduce the substantial costs of production and enhance the spread, functionality and appeal of multimedia content.

Recall Brian O'Leary (2012) and his argument that publishers should move from containers to context. While I would argue the nature of content framing means we can never wholly move on from containers (an unhelpful metaphor) O'Leary's context-oriented publishing has much to recommend it. He sees the New Publisher as not only publishing work but actively managing the context of consumption – in content-abundant scenarios, so the reasoning goes, context has equal if not more value than content itself. Content, he writes, 'is no longer just a product. It's part of a value chain that solves readers' problems' (O'Leary 2012, 15). Context is largely a question of metadata – it is about tagging, linking, well-crafted metadata, embracing open APIs, the central motif of contextual publishing. It chimes with Craig Mod's (2011) remixing of publishing's linear stages to posit a circular or 'writeable' publishing model (also known as a reverse value chain) in which publishing is – and derives additional benefit from – an ongoing interaction with a work. In his New Publisher talk, Stephen Page summed it up well: publishers should become a 'creative interface between readers and writers' (Page 2012). What does such a publisher look like? What kind of alliances, spin-offs, and re-organisations are needed to produce its workflow?

Publishers' relationships with writers are destabilised. Perhaps we will return to the era of what Bill Ryan (1991) calls performer managers, figures like David Garrick, Johann Wolfgang von Goethe, Jean Racine and George Frideric Handel, who combined the roles of business manager, impresario and artist before the separation of roles in the Industrial Revolution and beyond. J. K. Rowling might be the tip of the iceberg. Equally professional publishing may tend towards an after-the-fact finesse of already available content; as self-publishing tends towards the standard, so the place of traditional publishing shifts into a new structural role.

Responsive organisation design becomes beneficial as the landscape moves faster and more unpredictably than ever before. Publishers might begin to think like the 'lean start-ups' advocated by entrepreneur Eric Ries (2011). In essence, this means gearing their workflows around learning to an unprecedented degree. Ries argues effective start-ups have a goal of learning, as quickly as possibly, what the consumer wants and where the company adds value. This means not just putting products out there but measuring, learning and then acting in fast iterations – what he calls 'validated learning'. Mistakes are made, recognised and eliminated not as a by-product of work, but as its goal. All business assumptions are interrogated; innovation is, as a result, constant and the focus on the customer, the end user – the reader – is absolute.

Part of the problem for publishers is that their minimum viable product (MVP), the essence of a lean learning process, always comes too late, after significant investment (Munro 2013). Peer review and user feedback are parts of the publishing process, but nowhere near as much as for digital businesses, where techniques like A/B and multivariate testing dictate strategy. Publishers have no real equivalent of a beta product, instead always shipping a finished version with unproven demand. Even new books and series launched by big houses have a more ad hoc piloting process than in TV. Finding better MVPs, or at least better ways of iteratively releasing products without the full weight of sunk costs, would not only partially de-risk the process in tough times but gradually improve frames, models and means of amplification, through learning, in volatile and competitive digital markets. The alternatives are either doing nothing or continuing to learn the hard way. While responsive publishing would be an enormous cultural and organisational change, it could also be an exciting journey for readers. Publishers would benefit not just strategically but also from closer, more collaborative relationships with their end customers.

The benefit of an agile approach stems from the as yet unclear outlines of the New Publisher. In all likelihood, it will remain unclear for years to come. In such a situation, the strategy cannot and, returning to Christensen (1997), should not be outlined in advance. There is no point laying out detailed business or product plans here. Building conditions conducive to learning and pivoting is eminently sensible. Data, like curation, is easily parodied as faddish, but its value is evident in this kind of set up; the historical absence of rich data has meant publishers have struggled to measure and understand in depth their successes and failures. Rectifying the situation with data collection, mining and analysis offers a platform for robust experimentation, learning and thereby strategy formation. If better use of MVPs is one side of the equation, better use of data is the other.

Strides are already being made. New business units like Pearson Labs Catalyst and Macmillan's Digital Science are somewhere between venture capital fund, start-up incubator and in-house innovation hubs. Publishers have always been investment vehicles, so why not expand that scope? Focused on bleeding edge technology and buying wholesale into the usual start-up mantras of scalability, disruption and 'failing fast', they are far closer to seed accelerators like Y Combinator or TechStars than publishing imprints. The companies and products tend to be tools and services around content, rather than content suppliers. It's perfectly possible that eventually the original publishing arms will sit as small entities in much larger technology organisations. Whatever happens they act as skunkworks fostering disruptive innovation at a remove and providing a consistent stream of invaluable information and, if all goes to plan, revenue.

Only by experimenting can publishers alter their filtering, framing, amplification and modelling. Only through experimentation will difficult challenges be met: the move to access and the questions around a workable model across different media; how to harness value from attention like other digital and media organisations; how to shift into services instead of making products; how to reengineer the publishing process around the reader rather than the existing workflow and industry demands. We know these are how the core areas of publishing are evolving in a digital context. We just don't know where they will end up or whether the pincers of centralisation and fragmentation will be too strong.

Self-Definition

Publishing is accommodating. It always changes. Publishers consistently fail to grasp the long-term instability of their profession, which, behind the ur-image of the book, is turbulent and required liberal doses of adaptation, improvisation and flexibility. A measure of Buddhist outlook doesn't go amiss – to recognise change and transience as the basis for all things. Luckily most publishers, with their ever-changing stream of titles, writers, products and market conditions, are well poised in this regard.

Above all creating the New Publisher and meeting the digital challenge is not a business problem but a conceptual one. What is a publisher? If the answer for book publishers was, at any time, 'producers and publishers of books', they will undoubtedly struggle facing the kind of technological change that over the past two hundred years has become relatively normal. If they regard themselves as framers and amplifiers of content, content publishers in the largest sense, they have a much better chance of embracing the hard realities of technological and economic change. If publishers remember that the future of amplification is more important than their current business models, things look good. In general, publishers are smart, resilient and backed by an enviable track record of survival.

Nonetheless, existential questions are in the air: in 2012, Hachette produced a document outlining what it, as a publisher, did and why it was of value.[9] Companies don't tend to produce self-justifying missives for no reason. At root all this means becoming networks, not being the node on someone else's network. Publishers once *were* the key communications networks of society. Those days are long since over. The past fifty years have seen publishers getting steadily bigger through constant mergers and acquisitions. Seen in terms of the network, this increasing scale may be decisive in becoming true networks once again, not their victims.

Before the meaty business and strategic questions can be solved, first publishers must redefine their mission, their role and their identity. Thinkers like Bob Stein have made this argument for decades. CEOs routinely pay the idea lip service (Garside 2012). The best way of actually doing it is to have an underlying, anchoring account of publishing. The dangers of a misappropriation of identity are a lack of grip on the new technologies and practices undergirding new frames and amplifications and a lack of real understanding of the mechanics of new models (such as concentration in the network). If, as Douglas Rushkoff (2010) has argued, coding is the new literacy, publishers have some way to go before they are literate; which surely is their bread and butter?[10] History tells us when it wants, when it has the vision, publishing can change with resounding success.

Coda

The digital challenge is real. My concerns are not with the day-to-day activities of publishers, only the overarching narratives of publishing history and theory. Bearing this in mind, is there an alternate reality to digital publishing? I have already mentioned the layered nature of disintermediation and said the printed book is not going away.

---

9 See Greenfield (2011). The document makes for interesting reading and boils down to three key points: publishers are content curators, venture capitalists and distribution specialists – all still, they argue, needed today as much as ever.

10 This is a point echoed by Clay Shirky, who has called publishing a new literacy, not just useful but an essential skill in the twenty-first century (Keen 2010).

Publishers face decline and greater irrelevance more pressingly than they do extinction. Might that not be a viable future?

A case can be made. Technology can change slowly. Throughout the twentieth century there was a persistent overestimation new technology's impact and penetration (Edgerton 2006). The story of publishing is not one of uninterrupted technological growth, but includes backward steps and periods of stasis (Raven 2007); after all, the printing press barely changed in 300 years. Publishers didn't exactly jump at the new media of radio, cinema and television; and while they all occupied a large portion of the public, headspace didn't completely eat the book-publishing niche. Moreover there are serious questions about whether digital business models could ever work for publishing. At an extreme we are heading to nihilistic monopolies, all culture channelled through various mega-portals, Orwellian connotations and all. Monetisation of content becomes basically impossible; content is free; value accrues to the monopolies, not creators or other intermediaries; and the general fabric of cultural life is debased as a result of lack of sufficient quality control and artist incentivisation (Keen 2008; Levine 2011; Lanier 2013).

On the other hand, in this environment, there may be, in James Bridle's words, 'a new value of text'. When faced with a blizzard of multimedia all-singing all-dancing entertainment, the value of sitting down and reading grows. Cory Doctorow (2011) agrees – readers don't want bells and whistles but a good story, well told, with no distractions. There is a good argument that print production values become more, not less, important in digital environments.[11] The uniqueness, craft and physicality of a book are assets in this weightless and intangible world.

An alternative future can be mapped: focus on texts, reading and print, with sumptuous production and good old-fashioned editorial values. So far publishers have survived. Even grown. Most readers are quite happy with print books lining their shelves. The business model is sound.

Everything written here will be tested; this outline may be the best course, but it's unlikely. Content selection and content itself would both be worse if publishing is simply folded into technology or Big Media or left to pontificate on its long, slow obsolescence, as would happen if publishing collectively opted for something like this route. This isn't a *modus vivendi*; it's a full-scale retreat. I could be wrong, but there is an opportunity out there – and what are opportunities if not for the taking?

---

11 See for example Bosman (2011).

Conclusion

INSIDE THE CONTENT MACHINE

What makes publishing so interesting is its extraordinary diversity. This is a practice with history and geographical reach, crossing any number of essential human activities. For that reason this study can only ever hope to be partial. There is always more work – empirical, analytical, exegetical, normative – needed to get anywhere close to a full understanding. Throughout I have jumped from context to context, thinker to thinker. There will be those who argue it is impossible to generalise a wider notion of publishing from the local issues of my examples. Hopefully the spread of different examples goes some way to allaying their concerns. In addition, I would argue our social practices are, of course, always highly specific and specifically conditioned; any kind of high-level generalisation is a risky proposition requiring substantial ongoing work for verification. But to simply relativise everything and do away with deep, impactful and explanatory commonalities, the generative mechanisms producing our lives, is even more foolish. If we do so, we are missing the big picture; we may even be missing the fact there is a big picture to see in the first place!

Any account of publishing needs an anchoring theory of content. The account of content offered here is a sketch. Even when not stated explicitly, there will be various assumptions about what content is and how it works. Better, I believe, to state the understanding of content openly. However, to pretend we don't need a theory of content is to fail at the first hurdle. Moreover, we need a view of content explaining how publishing works over different modalities – the score to *Le Nozze di Figaro*, a Tin Pan Alley ballad and 'Gangnam Style' are all musical content and all are published. Can our conception of content connect the dots or does it view content atomistically, incapable of understanding why these very different things are all musical content and all publishable?

Such questions only grow in importance. In our universities the humanities remain in an epistemic crisis. Now they are actively under assault from the crudely instrumentalist criteria of hostile governments and funders. Ironically this occurs as intellectual property, the products of the publishing, creative, copyright or cultural industries, whatever you call them, become more and more central to national economies. Arts and humanities remain the best training for the agile mind and the delicate balance of commerce and taste needed to secure the future and relevance of this sector.

Areas like publishing studies and the analysis of categories like 'Content' and 'Publishing' have been unjustly neglected in favour of 'Literature' and 'Fine Art'. It seems only logical that they will surely, indeed rightly, become more prevalent in the academy. They are not only – to put it bluntly – a hedge against the terrible bias against the humanities, but are worthwhile forms of study in themselves. As the oxygen and engines of our cultural lives and increasingly economies, the real scandal is their comparative neglect.

Publishing as an intellectual problem is a rarefied concern for publishers themselves, which is why I don't pretend these arguments have immediate relevance. Staying afloat is hard enough without staring in the philosophical mirror. One might argue too much reflection is harmful, like a sportsmen becoming thoughtful at the crucial moment and so dropping the ball. I, for one, hope not.

Of course, publishing isn't just an intellectual problem. Primarily it is a practical one, how to sell, produce, distribute – frame and amplify – content according to pre-selected models. Yet as digital inroads are made and the Internet becomes a democratic publishing platform, publishing loses its gatekeeper status. Bit by bit, the role of publishing is eroded, and so the practical and the intellectual problems merge. In order to be a successful digital publisher you need to first understand the implications of digital publishing; for the die-hard traditionalist making this transition, this is unsettling.

This is important because publishing matters. Sure, publishers have not always behaved well. They have lied, cheated, robbed, cooked the books, tactically defaulted on debts; they have repeatedly sacrificed any principles at the altar of wealth; they have exploited authors and anyone else they can successfully get one over on; they have polluted the public sphere by publishing reams of damaging and objectionable material, either out of conviction or, probably worse, to make easy money; they have almost everywhere resisted technological, economic or organisational change with a staggering tenacity; they have erected monopolies and cartels to protect their interests; their exchanges are often, to quote James Raven, marked by 'bitterness and savagery' (2007, 364). Put another way, publishers are all too human: opportunistic, acquisitive, keen to survive, keener to thrive.

In spite of this, publishing is what creates our public sphere, our modes of discourse. For millennia publishing has been an essential social function, one of the keys to civilisation. It has underpinned our science and culture for centuries and arguably been midwife to their flourishing. A strong and variegated publishing environment helps create deliberative, reflective societies. Publishing has been both catalyst for change and the glue holding people together, a humble intermediary but one whose impact is incalculable. Publishing delimits the intellectual system of a society, encompassing its bookshops, universities, libraries, schools, newspapers, radio and televisions, hobbies and business. What happens to publishing really does matter, as it partly defines who we are, what we know and can know, what gets thought, written, read and done.

Thus, the question has never been about the security of the future of publishing as such. If anything, in the networked age publishing is more relevant and ubiquitous than ever. Rather, the question is about the legacy of those who got comfortable squatting on the word 'publisher'.

Publishing is the content machine inasmuch as a few simple operations are enough to constitute the act of publication. It is a social machine. One problem: the Machine Age has ended. It took a long time for steam-driven machines to find acceptance among book publishers, although they were pioneered by colleagues in the newspaper business. Luckily, at the time, competition for book publishers was not so much in evidence. Europeans at home might have had access to alcohol, a pack of cards, maybe some musical instruments, an open fire, each other – they didn't have tablets, a smart TV, a PC and a games console in addition to all of the above. Early publishers were not operating amid a deluge of published materials. Now, every year literally millions of books are published in English alone. Really publishing's redefinition means going from the Content Machine to the Content Algorithm. At a time as distant from us as we are from Gutenberg, a version of this book will probably be called just that.

In order to describe something in theoretical terms, it is necessary to abstract to a degree. When we talk of publishing in terms of framing and amplification, when we delineate a notion like models, we draw away from human beings. This gives the theoretical canvas. From a position inside the content machine however, it is almost comically absurd.

Above all people make publishing. And what people. There could hardly be more gregarious, colourful, insightful, curious, intelligent and, often, inspirational group in any other industry. Not all of them have been saints, but a huge number have been great characters. Viewing publishing in the abstract removes not only the exhilarating subjective aspects of publishing, but to some extent the extraordinary cast of charismatic characters driving the trade. So many great names are still with us, from Johannes Gutenberg to John Murray, Gaston Gallimard to Albert A. Knopf, Samuel Fischer to Giangiacomo Feltrinelli. Then of course there are the names that come to be associated with a house such as Siegfried Unseld at Suhrkamp Verlag or Tom Maschler at Jonathan Cape. Unfortunately this list reveals a sorry truth to publishing: for many years it was dominated by European and American men, many publishers run as little autocracies and fiefdoms as patriarchal as they were paternalistic. It also obscures the many hundreds of thousands of men and women behind those names, whose hard work, dedication, skill, professionalism and passion have been the heart and soul of the industry since the dawn of human civilisation. We can hope, expect and indeed see change.

As publishing contends with the blinking lights of a thousand data centres and the spartanly staffed offices of fearless start-ups, it becomes clearer than ever that what we think of as traditional publishing needs to deal with the inexorable expansion of virally powered systems feeding on network effects. It needs new frames and new models. If publishing is still going to be about people it will be different people: massed ranks of developers and social media mavens, shareholders and VCs, systems architects and software engineers, biz dev execs and chief information officers, UX ninjas and SEO consultants, angels and data scientists, brand designers, backend coding monkeys, and maybe the odd editor alongside a bunch of roles we can't even imagine yet. Yet that is what we must do: reimagine publishing, what it is, what it means, how it works. It's been done before; it will be done again. The real question is who will do the reimagining – publishers themselves or networks beyond their control? Time will tell.

BIBLIOGRAPHY

Adams, Thomas R. and Nicholas Barker. 2006. 'A Potencie in Life: Books in Society'. In *The Book History Reader*, edited by David Finkelstein and Alistair McCleery. 2nd ed. Abingdon: Routledge.

Adorno, Theodor. 1991. *The Culture Industry: Selected Essays on Mass Culture*. Abingdon: Routledge.

Altbach, Philip G. 1975. 'Publishing and the Intellectual System'. *Annals of the American Academy of Political and Social Science*. Vol. 421, *Perspectives on Publishing*. London: Sage Publications.

Anderson, Chris. 2009. *Free: How Today's Smartest Businesses Profit by Giving Something for Nothing*. London: Random House Business Books.

Arvidsson, Adam. 2006. *Brands: Meaning and Value in Media Culture*. Abingdon: Routledge.

Athill, Diana. 2000. *Stet: An Editor's Life*. London: Granta Books.

Barker, Nicolas. 2003. *Form and Meaning in the History of the Book: Selected Essays*. London: The British Library.

Barnard, John and D. F. McKenzie, eds. 2002. *The Cambridge History of the Book in Britain*. Vol. 4, *1557–1695*. Cambridge: Cambridge University Press.

Bellaigue, Eric de. 2004. *British Book Publishing as a Business since the 1960s: Selected Essays*. London: The British Library.

Benjamin, Walter. 2008. *The Work of Art in the Age of Mechanical Reproduction*. London: Penguin.

Benkler, Yochai. 2006. *The Wealth of Networks: How Social Production Transforms Markets and Freedom*. New Haven: Yale University Press.

Bennett, Tony, Lawrence Grossberg and Meaghan Morris, eds. 2005. *New Keywords: A Revised Vocabulary of Culture and Society*. Oxford: Blackwell.

Bhaskar, Michael. 2011. 'Towards Paracontent: Marketing, Publishing and Cultural Form in a Digital Environment'. *Logos: Journal of the World Publishing Community* 22.1.
_____. 2012. 'The Problem of Publishing'. *Logos: Journal of the World Publishing Community* 23.1.

Bhaskar, Roy. 1998. *The Possibility of Naturalism: A Philosophical Critique of the Contemporary Human Sciences*. 3rd ed. Abingdon: Routledge.

Bhaskar, Roy and Mervyn Hartwig. 2010. *The Formation of Critical Realism: A Personal Perspective*. Abingdon: Routledge.

Black, Michael. 2000a. *Cambridge University Press: 1584–1984*. Cambridge: Cambridge University Press.

————. 2000b. *A Short History of Cambridge University Press*. 2nd ed. Cambridge: Cambridge University Press.

Blagden, Cyprian. 1960. *The Stationers' Company: A History, 1403–1959*. London: Allen & Unwin.

Blum, Eleanor and Clifford Christians. 1981. 'Ethical Problems in Book Publishing'. *Library Quarterly* 51.2.

Bourdieu, Pierre. 1993. *The Field of Cultural Production: Essays on Art and Literature*. Cambridge: Polity Press.

————. 1996. *The Rules of Art: Genesis and Structure of the Literary Field*. Cambridge: Polity Press.

Boyle, James. 2008. *The Public Domain: Enclosing the Commons of the Mind*. New Haven: Yale University Press.

Brandt, Richard L. 2011. *One Click: Jeff Bezos and the Rise of Amazon.com*. London: Penguin.

Brantley, Peter. 2012. 'The New Missing Books'. *Publishing Research Quarterly* 28.3.

Briggs, Asa and Peter Burke. 2002. *A Social History of the Media: From Gutenberg to the Internet*. Cambridge: Polity.

Calabrese, Andrew and Colin Sparks, eds. 2004. *Toward a Political Economy of Culture: Capitalism and Communication in the Twenty-First Century*. Lanham, MD: Rowman & Littlefield.

Castells, Manuel. 2009. 'Communication, Power and Counter Power in the Network Society'. In *The Information Society: Critical Concepts in Sociology*, Vol. 1, *History and Perspectives*, edited by Robin Mansell. Abingdon: Routledge.

————. 2010. *The Rise of the Network Society*. 2nd ed. Chichester: Wiley-Blackwell.

Chartier, Roger. 1995. *Forms and Meanings: Texts, Performances, and Audiences from Codex to Computer*. Philadelphia: University of Pennsylvania Press.

Christensen, Clayton M. 1997. *The Innovator's Dilemma: When Technologies Cause Great Firms to Fail*. Boston: Harvard Business School Press.

Clifton, Rita, ed. 2009. *Brands and Branding*. London: Economist Books.

Clark, Giles and Angus Phillips. 2008. *Inside Book Publishing*. 4th ed. Abingdon: Routledge.

Collins, Paul. 2009. *The Book of William: How Shakespeare's First Folio Conquered the World*. New York: Bloomsbury.

Connolly, Marie, and Alan B. Krueger. 2006. 'Rockonomics: The Economics of Popular Music', edited by Bill Cope and Angus Phillips. *The Future of the Book in the Digital Age*. Oxford: Chandos Publishing.

Cope, Bill and Angus Phillips, eds. 2009. *The Future of the Academic Journal*. Oxford: Chandos Publishing.

Coupland, Douglas. 2010. *Marshall McLuhan: You Know Nothing of My Work!*. New York: Atlas & Co.

Darnton, Robert. 1979. *The Business of Enlightenment: A Publishing History of the Encyclopédie, 1775–1800*. Cambridge, MA: The Belknap Press.

————. 2006. 'What is the History of Books?'. In *The Book History Reader*, edited by David Finkelstein and Alistair McCleery. 2nd ed. Abingdon: Routledge.

————. 2009. *The Case for Books: Past, Present, and Future*. New York: Public Affairs.

Darnton, Robert and Daniel Roche, eds. *Revolution in Print: The Press in France 1775–1800*. Berkeley and Los Angeles: University of California Press.

Davies, Paul and Niels Henrik Gregersen, eds. 2010. *Information and the Nature of Reality: From Physics to Metaphysics*. Cambridge: Cambridge University Press.

Denison, D. C. 2010. *E-Publishers to Watch: 2010*. Berlin: Kindle Direct Publishing.

Delany, Paul. 2002. *Literature, Money and the Market: From Trollope to Amis*. Basingstoke: Palgrave.

Deleuze, Gilles and Félix Guattari. 2004. *A Thousand Plateaus: Capitalism and Schizophrenia*. London: Continuum Press.

Dusek, Val. 2006. *Philosophy of Technology: An Introduction*. Oxford: Blackwell.

Edgerton, David. 2006. *The Shock of the Old: Technology and Global History since 1900*. London: Profile Books.

Eisenstein, Elizabeth L. 1980. *The Printing Press as an Agent of Change*. Vols 1 and 2. Cambridge: Cambridge University Press.

Eliot, Simon and Jonathan Rose, eds. 2007. *A Companion to the History of the Book*. Oxford: Blackwell.

English, James F. 2005. *The Economy of Prestige: Prizes, Awards and the Circulation of Cultural Value*. Cambridge, MA: Harvard University Press.

Feather, John. 2005. *A History of British Publishing*. London: Routledge.

Febvre, Lucien and Henri-Jean Martin. 2010. *The Coming of the Book: The Impact of Printing 1450–1800*. 3rd ed. London: Verso.

Ferdinand, C. Y. 2004. 'Henry Herringman'. *Oxford Dictionary of National Biography*. Online (January 2008): www.oxforddnb.com/view/article/37538

Finkelstein, David and Alistair McCleery. 2005. *An Introduction to Book History*. Abingdon: Routledge.

———, eds. 2006. *The Book History Reader*. 2nd ed. Abingdon: Routledge.

Finlayson, James Gordon. 2005. *Habermas: A Very Short Introduction*. Oxford: Oxford University Press.

Foucault, Michel. 1980. *Language, Counter-memory, Practice: Selected Essays and Interviews*. Ithaca, NY: Cornell University Press.

Fyfe, Aileen. 2012. *Steam-Powered Knowledge: William Chambers and the Business of Publishing 1820–1860*. Chicago: University of Chicago Press.

Galloway, Susan and Stewart Dunlop. 2007. 'A Critique of Definitions of the Cultural and Creative Industries in Public Policy'. *International Journal of Cultural Policy* 13.1.

Genette, Gérard. 1997. *Paratexts: Thresholds of Interpretation*. Cambridge: Cambridge University Press.

Gibson, Chris and Natascha Klocker. 2004. 'Academic Publishing as "Creative Industry" and Recent Discourses of "Creative Economies": Some Critical Reflection'. *Area* 36.4.

Gleick, James. 2011. *The Information: A History, A Theory, A Flood*. New York: Pantheon.

Godine, David R. 2011. 'The Role and Future of the Traditional Book Publisher'. *Publishing Research Quarterly* 27.4.

Gomez, Jeff. 2008. *Print is Dead: Books in Our Digital Age*. Basingstoke: Palgrave.

Graeber, David. 2012. *Debt: The First 5,000 Years*. New York: Melville House.

Graham, Peter W. 2004. 'Byron and the Business of Publishing'. In *The Cambridge Companion to Byron*, edited by Drummond Bone. Cambridge: Cambridge University Press.

Greco, Albert N. 2005. *The Book Publishing Industry: Second Edition*. New Jersey: Lawrence Erlbaum Associates.

———, ed. 2009. *The State of Scholarly Publishing: Challenges and Opportunities*. New Brunswick, NJ: Transaction Publishers.

Greco, Albert N., Clara E. Rodriguez and Robert M. Wharton. 2007. *The Culture and Commerce of Publishing in the 21st Century*. Stanford: Stanford University Press.

Greenblatt, Stephen. 2011. *The Swerve: How the Renaissance Began*. London: The Bodley Head.

Griffin, Dustin. 1996. *Literary Patronage in England, 1650–1800*. Cambridge: Cambridge University Press.

Guthrie, Richard. 2011. *Publishing: Principles & Practice*. London: Sage Publications.

Habermas, Jürgen. 1992. *The Structural Transformation of the Public Sphere: Inquiry into a Category of Bourgeois Society*. Cambridge: Polity Press.

Halasz, Alexandra. 1997. *The Marketplace of Print: Pamphlets and the Public Sphere in Early Modern England*. Cambridge: Cambridge University Press.

Hallin, Daniel C. and Paolo Mancini. 2004. *Comparing Media Systems: Three Models of Media and Politics*. Cambridge: Cambridge University Press.

Hayles, N. Katherine. 2008. *Electronic Literature: New Horizons on the Literary*. Notre Dame, IN: University of Notre Dame Press.

Hesmondhalgh, David. 2002. *The Cultural Industries*. London: Sage Publications.

Hesmondhalgh, David and Sarah Baker. 2011. *Creative Labour: Media Work in Three Cultural Industries*. Abingdon: Routledge.

Hind, Dan. 2010. *The Return of the Public*. London: Verso.

Hinks, John and Catherine Armstrong, eds. 2005. *Printing Places: Locations of Book Production & Distribution since 1500*. New Castle, DE and London: Oak Knoll Press and The British Library.

Holub, Robert C. 2003. *Reception Theory: A Critical Introduction*. London: Routledge.

Howard, Nicole. 2009. *The Book: The Life Story of a Technology*. Baltimore: Johns Hopkins University Press.

Howard, Philip N. 2011. *Castells and the Media: Theory and Media*. Cambridge: Polity.

Howkins, John. 2001. *The Creative Economy: How People Make Money from Ideas*. London: Allen Lane.

Hu, Yang and Xiao Yang. 2010. *Chinese Publishing*. Cambridge: Cambridge University Press.

Isaacson, Walter. 2011. *Steve Jobs: The Exclusive Biography*. London: Little, Brown.

Jauss, Hans-Robert. 1982. *Toward an Aesthetic Reception*. Minneapolis: University of Minnesota Press.

Johns, Adrian. 1998. *The Nature of the Book: Print and Knowledge in the Making*. Chicago: University of Chicago Press.

———. 2009. *Piracy: The Intellectual Property Wars from Gutenberg to Gates*. Chicago: University of Chicago Press.

Iser, Wolfgang. 1978. *The Act of Reading: A Theory of Aesthetic Response*. London: Routledge & Kegan Paul.

Ito, Mizuko, Misa Okabe and Daisuke Matsuda, eds. 2005. *Personal, Portable, Pedestrian: Mobile Phones in Japanese Life*. Cambridge, MA: The MIT Press.

Jacobs, Nicholas. 1998. 'Trials and Triumphs of East German Publishing'. *New Left Review* i/231.

Jenkins, Henry. 2006. *Convergence Culture: Where Old and New Media Collide.* New York: New York University Press.

Jopson, Barney. 2012. *The Amazon Economy: FT Edits.* London: Portfolio Penguin.

Keen, Andrew. 2008. *The Cult of the Amateur: How Blogs, MySpace, YouTube and the Rest of Today's User-Generated Media Are Killing Our Culture and Economy.* London: Nicholas Brealey Publishing.

Kelly, Kevin. 1999. *New Rules for the New Economy: 10 Ways the Network Economy Is Changing Everything.* London: Fourth Estate.

Kirschenbaum, Matthew G. 2008. *Mechanisms: Media and the Forensic Imagination.* Cambridge, MA: The MIT Press.

Knowles, Elizabeth, ed. 2008. *The Oxford Dictionary of Modern Quotations.* Oxford: Oxford University Press.

Kovač, Miha. 2008. *Never Mind the Web: Here Comes the Book.* Oxford: Chandos Publishing.

Küng, Lucy, Robert G. Picard and Ruth Towse, eds. 2008. *The Internet and Mass Media,* London: Sage Publications.

Landow, George. 2006. *Hypertext 3.0: Critical Theory and New Media in an Era of Globalization.* Baltimore: Johns Hopkins University Press.

Lanham, Richard A. 2006. *The Economics of Attention: Style and Substance in the Age of Information.* Chicago: University of Chicago Press.

Lanier, Jaron. 2011. *You Are Not a Gadget: A Manifesto.* London: Penguin.

_____. 2013. *Who Owns the Future?.* London: Allen Lane.

Lashinsky, Adam. 2012. *Inside Apple: The Secrets Behind the Past and Future Success of Steve Job's Iconic Brand.* London: John Murray.

Latour, Bruno. 1993. *We Have Never Been Modern.* Cambridge, MA: Harvard University Press.

_____. 2005. *Reassembling the Social: An Introduction to Actor-Network-Theory.* Oxford: Oxford University Press.

Latour, Bruno, Graham Harman and Peter Erdelyi. 2011. *The Prince and the Wolf: Latour and Harman at the LSE.* Alresford: Zero Books.

Lemert, Charles and Ann Branaman, eds. 1997. *The Goffman Reader.* Oxford: Blackwell.

Lessig, Lawrence. 2004. *Free Culture: How Big Media Uses Technology and the Law to Lock Down Culture and Control Creativity.* New York: The Penguin Press.

_____. 2006. *Code: Version 2.0.* New York: Basic Books.

_____. 2009. *Remix: Making Art and Commerce Thrive in the Hybrid Economy.* London: Bloomsbury Academic.

Levine, Robert. 2011. *Free Ride: How the Internet Is Destroying the Culture Business and How the Culture Business Can Fight Back.* London: The Bodley Head.

Lewis, Jeremy. 2006. *Penguin Special: The Life and Times of Allen Lane.* London: Penguin.

Lih, Andrew. 2009. *The Wikipedia Revolution: How a Bunch of Nobodies Created the World's Greatest Encyclopedia.* New York: Hyperion.

Lowry, Martin. 1979 *The World of Aldus Manutius: Business and Scholarship in Renaissance Venice.* Oxford: Blackwell.

Floridi, Luciano. 2010. *Information.* Oxford: Oxford University Press.

Maclaran, Pauline et al., eds. 2009. *The SAGE Handbook of Marketing Theory.* London: Sage Publications.

Man, John. 2009. *The Gutenberg Revolution: How Printing Changed the Course of History*. London: Bantam Books.

Mansell, Robin, ed. 2009. *The Information Society: Critical Concepts in Sociology*, Vol. 1, *History and Perspectives*. Abingdon: Routledge.

Maschler, Tom. 2005. *Publisher: A Kind of Life*. London: Picador.

McGuire, Hugh and Brian O'Leary, eds. 2012. *Book: A Futurist's Manifesto: A Collection of Essays from the Bleeding Edge of Publishing*. Boston: O'Reilly Media.

McKee, Alan. 2005. *The Public Sphere: An Introduction*. Cambridge: Cambridge University Press.

McKenzie, D. F. 1999. *Bibliography and the Sociology of Texts*. Cambridge: Cambridge University Press.

McLuhan, Marshall. 2001. *Understanding Media: The Extensions of Man*. London: Routledge.

_____. 2011. *The Gutenberg Galaxy: Centennial Edition*. Toronto: University of Toronto Press.

McQuail, Denis. 2010. *McQuail's Mass Communication Theory*. 6th ed. London: Sage Publications.

Miller, Laura J. 2007. *Reluctant Capitalists: Bookselling and the Culture of Consumption*. Chicago: University of Chicago Press.

Mills, Sara. 1997. *Discourse*. London: Routledge.

Miège, Bernard. 1989. *The Capitalization of Cultural Production*. New York: International General.

Mod, Craig. 2011. *Post-artifact Publishing: Digital's Effect on How We Produce, Distribute and Consume Content*. Palo Alto, CA: Pre/Post.

_____. 2012. *Books in the Age of the iPad*. Palo Alto, CA: Pre/Post.

Moor, James. H. 2005. 'Why We Need Better Ethics for Emerging Technologies'. *Ethics and Information Technology* 7.2.

Moretti, Franco. 2007. *Graphs, Maps, Trees: Abstract Models for Literary History*. London: Verso.

Morris, Sally, Ed Barnas, Douglas LaFrenier and Margaret Reich. 2013. *The Handbook of Journal Publishing*. Cambridge: Cambridge University Press.

Murphy, Andrew. 2003. *Shakespeare in Print: A History and Chronology of Shakespeare Publishing*. Cambridge: Cambridge University Press.

Murray, Simone. 2006. 'Publishing Studies: Critically Mapping Research in Search of a Discipline'. *Publishing Research Quarterly* 22.4.

Naughton, John. 2012. *From Gutenberg to Zuckerberg: What You Really Need to Know About the Internet*. London: Quercus.

Norwich, John Julius. 2012. *A History of Venice*. London: Penguin.

Novak, Maxmillian E. and George R. Guffey, eds. 1984. *The Works of John Dryden: Plays*. Berkeley: University of California Press.

Nunberg, Geoffrey, ed. 1996. *The Future of the Book*. Berkeley: University of California Press.

OECD. 2010. *News in the Internet Age: New Trends in News Publishing*. Paris: OECD Publishing.

O'Leary, Brian F. 2011a. 'Context First: A Unified Field Theory of Publishing'. *Publishing Research Quarterly* 27.3.

_____. 2012. 'Context, Not Container'. In *Book: A Futurist's Manifesto: A Collection of Essays from the Bleeding Edge of Publishing*, edited by Hugh McGuire and Brian O'Leary. Boston: O'Reilly Media.

Orwell, George. 2008. *Books v. Cigarettes*. London: Penguin.

Owen, Peter, ed. 1995. *Publishing Now: A Definitive Assessment by Key People in the Book Trade*. 2nd ed. London: Peter Owen.

Pariser, Eli. 2011. *The Filter Bubble: What the Internet Is Hiding from You*. London: Viking.

Parry, Roger. 2011. *The Ascent of Media: From Gilgamesh to Google via Gutenberg*. London: Nicholas Brealey Publishing.

Patry, William. 2011. *How to Fix Copyright*. New York: Oxford University Press.

Pettegree, Andrew. 2010. *The Book in the Renaissance*. New Haven: Yale University Press.

Phillips, Angus. Forthcoming. *Turning the Page: The Evolution of the Book*. London: Routledge.

Plato. 2005. *Phaedrus*. London: Penguin.

Poe, Marshall T. 2011. *A History of Communication: Media and Society from the Evolution of Speech to the Internet*. New York: Cambridge University Press.

Postman, Neil. 2005. *Amusing Ourselves to Death: Public Discourse in the Age of Show Business*. 2nd ed. New York: Penguin.

Powell, Walter W. 1985. *Getting Into Print: The Decision-Making Process in Scholarly Publishing*. Chicago: University of Chicago Press.

Raven, James. 2007. *The Business of Books: Booksellers and the English Book Trade, 1450–1840*. New Haven and London: Yale University Press.

Reading at Risk: A Survey of Literary Reading in America. 2004. Washington DC: National Endowment for the Arts.

Reske, Christoph. 2000. *Production of Schedel's Nuremburg Chronicle*. Vol. 1. Wiesbaden: Harrasowitz.

Richardson, Brian. 1999. *Printing, Writers and Readers in Renaissance Italy*. Cambridge: Cambridge University Press.

Ricoeur, Paul. 2003. *The Rule of Metaphor*. London: Routledge.

Ries, Eric. 2011. *The Lean Startup: How Constant Innovation Creates Radically Successful Businesses*. London: Portfolio Penguin.

Rifkin, Jeremy. 2000. *The Age of Access: The New Culture of Hypercapitalism: Where All Life Is Paid for Experience*. New York: Putnam.

Rushkoff, Douglas. 2010. *Program or be Programmed: Ten Commands for a Digital Age*. New York: OR Books.

Ryan, Bill. 1991. *Making Capital from Culture: The Corporate Form of Capitalist Cultural Production*. Berlin and New York: De Gruyter.

Schama, Simon. 1979. 'Revolution and Enlightenment in France'. *London Review of Books* 1.5.

Schiffrin, André. 2001. *The Business of Books*. London: Verso.

_____. 2010. *Words and Money*. London: Verso.

Schmidt, Eric and Jared Cohen. 2013. *The New Digital Age: Reshaping the Future of People, Nations and Business*. London: John Murray.

Schweser, Carl. 1983. 'The Economics of Academic Publishing'. *Journal of Economic Education* 14.1.

Sher, Richard B. 2006. *The Enlightenment and the Book: Scottish Authors and Their Publishers in Eighteenth-Century Britain, Ireland and America*. Chicago: University of Chicago Press.

Shillingsburg, Peter L. 2006. *From Gutenberg to Google: Electronic Representations of Literary Texts*. Cambridge: Cambridge University Press.

Shirky, Clay. 2008. *Here Comes Everybody*. London: Penguin.

Siegel, Lee. 2008. *Against the Machine*. London: Serpent's Tail.

Siemens, Ray and Susan Schriebman, eds. 2007. *A Companion to Digital Literary Studies*, Oxford: Blackwell.

Siemens, Ray, John Unsworth and Susan Schriebman, eds. 2008. *A Companion to Digital Humanities*. London: Wiley-Blackwell.

Smith, Greg. 2006. *Erving Goffman*. Abingdon: Routledge.

Squires, Claire. 2007. *Marketing Literature: The Making of Contemporary Literature*. Basingstoke: Palgrave Macmillan.

St Clair, William. 2004. *The Reading Nation in the Romantic Period*. Cambridge: Cambridge University Press.

Stark, Gary D. 1981. *Entrepreneurs of Ideology: Neoconservative Publishers In Germany, 1890–1933*. Chapel Hill: University of North Carolina Press.

Steele, Colin. 2008. 'Scholarly Monograph Publishing in the 21st Century: The Future More than Ever Should Be an Open Book'. *Journal of Electronic Publishing* 14.2.

Stepanova, Masha. 2007. 'Disciplinary Duality: The Contested Terrain of Book Studies'. *Publishing Research Quarterly* 23.2.

Stetz, Margaret D. 2007. 'Publishing Industries and Practices'. In *The Cambridge Companion to the Fin de Siècle*, edited by Gail Marshall. Cambridge: Cambridge University Press.

Stevenson, Iain. 2010. *Book Makers: British Publishing in the Twentieth Century*. London: British Library Publishing.

Striphas, Ted. 2009. *The Late Age of Print: Everyday Book Culture from Consumerism to Control*. New York: Columbia University Press.

Suarez, Michael F. and H. R. Woudhuysen, eds. 2010. *The Oxford Companion to the Book*. Vols 1 and 2. New York: Oxford University Press.

Suber, Peter. 2012. *Open Access*. Cambridge, MA: The MIT Press.

Sutherland, John. 1988. 'Publishing History: A Hole at the Centre of Literary Sociology'. *Critical Inquiry* 14.3.

———. 2007. *Bestsellers*. Oxford: Oxford University Press.

Swartz, David. 1997. *Culture & Power: The Sociology of Pierre Bourdieu*. Chicago: University of Chicago Press.

Taylor, Paul A. and Jan L. L. Harris. 2008. *Critical Theories of Mass Media: Then and Now*. Maidenhead: Open University Press.

Tebbel, John. 1987. *Between Covers: The Rise and Transformation of Book Publishing in America*. New York: Oxford University Press.

Thompson, John B. 1995. *The Media and Modernity: A Social Theory of the Media*. Cambridge: Polity.

———. 2005. *Books in the Digital Age*. Cambridge: Polity.

———. 2010. *Merchants of Culture: The Publishing Business in the Twenty-First Century*. Cambridge: Polity.

Throsby, David. 2001. *Economics and Culture*. Cambridge: Cambridge University Press.

Todorov, Tzvetan. 1990. *Genres in Discourse*. New York: Cambridge University Press.

Tuten, Tracy L. 2008. *Advertising 2.0: Social Media Marketing in a Web 2.0 World*. Santa Barbara, CA: Greenwood Press.

Twain, Mark. 1935. *Mark Twain's Notebook*. New York: Harper and Brothers.

Unwin, Stanley. 1960. *The Truth About a Publisher: An Autobiographical Record*. London: Unwin Brothers.

Weedon, Alexis. 2003. *Victorian Publishing: The Economics of Book Production for a Mass Market, 1836–1916*. Hampshire: Ashgate.

Wikström, Patrick. 2009. *The Music Industry: Music in the Cloud*. Cambridge: Polity.

Willes, Margaret. 2010. *Reading Matters: Five Centuries of Discovering Books*. London: Yale University Press .

Williams, Raymond. 1983. *Keywords: A Vocabulary of Culture and Society*. London: Flamingo.

_____. 2003. *Television: Technology and Cultural Form*. 3rd ed. London: Routledge.

_____. 2005. *Culture and Materialism: Selected Essays*. London: Verso.

Williams, Dimitri. 2002. 'Structure and Competition in the U.S. Home Video Game Industry'. *International Journal of Media Management* 4.1.

Weel, Adriaan van der. 2011. *Changing Our Textual Minds: Towards a Digital Order of Knowledge*. Manchester: Manchester University Press.

Werschler, Darren. 2011. 'News That Stays News: Marshall McLuhan and Media Poetics'. *Journal of Electronic Publishing* 14.2.

Winchester, Simon. 2003. *The Meaning of Everything: The Story of the Oxford English Dictionary*. Oxford: Oxford University Press.

Wu, Tim. 2011. *The Master Switch: The Rise and Fall of Information Empires*. London: Atlantic.

Zittrain, Jonathan. 2008. *The Future of the Internet: And How to Stop It*. London: Allen Lane.

Online Material

Alizadeh, Ali. 2011. 'The Death of the Book, and Other Utopian Fantasies'. *Overland*, 30 June 2011. Online: http://overland.org.au/2011/06/meanland-the-death-of-the-book-and-other-utopian-fantasies/ (accessed 21 August 2013).

Anderson, Chris and Michael Wolf. 2010. 'The Web is Dead. Long Live the Internet'. *Wired*, 17 August. Online: http://www.wired.com/magazine/2010/08/ff_webrip/all/1 (accessed 21 February 2012).

Anderson, Kent. 2012. 'Are We a Service or a Product Industry?' Scholarly Kitchen, 14 May. Online: http://scholarlykitchen.sspnet.org/2012/05/14/ask-the-chefs-are-we-a-service-industry-or-a-product-industry/ (accessed 15 May 2012).

Baron, Dennis. 2011. 'Content-Free Prose: The Latest Threat to Writing or the Next Big Thing'. The Web of Language, 25 June. Online: http://illinois.edu/blog/view/25/54474?displayType=month&displayMonth=201106 (accessed 27 June 2011).

Bernius, Matthew. 2010. '"A Canon" of Publishing & Reading'. MattBernius. com, 22 October. Online: http://www.mattbernius.com/a-shot-at-a-canon-of-publishing/ (accessed 6 August 2012).

Bhaskar, Michael. 2011. 'Digital Publishing Start-Ups'. Google Docs, 28 November. Online:https://docs.google.com/document/d/1vcPBUincOjwgIQBjq_qhMPb9 QYitgeyl6gQUM1hWQUw/edit (accessed 29 December 2012).

Brantley, Peter. 2012. 'Back Doors to Transformation'. *Publishers Weekly*, 30 January. Online: http://blogs.publishersweekly.com/blogs/PWxyz/2012/01/30/back-doors-to-transformation/ (accessed 30 January 2012).

Bridle, James. 2011. 'On the New Value of Text'. Booktwo, 5 October. Online: http://booktwo.org/notebook/the-new-value-of-text/ (accessed 6 October 2011).

_____. 2012. 'Literature Needs Much More than Ebooks'. *Wired*, 12 April. Online: http://www.wired.co.uk/magazine/archive/2012/05/ideas-bank/literature-needs-much-more-than-ebooks (accessed 21 April 2012).

Bosman, Julie. 2011. 'Selling Books by Their Gilded Covers'. *New York Times*, 4 December. Online: http://www.nytimes.com/2011/12/04/books/publishers-gild-books-with-special-effects-to-compete-with-e-books.html?_r=1&pagewanted=all (accessed 4 December 2011).

Bosman, Julie and Jeremy W. Peters. 2011. 'In E-Books Publishers Have Rivals: News Sites'. *New York Times*, 19 September. Online: http://www.nytimes.com/2011/09/19/business/media/in-e-books-publishing-houses-have-a-rival-in-news-sites.html?_r=2& (accessed 6 October 2011).

Brockes, Emma. 2012. Interview with Maurice Sendak. *Believer*, November. Online: http://www.believermag.com/issues/201211/?read=interview_sendak (accessed 30 December 2012).

Butler, Kirstin. 2011. '7 Platforms Changing the Future of Publishing'. Brainpickings, 28 June. Online: http://www.brainpickings.org/index.php/2011/06/28/7-publishing-platforms/ (accessed 30 June 2011).

Byrne, David. 2007. 'David Byrne's Survival Strategies for Emerging Artists – and Megastars'. *Wired*, 18 December. Online: http://www.wired.com/entertainment/music/magazine/16-01/ff_byrne?currentPage=all (accessed 31 May 2011).

Caron, Frank. 2008. 'Gaming Expected to Be a $68 Billion Business by 2012'. Ars Technica, 18 June. Online: http://arstechnica.com/gaming/2008/06/gaming-expected-to-be-a-68-billion-business-by-2012/ (accessed 13 December 2011).

Carr, Nicholas. 2011. 'Books that Are Never Done Being Written'. *Wall Street Journal*, 31 December. Online: http://online.wsj.com/article/SB100014240529702038 93404577098343417771160.html (accessed 3 January 2012).

_____. 2012. 'Power to the Data!'. Rough Type, 27 January. Online: http://www.roughtype.com/?p=1572 (accessed 24 June 2013).

Carr, Nicholas and Clay Shirky. 2013. 'Containers and Their Contents'. Rough Type, 3 January. Online: http://www.roughtype.com/?p=2315#comments (accessed 13 February 2013).

Charman-Anderson, Sue. 2012. 'Million Dollar Book Proves Kickstarter Model'. Forbes, 20 February. Online: http://www.forbes.com/sites/suwcharmananderson/2012/02/20/million-dollar-book-proves-kickstarter-model-now-authors-just-need-the-reach/ (accessed 21 February 2012).

Cheshire, Tom. 2011. 'How Rovio Made Angry Birds a Winner'. *Wired*, 7 March. Online: http://www.wired.co.uk/magazine/archive/2011/04/features/how-rovio-made-angry-birds-a-winner?page=all (accessed 20 March 2012).

———. 2012. 'Tumbling on Success: How Tumblr's David Karp Built a £500 Million Empire'. *Wired*, 2 February. Online: http://www.wired.co.uk/magazine/archive/2012/03/features/tumbling-on-success?page=all_ (accessed 29 February 2012).

Christensen, Clayton. 2012. 'Mastering the Art of Disruptive Innovation in Newspapers'. Harvard Nieman Labs, 17 October. Online: http://www.nieman. harvard.edu/reports/article/102798/Breaking-News.aspx#part1 (accessed 22 October 2012).

Christie's. 2012. 'The Birds of America Lot'. Christies.com, January. Online: http://www.christies.com/lotfinder/audubon-john-james-ithe-birds-of/5525248/lot/lot_details.aspx?from=searchresults&intObjectID=5525248&sid=c6ec2e78-b1b2-434c-89c1-4806642dda25 (accessed 16 February 2012).

Clark, Alex. 2011. 'The Lost Art of Editing'. *Guardian*, 11 February. Online: http://m.guardian.co.uk/books/2011/feb/11/lost-art-editing-books-publishing?cat=books&type=article (accessed 6 May 2012).

Cole, William Rossa. 1989. 'No Author is a Man of Genius to His Publisher'. *New York Times*, 3 September. Online: http://www.nytimes.com/1989/09/03/books/no-author-is-a-man-of-genius-to-his-publisher.html (accessed 30 December 2012).

Darnton, Robert. 2000a. 'Extraordinary Commonplaces'. *New York Review of Books*, 21 December. Online: http://www.nybooks.com/articles/archives/2000/dec/21/extraordinary-commonplaces/ (accessed 5 January 2012).

———. 2000b. 'Presidential Address: An Early Information Society: News and the Media in Eighteenth-Century Paris'. *American Historical Review* 105.1:78pars. Online: http://www.historycooperative.org/journals/ahr/105.1/ah000001.html (accessed 14 November 2011).

———. 2009. 'Google & the Future of Books'. *New York Review of Books*, 12 February. Online: http://www.nybooks.com/articles/archives/2009/feb/12/google-the-future-of-books/ (accessed 27 November 2011).

Darnton, Robert and Rhys Tranter. 2012. 'Do Books Have a Future? An Interview with Robert Darnton'. A Piece of Monologue, 4 January. Online: http://www.apieceofmonologue.com/2012/01/robert-darnton-interview-google-books.html (accessed 6 January 2012).

Doctorow, Cory. 2011. 'Publishers and the Internet: A Changing Role?'. *Guardian*, 30 June. Online: http://www.guardian.co.uk/technology/2011/jun/30/publishers-internet-changing-role/print (accessed 30 June 2011).

Economist. 2011. 'Social Media in the Sixteenth Century: How Luther Went Viral'. *Economist*, 17 December. Online: http://www.economist.com/node/21541719 (accessed 31 December 2011).

———. 2012. 'The Price of Information: Scientific Publishing'. *Economist*, 4 February. Online: http://www.economist.com/node/21545974?frsc=dg|a (accessed 5 February 2012).

Edwards, Ralph. 2006. 'The Economics of Game Publishing'. IGN, 6 June. Online: http://uk.ign.com/articles/2006/05/06/the-economics-of-game-publishing (accessed 6 December 2011).

ESA. 2011. 'Essential Facts About the Computer and Video Game Industry 2011'. ESA. Online: http://theesa.com/facts/pdfs/ESA_EF_2011.pdf (accessed 20 March 2012).

Esposito, Joe. 2011. 'Ebooks and Their Containers: An Evolving Bestiary'. Scholarly Kitchen, 18 January. Online: http://scholarlykitchen.sspnet.org/2011/01/18/e-books-and-their-containers/ (accessed 18 January 2011).

———. 2013. 'The Personality of a Publisher'. Scholarly Kitchen, 3 June. Online: http://scholarlykitchen.sspnet.org/2013/06/03/the-personality-of-a-publisher/ (accessed 4 June 2013).

Fish, Stanley. 2012. 'The Digital Humanities and the Transcending of Mortality'. *New York Times*, 9 January. Online: http://opinionator.blogs.nytimes.com/2012/01/09/the-digital-humanities-and-the-transcending-of-mortality/?ref=opinion (accessed 11 January 2012).

Garside, Juliette. 2012. 'Victoria Barnsley: "We Can't Think of Ourselves as Book Publishers Any More"'. *Guardian*, 26 August. Online: http://www.guardian.co.uk/media/2012/aug/26/victoria-barnsley-harpercollins-cant-think-book-publishers (accessed 20 January 2012).

Gauthier, Gary. 2011. 'Reasons Not to Self-Publish: A Fallacy is Exposed'. Jennyhansenauthor.wordpress.com, 16 December. Online: http://jennyhansenauthor.wordpress.com/2011/12/16/reasons-not-to-self-publish-by-gary-gauthier/ (accessed 19 December 2011).

Godin, Seth. 2010. 'The Domino Project'. Sethgodin.typepad.com, 8 December. Online: http://sethgodin.typepad.com/seths_blog/2010/12/the-domino-project.html (accessed 7 February 2012).

Greenfield, Jeremy. 2011. 'Leaked: Hachette Document Explains Why Publishers Are Relevant'. Digital Book World, 6 December. Online: http://www.digitalbookworld.com/2011/leaked-hachette-explains-why-publishers-are-relevant/ (accessed 13 December 2011).

Harris, Jonathan. 2008. 'A Brief History of the Pre Internet Music Business'. Scribd.com. Online: http://www.scribd.com/doc/4067086/A-Brief-History-of-the-Pre-Internet-Music-Business#open_download (accessed 22 September 2011).

Hellman, Eric. 2011. 'In Defense of the Book as a Container'. Teleread, 11 April. Online: http://www.teleread.com/paul-biba/in-defense-of-the-book-as-a-container-by-eric-hellman/ (accessed 11 April 2011).

Hui, Sylvia. 2010. 'Oxford English Dictionary Could Go Out of Print Thanks to the Internet'. Huffington Post, 30 August. Online: http://www.huffingtonpost.com/2010/08/30/oxford-english-dictionary_1_n_698588.html (accessed 4 April 2012).

Jaschik, Scott. 2012. 'Kill Peer Review or Reform It?'. *Inside Higher Ed*, 6 January. Online: http://www.insidehighered.com/news/2012/01/06/humanities-scholars-consider-role-peer-review (accessed 10 January 2012).

Jenkins, Henry. 2011. 'Introduction to Communications'. Henryjenkins.org, 10 January. Online: http://henryjenkins.org/2011/01/introduction_to_communications.html (accessed 11 January 2011).

Jha, Alok. 2012. 'Wellcome Trust Joins "Academic Spring" to Open Up Science'. *Guardian*, 9 April. Online: http://www.guardian.co.uk/science/2012/apr/09/wellcome-trust-academic-spring (accessed 10 April 2012).

JISC. 2011. 'Digital Monograph Technical Landscape Study'. JISC, December. Online: http://jiscpub.blogs.edina.ac.uk/final-report/#43 (accessed 10 January 2012).

———. 2012. 'OAPEN-UK Focus Group Findings'. OAPEN, 3 February. Online: http://oapen-uk.jiscebooks.org/2012/02/03/oapen-uk-focus-group-findings/ (accessed 6 February 2012).

Johnson, Steven. 2010. 'The Glass Box and the Commonplace Book'. Stevenberlinjohnson.com, 23 April. Online: http://www.stevenberlinjohnson.com/2010/04/the-glass-box-and-the-commonplace-book.html (accessed 5 January 2012).

Jones, Philip. 2011. 'Global Publishing Back on the Front Foot'. *Bookseller*, 20 June. Online: http://www.thebookseller.com/news/global-publishing-back-front-foot.html (accessed 3 November 2012).

Keen, Andrew. 2010. 'Can the Internet Save the Book?'. Salon, 9 July. Online: http://www.salon.com/2010/07/09/clay_shirky/ (accessed 8 December 2010).

Kelly, Keith. 2011. 'Amazon's Publishing Push Is Raising Eyebrows'. *New York Post*, 25 May. Online: http://www.nypost.com/p/news/business/amazon_publishing_push_is_raising_wiJw12c25HG7L9PSt2RVrM (accessed 31 May 2011).

Kelly, Kevin. 2011. 'What Books Will Become'. kk.org, 15 April. Online: http://www.kk.org/thetechnium/archives/2011/04/what_books_will.php (accessed 18 April 2011).

König, Thomas. 'Frame Analysis: A Primer'. Restore. Online: http://www.restore.ac.uk/lboro/resources/links/frames_primer.php (accessed 12 March 2012).

———. 'Introduction to Frame Analysis'. ccsr.ac.uk. Online: http://www.ccsr.ac.uk/methods/publications/frameanalysis/ (accessed 12 March 2012).

Lafarge, Paul. 2011. 'Why the Book's Future Never Happened'. Salon, 4 October. Online: http://www.salon.com/2011/10/04/return_of_hypertext/singleton/ (accessed 6 October 2011).

Lewis-Kraus, Gideon. 2009. 'The Last Book Party'. *Harper's Magazine*, March. Online: http://harpers.org/archive/2009/03/the-last-book-party/ (accessed 7 October 2011).

Linn, Don. 2011. 'Key Issues in Contemporary Publishing'. BaitnBeer. Online: http://www.baitnbeer.com/content/what-men-and-women-talk-about-when-they-talk-about-publishing-part-2 (accessed 20 June 2011).

Lovink, Geert et al. 2011. 'I Read Where I Am'. Ireadwhereiam.com. Online: http://www.ireadwhereiam.com/ (accessed 15 June 2011).

McKenna, Laura. 2012. 'Locked in the Ivory Tower: Why JSTOR Imprisons Academic Research'. *Atlantic*, 20 January. Online: http://www.theatlantic.com/business/print/2012/01/locked-in-the-ivory-tower-why-jstor-imprisons-academic-research/251649/ (accessed 23 January 2012).

Matthew Adkins, G. 2012. 'Censorship and the State in the French Enlightenment'. H-net.org, October. Online: https://www.h-net.org/reviews/showrev.php?id=36802 (accessed 19 November 2012).

Merholz, Peter. 2009. 'Innovation and the Highlander Principle'. *Harvard Business Review*, 22 September. Online: http://blogs.hbr.org/merholz/2009/09/innovation-and-the-highlander.html (accessed 14 February 2012).

Miller, Matthew. 2012. 'Android Tablet Marketshare up 10%'. Zdnet. 27 January. Online: http://www.zdnet.com/blog/mobile-gadgeteer/android-tablet-market-share-up-10-ipad-down-10-through-2011/5430 (accessed 3 February 2012).

Moor, Robert. 2012. 'Bones of the Book'. *n+1*, 27 February. Online: http://nplusonemag.com/bones-of-the-book (accessed 8 March 2012).

Morrison, Ewan. 2011. 'Are Books Dead and Can Authors Survive?'. *Guardian*, 22 August. Online: http://www.guardian.co.uk/books/2011/aug/22/are-books-dead-ewan-morrison (accessed 4 January 2012).

_____. 2012. 'The Self-Epublishing Bubble'. *Guardian*, 30 January. Online: http://www.guardian.co.uk/books/2012/jan/30/self-e-publishing-bubble-ewan-morrison (accessed 30 January 2012).

Morse Library. 2003. 'Nuremberg Chronicle: About this Book'. Beloit College. Online: http://www.beloit.edu/nuremberg/inside/about/printer.htm (accessed 18 November 2011).

Munro, Mat. 2012. 'Lean Publishing'. Medium.com, 30 June. Online: https://medium.com/p/2ee7d1305f79 (accessed 2 July 2013).

Nash, Richard. 2013. 'What Is the Business of Literature?'. *Virginia Quarterly Review*. Online: http://www.vqronline.org/articles/2013/spring/nash-business-literature/ (accessed 21 March 2013).

Nawotka, Ed. 2012. 'Combining the Television and Publishing Mindset'. Publishing Perspectives, 31 January. Online: http://publishingperspectives.com/2012/01/combining-the-television-and-publishing-mindset/ (accessed 31 January 2012).

New York Times. 1986. 'Cass Canfield, a Titan of Publishing, is Dead at 88'. *New York Times*, 28 March. Online: http://www.nytimes.com/1986/03/28/obituaries/cass-canfield-a-titan-of-publishing-is-dead-at-88.html?pagewanted=2 (accessed 21 August 2013).

Norman, Jeremy. 2004. 'From Cave Paintings to the Internet: Chronological and Thematic Studies on the History of Information and Media'. History of Information. Online: http://www.historyofinformation.com/ (accessed 8 March 2012).

O'Leary, Brian. 2011b. 'Thinking about Tomorrow'. Magellan Media Partners, 27 June. Online: http://www.magellanmediapartners.com/index.php/mmcp/article/thinking_about_tomorrow/ (accessed 27 June 2011).

Page, Stephen. 2012. 'The Way Ahead for Publishing'. *Guardian*, 13 January. Online: http://www.guardian.co.uk/books/2012/jan/13/way-ahead-publishing-ebooks-stephen-page (accessed 13 January 2012).

Popova, Maria. 2011. 'Merchants of Culture: A Meditation on the Future of Publishing'. Brainpickings, 2 February. Online: http://www.brainpickings.org/index.php/2011/02/02/merchants-of-culture-future-of-publishing/ (accessed 6 July 2011).

_____. 2012. 'Manuel Lima on the Power of Knowledge Networks in the Age of Connectivity'. Brainpickings, 6 January. Online: http://www.brainpickings.org/index.php/2012/01/06/manuel-lima-the-power-of-networks/ (accessed 17 January 2012).

PricewaterhouseCoopers. 2010. 'Turning the Page: The Future of Ebooks'. PricewaterhouseCoopers. Online: http://www.pwc.com/en_GX/gx/entertainment-media/pdf/eBooks-Trends-Developments.pdf (accessed 13 January 2011).

Rivera, Jeff. 2011. 'Seth Godin's Domino Project: Can It Beat the Big Six'. Publishing Perspectives, 17 June. Online: http://publishingperspectives.com/2011/06/seth-godin-domino-project-beat-big-six/ (accessed 20 June 2011).

Runciman, David. 2009. 'Like Boiling a Frog'. London Review of Books, 28 May. Online: http://www.lrb.co.uk/v31/n10/david-runciman/like-boiling-a-frog (accessed 27 August 2012).

Saffo, Paul. 1998. 'DisinterREmediation: Longer, Not Shorter, Value Chains Are Coming'. Saffo.com. Online: http://www.saffo.com/essays/disinteremediation-longer-not-shorter-value-chains-are-coming/ (accessed 14 December 2012).

Schiffrin, André. 2012. 'How Mergermania is Destroying Book Publishing'. Nation, 17 November. Online: http://www.thenation.com/article/171508/how-mergermania-destroying-book-publishing (accessed 20 November 2012).

Schmid, John. 1996. 'An East German Publishing Coup'. New York Times, 7 October. Online: http://www.nytimes.com/1996/10/07/business/worldbusiness/07iht-pub.t.html (accessed 3 September 2012).

Shatzkin, Mike. 2012. 'Trying to Explain Publishing, or Understand It, Remains a Great Challenge'. Idea Logical Company, 31 October. Online: http://www.idealog.com/blog/trying-to-explain-publishing-or-understand-it-often-remains-a-great-challenge/ (accessed 1 November 2012).

Shirky, Clay. 2002. 'Weblogs and the Mass Amateurisation of Publishing'. Shirky.com, 3 October. Online: http://www.shirky.com/writings/weblogs_publishing.html (accessed 5 January 2012).

_____. 2009. 'Newspapers and Thinking the Unthinkable'. Shirky.com, 13 March. Online: http://www.shirky.com/weblog/2009/03/newspapers-and-thinking-the-unthinkable/ (accessed 31 January 2012).

_____. 2012. 'How We Will Read'. Findings, 5 April. Online: http://blog.findings.com/post/20527246081/how-we-will-read-clay-shirky (accessed 10 April 2012).

Singer, Adam. 2012. 'Get Content-Centric, or Be Disrupted in Search and Social'. Thefuturebuzz.com, 2 February. Online: http://thefuturebuzz.com/2012/02/02/content-centric/ (accessed 6 February 2012).

Singh, Anita. 2012. 'Jonathan Franzen: E-Books Are Damaging Society'. Daily Telegraph, 29 January. Online: http://www.telegraph.co.uk/culture/hay-festival/9047981/Jonathan-Franzen-e-books-are-damaging-society.html (accessed 30 January 2012).

Smith, Kelvin. 2012. 'The Future of Publishing Is in the Cupboard under the Stairs'. Bookbrunch, 31 July. Online: http://www.bookbrunch.co.uk/article_free.asp?pid=the_future_of_publishing_is_in_the_cupboard_under_the_stairs (accessed 1 August 2012).

Sourcebooks. 2012. 'Sourcebooks Announces Agile Publishing Model'. Sourcebooks. Online: http://www.sourcebooks.com/blog/sourcebooks-announces-agile-publishing-model.html (accessed 30 January 2012).

Stray, Jonathan. 2011. 'What Should the Digital Public Sphere Do?'. Jonathanstray.com, 29 November. Online: http://jonathanstray.com/what-should-the-digital-public-sphere-do (accessed 1 December 2011).

Stone, Brad. 2012. 'Amazon's Hit Man'. Business Week, 25 January. Online: http://www.businessweek.com/magazine/amazons-hit-man-01252012.html (accessed 26 January 2012).

Streitfield, David. 2012. 'Erasing the Boundaries'. *New York Times*, 13 February. Online: http://www.nytimes.com/2012/02/13/technology/keeping-consumers-on-the-digital-plantation.html?_r=3&ref=technology& (accessed 13 February 2012).

Stross, Randall. 2010. 'Failing Like a Buggy Whip Maker? Better Check Your Simile'. *New York Times*, 10 January. Online: http://www.nytimes.com/2010/01/10/business/10digi.html?_r=1&adxnnl=1&adxnnlx=1356718069-A/XcP973zMkyZAlzM9j54A (accessed 16 July 2012).

Sun, Helen. 2011. 'How Freemium Self-Publishing Is Taking Over in China'. Publishing Perspectives, 1 November. Online: http://publishingperspectives.com/2011/11/freemium-self-published-fiction-china/ (accessed 18 January 2012).

Sutherland, John. 2012. 'Paper Promises'. *Literary Review*. Online: http://www.literaryreview.co.uk/sutherland_06_12.php (accessed 12 June 2012).

Taylor, Mike. 2012. 'Academic Publishers Have Become the Enemies of Science'. *Guardian*, 16 January. Online: http://www.guardian.co.uk/science/2012/jan/16/academic-publishers-enemies-science (accessed 17 January 2012).

Thadeusz, Frank. 2010. 'The Real Reason for Germany's Industrial Expansion?: No Copyright Law'. *Der Spiegel*, 18 August. Online: http://www.spiegel.de/international/zeitgeist/no-copyright-law-the-real-reason-for-germany-s-industrial-expansion-a-710976.html (accessed 23 January 2012).

Thibault. 2010. 'Search Engine Share by Country'. Them.pro, 27 July. Online: http://www.them.pro/Search-engine-market-share-country (accessed 21 February 2012).

Thompson, John B. and William Cole. 2010. 'Is Publishing Doomed?'. *Brooklyn Rail*, 5 November. Online: http://www.brooklynrail.org/2010/11/express/is-publishing-doomed-john-b-thompson-with-williams-cole (accessed 2 July 2012).

Updike, John. 2006. 'The End of Authorship'. *New York Times*, 25 June. Online: http://www.nytimes.com/2006/06/25/books/review/25updike.html?pagewanted=all&_r=0 (accessed 4 January 2012).

Warren, John W. 2010. 'The Progression of Digital Publishing: Innovation and E-volution of E-Books'. *International Journal of the Book*, Rand. Online: http://www.rand.org/content/dam/rand/pubs/reprints/2010/RAND_RP1411.pdf (accessed 8 December 2010).

Wasserman, Steve. 2012. 'The Amazon Effect'. *Nation*, 29 May. Online: http://www.thenation.com/article/168125/amazon-effect# (accessed 31 May 2012).

Wolf, Gary. 1996. 'The Wisdom of Saint Marshall, the Holy Fool'. *Wired*, January 1996. Online: http://www.wired.com/wired/archive/4.01/saint.marshal_pr.html (accessed 31 January 2011).

Wolf, Michael. 2011. 'Why 2012 Will Be the Year of the Artist-Entrepreneur'. Giga Om, 29 December. Online: http://gigaom.com/2011/12/29/why-2012-will-be-year-of-the-artist-entrepreneur/ (accessed 29 December 2011).

Yourgrau, Barry. 2009. 'Thumb Novels: Mobile Phone Fiction'. Keitai-shosetsu. Online: http://www.keitai-shosetsu.com/ (accessed 6 February 2012).

Zittrain, Jonathan. 2001. 'The Personal Computer Is Dead'. Harvard Law, 30 November. Online: http://www.law.harvard.edu/news/2011/11/30_zittrain-the-personal-computer-is-dead.html (accessed 1 December 2011).

INDEX

Printed in the USA
CPSIA information can be obtained
at www.ICGtesting.com
JSHW082202140824
68134JS00014B/382

9 780857 281111